Escape through the Balkans

Next page: Photograph of Irene
Grünbaum (right), circa 1940–50.

Escape through the Balkans

The Autobiography of Irene Grünbaum

Translated and edited with an introduction by Katherine Morris

University of Nebraska Press, Lincoln and London

Library of Congress
Cataloging-in-
Publication Data.
Grünbaum, Irene,
1909–1983. Escape
through the Balkans:
the autobiography
of Irene Grünbaum /
translated and
edited by Katherine
Morris.   p.   cm.
ISBN 0-8032-2161-4
(cl : alk. paper).
1. Grünbaum, Irene,
1909–1983. 2. Jews —
Persecutions—Balkan
Peninsula. 3. Holocaust,
Jewish (1939–1945)—
Balkan Peninsula—
Personal narratives.
4. Balkan Peninsula—
Ethnic relations.
I. Title. DS135.B33G78 1996
940.53'18'092—DC20 [B]
95-24598 CIP

CONTENTS

PREFACE

Finding Irene Grünbaum's autobiography was serendipitous. About five years ago I started collecting material on Jewish women who had immigrated to Brazil during the Nazi era, so I wrote to several archives in Germany and Austria. The Institute of Austrian Resistance in Vienna responded by sending me Irene Grünbaum's memoir, a 150-page manuscript containing no title, no chapter headings, and no paragraph indentions. I glanced through it hoping to find something about her life in Brazil and encountered only one sentence on this subject, so it languished in my apartment.

I was working on other research, but occasionally I would pick up Grünbaum's memoir. As I read more, I became intrigued. What struck me was her point of view—which was quite different from that of a man—and how she dealt with the problems a woman faces when traveling alone. The pace of the narrative, the colorful characters she encountered, and her courage heightened my interest.

Although *Escape through the Balkans* reveals what Irene Grünbaum experienced during the war, much of what she did before moving to the Balkans and after immigrating to Brazil remains a mystery. Two letters, one written by the late Rabbi Fritz Pinkuss in 1992 and the other written by the author in 1966, provide a brief sketch. Irene Grünbaum was born Irene Levi in Darmstadt, Germany, in 1909. She was married to Bobby Eskenazi, a jewel merchant, and living in Belgrade when the Germans invaded the Balkans. He perished in a death camp during the war. After immigrating to Brazil in 1947, Irene married Harry Grünbaum, an engineer. From 1956 to 1965 she worked for the Hebrew Immigrant Aid Society as a social worker. Her job during these years included greeting and counseling several thousand Jewish immigrants who arrived at the port of Santos. She died in São Paulo in 1983.

I would like to thank Andrew Bulgin and Lori Batten for reading early sections of the manuscript. Susan Zuccotti's careful editing and constructive criticism were particularly helpful, and Ezra Mendelsohn provided insightful suggestions for the introduction. I would also like to acknowledge Maria H. S. Choi for sending me photographs and information about the author.

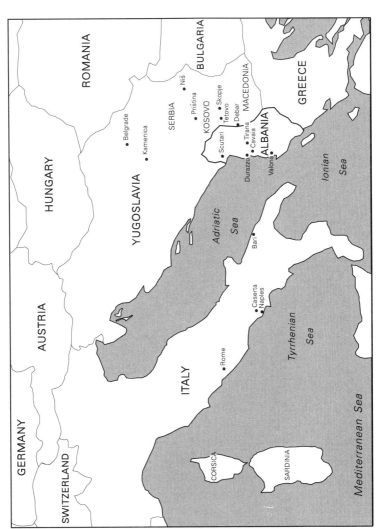

Southern Europe in Grünbaum's time, 1941–1947

INTRODUCTION

In Belgrade, Serbia, on 6 April 1941 at 6:00 A.M., Irene Grünbaum was awakened from a restless sleep by a bomb. Many more bombs were to follow. *Escape through the Balkans* is her story of the Nazi invasion and civil war and how these events changed her life forever. Grünbaum's odyssey began in Belgrade. After the war broke out in Yugoslavia she fled to Bulgarian-occupied Macedonia, and later, as one of the few survivors of the blockade in Skopje, she escaped to Albania. Soon after the Allied victory in Europe she flew to Rome, where she stayed for one and a half years before emigrating to Brazil.

Grünbaum's manuscript vividly portrays the individual faces of Jews, Christians, Muslims, Germans, Allies, and Partisans in the intense wartime confusion. Some of the most memorable are the Serbs and Muslims who helped her. The Serbs were often sympathetic to the plight of the Jews during World War II, a noteworthy fact given that today Serbs are most often portrayed as the bullies in the Balkan war. Furthermore, the Muslims of Albania and Macedonia helped Grünbaum as well as other Jews—again, a particularly fascinating fact today.

Irene Grünbaum's Balkan chronicle is a unique contribution to the field of Holocaust history. Very little primary source material is available in English on the persecution of Jews in Yugoslavia, and still less on the deportation of Jews from Skopje, Macedonia. And there is almost nothing in English about the situation of the Jews in Albania.

Two distinct Jewish communities thrived in the Balkan Peninsula long before the interwar period: the Sephardic and the Ashkenazic Jews, who had emigrated from the former Ottoman territories and from the former Hapsburg territories, respectively. The Ottoman Empire welcomed the Sephardim after they were expelled from Christian Spain in 1492. The majority initially settled in Salonika (Thessalonica) and Istanbul, but by about 1550 their descendants began to move into such cities as Belgrade in Serbia, Sarajevo in Bosnia, and Skopje in Macedonia. In contrast, a large number of Ashkenazim from the Hapsburg areas emigrated to the southern Balkans as late as the nineteenth century. By midcentury many of these had joined the Neologue, a reform group that advocated less traditional Orthodox beliefs and more integrationist attitudes. Most of the Neologue Jews spoke German or Hungarian instead of Yiddish.[1]

Following World War I, circumstances were generally favorable for the Jewish minority in Yugoslavia until shortly before World War II. Any anti-Semitism that existed was usually targeted against Jews in the former Hapsburg territories rather than in the Serbian or Ottoman areas. In the 1920s and 1930s the Yugoslavian government was fundamentally controlled by the Serbs. They saw the local Jews as patriots because many had served in the Balkan wars and in World War I. Bosnian and Croatian Jews had also fought in World War I, in the Austro-Hungarian army, but since the Jews of Belgrade were often chosen to represent all Yugoslav Jewry in affairs of state, they were considered special.[2]

Thus, any anti-Jewish feeling was usually directed against the Ashkenazim, or German- or Hungarian-speaking Jews, who were recent immigrants and considered foreign, rather than against the Sephardim, or Ladino-speaking Jews, who had been in the Balkans for centuries and were considered natives.[3] An example of bureaucratic discrimination against the Ashkenazim occurred shortly after World War I, when local authorities, chiefly in Bosnia but also in Croatia, expelled "foreigners," or recent Ashkenazic immigrants who had been citizens of the Hapsburg monarchy.[4]

Although conditions were fairly stable for the Jews in interwar Yugoslavia, both because the government had a friendly policy toward them and because the Jews constituted a small percentage of the population, anti-Jewish sentiment gradually became stronger in the 1930s both at home and abroad. German economic and political issues, such as the German-Yugoslavian trade agreement of 1 May 1934, helped sustain close dependence on Berlin despite Yugoslavia's formal neutrality.[5] After the Anschluss in 1938, with the expulsions and emigration of Austrian Jews, the favorable situation for the Jews of Yugoslavia waned.

As Irene Grünbaum illustrates, in 1941 things changed radically for Yugoslav Jews. The sentiment of the Yugoslav people notwithstanding, on 25 March 1941 the Yugoslavian government signed the Tripartite Pact, allying itself with the Axis. This provoked a military putsch. On 27 March General Dušan Simović led a bloodless coup d'état in opposition to the government's pro-German stance. When Hitler heard about the demonstrations in Belgrade against the pact, he decided to attack. The invasion was quick. On 6 April the Germans bombed Belgrade, and in less than two weeks the Yugoslavian armed forces surrendered: General Kalafatovich signed the capitulation on 17 April.[6] Even the German command was surprised by how rapidly the Yugoslavian army fell.[7]

Immediately following the German occupation, the Axis powers reorganized and carved up the country of Yugoslavia: Hungary took its pre-1919 territories of Baranja and Bačka; Bulgaria occupied the Yugoslavian sections of Macedonia; Germany and Italy divided Slovenia; Italy claimed Montenegro, Dalmatia, and a part of Bosnia-Hercegovina; and an Albanian government was set up in the Kosovo area. Serbia became a German puppet state. The Independent State of Croatia, which included Bosnia and Hercegovina, was proclaimed. However, despite its alleged independence, Croatia was divided between two occupying powers whose spheres of influence ran from north to south: Italy controlled the western half, and Germany the eastern half. By the time the Germans invaded the Soviet Union on 22 June 1941, all the Balkan states were entangled in the war.[8]

Hitler, an Austrian, shared the disdain of the Hapsburg elite for the peoples of the Balkans, especially Serbs. He degraded Jews, Russians, Serbs, and Roma (gypsies) to a subhuman status and promoted enmities that had existed there for centuries.[9] The German army committed atrocities and merely stood by as ethnic groups murdered and mutilated one another. Over the course of the war, however, the Balkans became a quagmire for the Wehrmacht—they were not used to guerrilla warfare, the complexities of Balkan politics, or the terrain.

Foreign occupation and partition created chaos in Yugoslavia, which soon was the site of a bloody civil war. The Ustasha, or Croatian fascists, led by Ante Pavelić, fought with Germans and Muslims against the Serbs. The Yugoslav colonel Draža Mihailović, who had not accepted the surrender of the Yugoslav armed forces, formed guerrilla bands of Chetniks in southwest Serbia. The Chetniks were closely associated with King Peter and the government in exile and were almost exclusively Serbian. Thus, they were usually anticommunist and anti-Croat. The Ustasha, assisted by Muslims, killed Serbs, and the Serbs, especially the Chetniks, retaliated. Throughout Croatia Catholics and Muslims fought against Serbian Orthodox and Jews. The summer of 1941 was a bloodbath in which the Ustasha burned villages and murdered thousands of Serbs and Jews.

Loyalties became difficult to discern. Noncommunist Serbs and many civilians sought protection in the Italian-occupied zone to escape Croatian brutality and German reprisals.[10] The Croatians, who were Italy's allies, were looking more like enemies. In contrast, the Serbs, enemies of Italy, were looking more like friends. To add to the confusion, the civil war wreaked havoc on the ethnically diverse population. Although the Chetniks initially fought against the Germans and the Ustasha, they ended up fighting the Partisans, the communist forces headed by Joseph Broz (Tito).[11]

For the Jews in Serbia all this spelled disaster, and it began almost immediately. On 30 May 1941, the first decisive steps of the systematic destruction of the Jewish population were taken: the military administration defined what a Jew was, demanded the removal of Jews from the professions and public service, started registration of Jewish property, introduced forced labor, forbade the Serbian population from hiding Jews *(Beherbergungsverbot)*, and ordered all members of the Jewish community to wear the yellow Star of David.[12]

Most unfortunately, the Nazis often linked Jews with communists in war-torn Serbia. After the Germans invaded the Soviet Union in June 1941, communists in German-occupied Serbia orchestrated an uprising there, to which the Germans responded by requiring Jews in Serbia to supply forty hostages weekly. The first reprisal executions in late June were against "Communists and Jews."[13]

These drastic measures by the Nazis did not, however, stem the resistance. According to Ernst Wisshaupt, the German army staff archivist, life was cheap in the Balkans: "Even with the most unrestricted reprisal measures— up until the end of August a total of approximately 1,000 communists and Jews had been shot or publicly hanged and the houses of the guilty burned down—it was not possible to restrain the continual growth of the armed revolt."[14] By 10 October 1941 the general reprisal policy, as developed by General Franz Böhme's staff, was to execute one hundred hostages for each German killed.[15] The draft stated that all communists and all Jews were to be seized. Thus, the slaughter of male Jews in Serbia was accomplished as part of the Wehrmacht reprisal policy.[16]

The Bulgarian attitude toward the war and toward the Jews was opportunistic.[17] The Bulgarians viewed Jews merely as commodities to be traded for political gain and did not share the German attitude about the "Jewish problem." At first their anti-Jewish ordinances were too slow for Berlin—not enough Jews were being deported. However, the Germans found a way to exterminate more Jews in Bulgaria. *Hauptsturmführer* Theodor Dannecker, a representative of Adolf Eichmann, *Obergruppenführer* responsible for the *Endlösung*, or Final Solution, arrived in Bulgaria in January 1943 with the mission of expelling as many Jews as possible. Commissar Aleksandar Belev of the Commissariat for Jewish Problems helped deport twenty thousand Jews—eight thousand from Macedonia, six thousand from Thrace, and six thousand from Old Bulgaria. In a sweeping exportation, Macedonian Jews were rounded up and sent to Treblinka on three trains.[18]

On 22 February 1943 a written authorization, the "Agreement for the removal of the first group of 20,000 Jews to the eastern German territories," was drafted. Aleksandar Belev signed for Bulgaria and Theodor Dannecker for Germany. A partial excerpt reads: "Upon the approval of this agreement by the Ministerial council of Bulgaria, the deportation of 20,000 Jews will be undertaken, regardless of the person's age or sex. The Reich is prepared to receive these Jews into its eastern provinces. . . . The Bulgarian Ministry of the Interior will guarantee that the transports consist only of Jews. . . . The Jews are not permitted to carry with them any arms, poison, foreign currency, precious metals, etc."[19]

The deportations of Jews from Skopje in March 1943 are always referred to as the exception to the otherwise excellent record of Bulgarian protection of the Jews. Bulgarian historians claim with pride that Bulgaria was the only country in Europe that did not hand Jews over to the Führer. However, Jews from Thrace, Macedonia, and Pirot, the "newly liberated lands," were deported and killed.[20] Why such a discrepancy? Some interpret this as a form of colonial politics toward the newly acquired territories. This had been a pattern in such Eastern European countries as Hungary and Romania, where the attitude that a country's own Jews were more important than another country's Jews predominated. This attitude also prevailed in Bulgaria: the Bulgarian government sacrificed the Jews from the annexed territories in order to save the Jews of Bulgaria.[21] When, however, Bulgaria was pushed to hand over more Jews, it refused. The German satellite feared Anglo-American reprisals, such as the bombardment of Sofia, and its worsening political position as an Axis partner.[22] Thus, the Bulgarian Jews were saved because the Jews of Macedonia and Thrace were sacrificed and because Germany suffered increasing major defeats in the war, such as in the battle of Stalingrad.

The situation in Albania was different. After centuries of Turkish rule, Albania had proclaimed its independence in 1913. During World War I it was occupied in the north by the Central Powers and in the south by Italy. Albania became an independent state in 1919, which Italy recognized on 8 August of that year. Amidst domestic unrest in 1925 Ahmed Zog initiated a coup, and he declared himself king in 1928. He changed the constitution, and in 1931 he tried to limit Italian influence.

Zog proved himself successful in this attempt until March 1939, when Hitler carved up Czechoslovakia. Benito Mussolini, Italy's fascist dictator, stated furiously: "Every time Hitler occupies a country he sends me a message."[23] In order to prove his power within the Axis, Mussolini annexed Albania in April 1939. Zog rejected the terms, and the Italian army invaded the country. Albania remained nominally Italian until late in the war.[24]

Il Duce's triumphs were short-lived. Allied paratroops landed in Sicily on 10 July 1943: Italy had lost the war. In order to avoid further disaster, Italy agreed to an armistice with the Allies and capitulated on 8 September 1943.

What did this mean for the Jews? Italy's attitude toward Germany and the

Jews during the war was incongruous. Italy's anti-Semitic legislation was less drastic than Germany's, although the Italians were not unreceptive to Nazi doctrine.[25] In *The Reawakening*, Primo Levi describes the inmates who remained in Auschwitz after the Russian liberation in January 1945. One, Olga, was a Jewish Croat partisan who had fled in 1942 to Piedmont, Italy, where she had found "a brief peace in the paradoxical Italy of those years, officially anti-Semitic."[26]

The inconsistency in Italy's behavior toward the Jews is best illustrated by the measures of the Italian army, foreign ministry, and diplomatic corps to protect Jews in the Italian-occupied territories.[27] For example, in the summer of 1942 a group of senior officers and Italian diplomats saved a few thousand Jews. The Jews, who were mostly Croatian, had fled the murderous Ustasha in 1941 and were living in the Italian-occupied zone under the protection of the Royal Italian Army. In 1942 Germany demanded that they be handed over, and Mussolini consented. But a few Italian generals and diplomats refused to cooperate.[28]

The Italians often overlooked anti-Jewish discrimination in Italy and tended to sympathize with the plight of the Jews. Even though anti-Semitism became part of the official government ideology in 1938, the Italians tended to be less ruthless in their actions toward the Jews than their German counterparts. This would explain why Jews remained relatively unmolested in Italian-occupied Albania until 1943. According to Jonathan Steinberg, "Until the sudden armistice on 8 September 1943 ended the Axis partnership no Jew under the protection of the Italian forces was ever surrendered to the Germans, the French, the Croatians, or anybody else."[29]

After Italy capitulated, the Germans began to occupy Albania and the Jewish community panicked. The unique situation created by the Italian occupation came to an end when the Nazis marched in. Very little is known about the Holocaust in Albania. Grünbaum mentions the Jews who remained in Albania after 8 September: "The approximately three hundred Jews who were still in Albania searched for protection and a place to hide" ("Tirana Revisited"). Although the exact number of Jews residing in Albania during the war is not known, there is information about expulsions of Jews from Albania late in the war.

The commanding general in Albania described a large deportation of Jews in April 1944, carried out by the SS division Skanderbeg, or Albanian collaborators. They arrested 300 Jews in Priština (Kosovo) who were subsequently deported to Bergen-Belsen.[30] Later that year, between 28 May and 5 July, they incarcerated 510 "Jews, Communists, partisans, and suspicious persons" in the Albanian area, later deporting 249 from this group.[31]

After Mussolini was overthrown on 25 July 1943, the Germans marched into Albania, and in late summer they seized larger towns and forced the Partisans into rural areas. Although their policies were particularly harsh in the regions where the guerrillas had been active, they moderated their actions to gain the acceptance of the people.[32] Then they concentrated on forming political alliances that would encourage animosity among Albanian factions.[33] Even though the Nazis knew that the Albanians resisted them bitterly and did not believe that the Axis would win, they publicly recognized Albanian "independence," insisting that they would help the country revolt against Italian oppression. A regency was appointed, and Albania was declared neutral. Beyond where lines of defense and communication were concerned, the Germans did not meddle much with the country's administration.

They did, however, openly support Albania's acquisition of Kosovo. Hitler had given this former Yugoslavian province to Mussolini in 1941. Kosovo had a large Albanian population that had suffered economic and political discrimination under the Serbs after World War I.[34] The idea of union with Kosovo was well received by Albania initially; however, in the latter part of World War II "ethnic Albania" became a source of bitter contention between the nationalists and communists. The communist resistance movement was influenced by the Yugoslavs, who would not be sympathetic to relinquishing territory to Albania. The Skanderbeg SS division tried to deport and exterminate the Serbs in the Kosovo region.[35]

One of the results of the Italian surrender was the flow of weapons into Partisan hands. Albania became an arms depot. The circumstances in Albania illustrate how desperate and volatile the political situation was after the Italian capitulation; it was confusing for the native population and even more so for refugees. A civil war broke out between the communists and their main political opponents, the guerrillas of the Balli Kombëtar, or National Front. The communists began to liquidate their enemies. Hideous atrocities and massacres followed, and there was great confusion about whom the Allies should support. As one author put it, "In the conditions prevailing in Albania in 1943–44 the task of deciding who was and who was not fighting the enemy at any given moment would probably have defeated Solomon himself."[36]

Like their comrades in Yugoslavia, the Albanian communists knew that they faced two enemies: their domestic political opponents on the one hand and the Germans on the other. Also like the Yugoslav communists, they were in a better position than the other Partisans to fight such a battle. Hence, they were able to secure more supplies from the Allies, leaving fewer available to the Balli Kombëtar and the royalists. International events also aided the Albanian communists. Shortly after the meeting between Churchill, Roosevelt, and Stalin in Teheran in November 1943, Britain decided to cease military aid to Draža Mihailović's Chetniks and give full support to Tito's Partisan movement.

The decision was a practical one and is best summarized by a conversation between Prime Minister Winston Churchill and Brigadier Fitzroy Maclean, the head of the Allied military mission to Tito's headquarters. After Maclean expressed his fears that the Yugoslav Partisans would set up a communist regime when hostilities ceased, Churchill asked him whether he planned to make Yugoslavia his home after the war. Maclean assured him that he had no intention of doing so. To which Churchill replied, "Neither do I. And, that being so, the less you and I worry about the form of government they set up, the better. That is for them to decide. What interests us is, which of them is doing most harm to the Germans?"[37]

This shift in policy was encouraging for the communist Partisans in Albania, who heard about the developments from their Yugoslav comrades.[38] Yugoslavia had become a kind of communist model, and Yugoslav communists instructed the Albanians on how to organize and recruit for the Albanian communist party. This party became known as the National Liberation Movement, or LNC, in Albanian. Its leader was Enver Hoxha, who worked closely with Tito. Even though members of the LNC came from various political persuasions, the communists dominated.[39]

The Allies funded the more radical, left-wing resistance groups in order to win the war; political problems could be solved later. Because the Germans either destroyed the government armies or made allies of them in their initial Balkan battles, the resistance forces in Yugoslavia, Greece, and Albania became the strongest national troops. In this manner, the German army changed the face of Yugoslavia: new communist regimes created by organized resistance movements replaced the old regimes. At the end of the war the Partisan Left, aided by the Soviet Union, dominated the new system.[40]

Escape through the Balkans is the story of how a Jewish woman escaped the Nazis. Admittedly, Grünbaum did not spend a prolonged period in a death camp; nonetheless, her memoir has much in common with the memoirs of those who did. Survivors of terrible tragedies such as the Holocaust share certain characteristics—the most notable being the desire to bear witness to the ordeal. Studies have shown that this wish arises from a need to keep the memory of the victims alive.[41] Often survivors view silence about their experiences as a form of complicity, a way of submitting to the perpetrator.

Although Irene Grünbaum could not be compared to Primo Levi or other writers such as Giuliana Tedeschi, Ida Fink, or Charlotte Delbo, who spent years in concentration camps, her story of seeking refuge in the Balkans does add something unique to the body of survival literature. Many of Grünbaum's horrific experiences resulted from the same evil that produced other narratives. Although her situation was not as desperate, she was nevertheless in constant danger, and death was always a possibility.

Grünbaum's narrative has much in common with the growing corpus of Holocaust testimony. One similarity between her memoir and others is that she often views her experience as part of the experience of all Jews. For example, when she describes her own situation she almost always relates what was happening to the other Jews. Another similarity is that she focuses on the present: living in the here and now enabled her and many like her to endure years of hardship. Grünbaum also manifests a kind of survivor's instinct or skill, an ability to act, as Terrence Des Pres wrote of survivors, "spontaneously and correctly during times of protracted stress and danger."[42]

Often she relies on her survival skills to get through deadly situations. This kind of talent is not related to race, class, gender, or education. One survivor of Treblinka maintained that "it wasn't ruthlessness that enabled an individual to survive—it was an intangible quality, not particular to educated or sophisticated individuals. Anyone might have it. It is perhaps best described as an overriding thirst—perhaps, too, a talent for life, and a faith in life."[43]

The autobiography of Irene Grünbaum is the story of a survivor. What exactly was it that allowed her to escape while her family did not? Was it, as she states herself, an ingenuity she inherited from her ancestors? Was it her ability to think quickly and to react properly in the most dangerous situations? Or was it her proficiency in several languages (German, Serbian, French, English)? Did she fare well because she had no children to hinder her? Was it her connections with Christians, Muslims, and Jews? Or was it just blind luck?

Irene Grünbaum's determination to live manifests itself throughout the narrative. Twice she slips into the most dangerous of states—indifference. Ironically, this fatal unconcern is strongest in Italy after the war. She realizes this and tells herself that she has to keep going, to keep trying. "Was I not happier than the many nameless ones who were rotting somewhere? Was it not my duty to live, to fight, to tell about what had happened?" ("Breakdown").

The recent hostilities in the former Yugoslavia have revived public interest in that part of the world. Irene Grünbaum's memoir reveals the complexity of the situation in the Balkans during World War II, the problems of which are relevant to our understanding of current events. Many political analysts refer to the interethnic rivalries of World War II in an attempt to explain the present-day carnage.

In addition to the losses incurred in the resistance and civil war from 1941 to 1945, masses of civilians were slaughtered. Germans massacred tens of thousands in Serbia, the Ustasha killed the Serbian inhabitants in Bosnia and Croatia, and the Serbian Chetniks murdered Muslim civilians in Bosnia and Montenegro. Hungarians butchered Serbs in Vojvodina, and most of the Jews in Yugoslavia were exterminated. Communist Partisans ruthlessly destroyed their opponents in their fight for power and social change. The list goes on. Statistics of these massacres are often manipulated for political gain in the present conflict.[44] For example, the Serbian government and the Serb-run Yugoslavian army have exaggerated the number of Serbs massacred by fascist Croats to justify their war against Croatia.

Serbia has also falsified historical fact to create historical fiction—the myth of Kosovo, for example. The Turks defeated the Serbs and other Slavs in the battle of Kosovo in 1389. Although the medieval battle was real, its modern interpretation is not. The Serbs now regard Kosovo as the cradle of their civilization, representing their five-hundred-year struggle against the Ottoman Turks. For the Serbs, the battle of Kosovo symbolizes Turkish or Muslim oppression, just as the Ustasha atrocities of this century symbolize Croatian oppression. Serbian president Slobodan Milošević has exploited and magnified these conflicts in his campaign against the Muslims and Croats. Often Kosovo is used to foment anti-Albanian sentiment among the Serbs, who are a minority in that province.

Since the demise of the communist party in Albania in 1990 and Macedonia's declaration of sovereignty in 1991, the conflict over Kosovo has riveted new attention on these geographic regions in the southern Balkans. Kosovo, the formerly autonomous province on Macedonia's northwestern border, is witnessing the deteriorating situation of its Albanian majority, which could destabilize the border country of Albania and the republic of Macedonia. The Kosovo Albanians are a repressed group in the Republic of Serbia; they are poor, agrarian, and Muslim, with the highest birthrate in Europe.[45] Sali Berisha, the president of Albania, has asserted his support for ethnic Albanians in Serbia and Macedonia and has publicly warned that Albania will not remain passive if fighting breaks out in Kosovo.[46] The Albanian communities in western Macedonia, in Kosovo, and in Albania proper all have national aspirations; however, Serbia, Greece, and Macedonia are adamantly opposed to Albanian unification. The Serbian forces and the federal army fighting in Croatia and Bosnia and the Serbian suppression of Albanians do not bode well for the future. Many fear that the current conflict could eventually affect all countries with large Albanian populations—Macedonia, Montenegro, Serbia, and Albania.

The Nazi invasion created misery for the people living in the culturally diverse Balkan Peninsula, and this violent suffering has, sadly, reappeared with the collapse of communism. Although Irene Grünbaum does not name specific political parties or Partisans in the chaos of war, she nevertheless narrates a compelling story of how individual Muslims, Christians, and Jews were able to overcome their ethnic hatred and ancient rivalry—and how human compassion can sometimes transcend both.

Serbia and Macedonia

PRELUDE

Brazil, Rio de Janeiro—how I love this country and this city, how deeply I feel that it is home, in spite of everything, in spite of the contradiction of my homelessness. I want to try to describe the events of the last few years, which left me without a country, without a family, without fortune, without anything but my mind and my courage. I want to describe the years of misery, of persecution, of my escape and my rescue. Where shall I begin? Shall I describe how serenely and happily I lived in Belgrade with my husband Bobby? How nice my small home was, how good my marriage was, how I believed that life would continue so forever?

No, it didn't continue forever, it couldn't go on forever, because Hitler had decided the fate of millions of people, including mine, because I'm a Jew, a child of Jewish parents and married to a Jew. How well I remember 23 March 1941. Revolution in Yugoslavia! The people are beside themselves. They are screaming in the streets: *Bolje rat nego pakt*, better a war than a pact with the Germans. They would have it soon. By the morning of 6 April the war had already begun. I couldn't sleep that Saturday night. Fear and panic seized all of us. The brutal surprise attack that followed was worse than we had imagined, and its aftermath was more horrifying than we had dreamed in our most hideous nightmares.[1]

BOBBY

I still remember Bobby buying a backpack on Saturday evening, a nice expensive one with leather trim. It cost 950 dinars, and I was outraged at the expenditure. Bobby was as proud as a schoolboy of his backpack, but he didn't need it. The backpack was left behind because we didn't have time to pack it. On Sunday morning our bad luck began. It began early. We heard the exercise hour, recipes, and folk music on the radio. It was 6:00 A.M. when the first bomb fell on Belgrade.

We sprang out of bed! We did not immediately understand what had happened. Was it a blast? Was it an explosion? Was it one of the many military exercises? We weren't in doubt for long. While the bombs fell in short intervals, we heard the radio announcer say, "Attention! Attention! The enemy is bombing Belgrade! Go to the basement!" We didn't just *go* to the basement: I think we *flew* to the basement, and each new bomb was accompanied by fear and dread. Would we survive it? Was the house falling down on us? Would we become cripples? Never before that time, and never again, have I been so afraid. On that sixth day of April 1941, that day that is so emblazoned in my memory, I was only a creature fearing death. It was the day I lost my home, the day I was in my apartment, the place I had created with love, for the last time. It was 6 April, the day I was thrown into the street, the beginning of my exile.

It was about ten o'clock when we left the house. We wanted to see if Bobby's brother, his wife, and his mother-in-law were still alive. We wanted to go farther and farther away from the bombs. We wanted to get out of Belgrade.

What did the city look like? We saw corpses everywhere. Damaged streetcars were scattered like broken toys, houses were without roofs, and the city was on fire. We ran farther, past the marketplace, where we caught sight of dead women, their baskets containing apples, vegetables, and eggs overturned. And there was blood—there was blood everywhere.

Finally we reached my sister-in-law's house. She was already standing at the door, my poor sister-in-law, who was always so elegant and who always made a point of being a "lady," even under these horrible circumstances. She wore a grotesque-looking hat and carried a suitcase.

We moved faster and faster, wanting to reach the Kasino Kino, where Bobby's brother, the manager, felt "at home." He proudly described the shelter, with its seven concrete slabs covering the basement, as sturdy. We arrived and discovered that the shelter was a bar. There were sofas, recesses, and a counter. Many people were already there. Many had come from the street, and others were already homeless. The bombardment started again soon and lasted until Monday morning. Then suddenly—I don't know how—came the news that the "storm" was over and the "punishment" at an end. There was handshaking and hugging, and then we left the basement to go home alone, without our husbands: they had left in the middle of the night to go to a general meeting.

We didn't get far before we saw the rubble, the corpses, and the unlocked houses and stores, with their goods lying in the street. We were astounded when we heard the bombs once again over our heads, and we ran quickly into the Majestic Hotel. There we found more noise and more moaning, more screaming children, and more wounded dragged from the street than at the Kasino. We lived through another day and night of terror. Around morning I made up my mind to get out of that hell at any cost, even if the bombs hit me on the street. My nerves couldn't take it.

Our friend Alexander huddled near me with his pretty young French wife and his daughter Nadine. "Alex," I said, "we must get out of the city or we'll die. Oh, if only we had a car!" Alex, who was holding his small daughter in his arms, suddenly gave her to me and said, "Wait, I'll see if the garage next-door is open." It *was* open, and the doors and windows of the house had been damaged by a bomb blast. It was three o'clock in the morning when Alex "borrowed" a car from the garage. Shivering, his wife and daughter, my sister-in-law, her mother, and I waited impatiently on the street while Alex worked on the car. Finally it started.

We drove, and what a ride it was! Knez-Mihailova, the main street, was ablaze; dogs and cats gone wild cried and barked in the streets. We didn't see anything—we didn't want to see anything. We only wanted one thing: to get out of the inferno and drive to a nearby village. Floods of people were in the streets that led out of the city. Fearing death, everyone fled Belgrade with horror in their eyes.

We were doing well. We had a "borrowed" car, the odds were on our side, and we were moving forward as fast as we possibly could through the crowd. But we had traveled for perhaps an hour when our car was stopped by a Serbian officer. What could we do? Our vehicle was seized, and we had an exhausted old woman, a small child, and a pregnant woman with us. But we were lucky: the officer had to go to the small town of Kamenica to look for his wife, and he only wanted us to take him there.[1] We were pleased. He sat on my knees because there was no room left in the car. Other passengers, older people whom we had picked up on the way, were riding on the footboards on both sides of the car.

We arrived at Kamenica, and with the help of our officer we found a "room" at the home of a farm woman. Alex left us because he had to go to his commanding officer to place the "borrowed" car at the disposal of the state. We made ourselves at home while our hostess placed straw and horse blankets at our disposal. We were freezing. Before long we had lice and fleas in abundance, and we were starving. The villagers didn't want to sell anything, because they were afraid of starvation, but it didn't matter: we were away from the bombs.

We planned how we would live here and calculated that we would stay a year in Kamenica, perhaps longer. In a year the war would surely be over, and perhaps our "free city" of Belgrade would be peaceful much sooner and we could go home. The center of action could never be in Belgrade, the "free city." At any rate, we were able to go home sooner than expected, because it didn't last a year—only ten days. We set out on our journey back.

Yugoslavia was already occupied by the Germans. Still, none of us understood the implications of this. Occupation of the country? Of course it was horrible, and certainly there would be price increases, economic measures, and forced labor, but our lives were saved. The soldiers went home to their wives, children, and mothers—they had survived.

My sister-in-law had befriended a farmer who had an ox-drawn vehicle. He promised to take us to the train station, where the tracks were still intact, so we climbed into the vehicle, which was not luxurious. Soon Nadine screamed, and her mother complained of pain. We feared a premature birth on a country road. Our elderly aunt cried, and the rest of us sat silently, observing the countryside.

There was much to see: dead, bloated horses and torn, tattered solitary soldiers, often wounded, plodding along. It was the retreating Yugoslavian army.[2] And we saw something else, the entry of the German army: tanks, tanks, tanks, columns of German armor—there was no end to it. We arrived at our train station, but there were no trains. We couldn't go any further because our three unfit passengers, the mother and her daughter and aunt, had gone on strike. They were exhausted and unable to walk. I was sick. I had bloody diarrhea, and when I ran to use the bathroom every two minutes, you could follow my tracks, I was bleeding so horribly.

We weren't the only ones waiting for a train, and the other homeless people weren't any better off. Children bawled and mothers looked for their children; it was chaos. Finally, the next day a train came through that was transporting soldiers back from the front. There was great joy among the soldiers and among ourselves. "Come here, sisters," they called, and they helped us into an animal cart, gave us *rakija* [brandy], which we drank from the bottle, and took Nadine in their arms. They were our friends.

We arrived in Belgrade around noon. The train station was no longer there. We climbed over rubble and stones and came to the street. The first thing we noticed were huge yellow posters hanging on the walls that read, "ALL JEWS ARE REQUIRED TO REPORT TO THE TASMAJDAN ON 19 APRIL AT 7:00 A.M. THOSE WHO DO NOT REGISTER WILL BE SHOT. SIGNED, THE GERMAN COMMANDER'S OFFICE."[3]

I turned pale. It was already noon on 19 April: we would be shot! I knew the Germans. I was born and raised in Germany and had already lost all of my loved ones—my sisters and their husbands and children—to the German concentration camps.[4] "Come back," I urged the others. "Let's run away. It doesn't matter where—back to a village." I couldn't think clearly. Was there escape from the Germans in a village somewhere? My sister-in-law took charge of the situation. "No," she stated flatly, "we can't go back. Let's go to my apartment and decide what we should do. Mother can't go any farther."

We set off with fear in our hearts. The door to my sister-in-law's apartment was wide open. Doors and windows were broken, and trash and furniture had been strewn about by the explosions. I was thirsty and there was no water, so I went to my neighbor and asked her for some. She gave me wine. "There is no water," she said. "The water pipes were destroyed by the bombs." Then she asked, "Why are you here? You're a Jew, and Jews will be shot!"

I dragged myself back to our apartment, incapable of thinking clearly. My sister-in-law decided that we three women should go to the Tasmajdan, leaving her elderly mother and the child at home. We started out on the difficult trip. On the way, we saw Jews who were already returning; they assured us that we need only register.

A crowd of some fourteen thousand Jews stood at the Tasmajdan. The young, the old, the sick, and children were all herded together there like animals, awaiting their fate. Why did no one resist? We got in line with the others. I gripped my sister-in-law's hand and looked to her for protection and strength because she seemed so calm. We waited for hours. It went very slowly. Birds were circling above us, shrieking horribly. They flew so close that we could almost feel them on our heads.

German girls in uniform were standing on the terrace of the office building, amused by the free spectacle. They laughed, made jokes, now and then shouting something to silence the crowd. "Quiet, or we'll have bombs thrown on you, you pack of Jews," and similar statements. Our helplessness pleased them. I was overcome with an intense hatred and would have gladly strangled each one of those girls, each one of those animals hiding behind a uniform. For me there was nothing human, and certainly nothing womanly, about them.

It was at the Tasmajdan that I found Bobby again! My husband's cousin, a small girl, saw me in the crowd and screamed loudly, "Auntie! Auntie Irene! You're still alive? Uncle Bobby has been looking for you for days, and we all thought that you were dead. How happy he'll be! I'll go get him: he's over there."

I wanted to get away from the crowd and elbowed my way through, stepped on people's feet, whereupon they screamed. It was so crowded, and each person was so concerned with himself, that no one had the patience to consider others. Nevertheless, I finally succeeded in getting away from the crowd. I saw Bobby. Was this soldier in a dirty uniform with a gray, unshaven face my husband? "Bobby!" I screamed and rushed toward him. For the first time in my life I fainted. I don't know whether it was from joy, weakness, hunger, or fear. At any rate, someone gave me something to smell and the dizziness went away. Bobby took me outside. "Come," he said. "You'll register tomorrow morning. Not everyone can register today." I was led away without protest.

Big, vacant transport vehicles were parked in front of the entrance. The driver smelled a business deal. "How much do you want for a ride to the Dušanova Ulica?" Bobby asked. The driver demanded an enormous price. "Good," replied Bobby. "Then you'll at least have to take more passengers." In no time the wagon was full of old people, a few pregnant women, and a blind man. We rode through the city, to the amusement of a few drunken soldiers, who screamed, "Look at the Jews! Where are they going?" Even today I can hear the voice of a very young soldier screaming, "Look! They're going to the guillotine like Marie Antoinette! We'll cut off their heads!" A few days later I registered and, like all the other Jews, received a yellow armband bearing the Star of David. We had to wear them so that everyone could identify us from a distance as Jews.

It was the beginning of hard times: Belgrade lay in ruins, there was neither water nor electricity, thousands of corpses were lying under the rubble, and the city stank to high heaven. The Jews were ordered to clean up the city and to remove corpses from the debris. Every morning they went to work, and every evening they returned filthy and exhausted, describing with horror what they had experienced during the day. They mentioned who in the group had been beaten, whose stomach or buttocks had been kicked by the soldiers. Struggling to their feet, they would resume their work, expecting at any moment a bullet in response to a whim of the overseer.

The general population of Belgrade suffered almost as much as the Jews. They helped where they could, visited their old friends, brought bread and flour, and did some shopping. The Jews were only allowed to shop between noon and one o'clock. At this time it was almost impossible to find anything, because the food supply began to run short and the farmers didn't bring anything else into the city. Everyone was afraid of starvation. But even worse was the lack of water. How could one cook? How could one take a bath?

Cleaning the apartment and washing clothes was unthinkable. When Bobby and his brothers came home in the evening, they washed their hands in a lysol solution that we had acquired.

I always shuddered when I went to bed. I smelled the odor of corpses and saw before my eyes scenes recalling what had happened during that day's difficult, wretched labor. I was scared!

Typhus was already in the city. Toilets could no longer be used; instead every family had a pail that they took each morning to a big park, where they emptied it into a lime pit. This lasted three weeks, and there was still no water. I had to go to the Danube to fetch water, standing in line under the watchful eye of the German guards. Once, when I finally got to the front of the line after a long, long wait, a soldier screamed, "Go back Jew! There is no water for Jews!" I turned back, and an old Serbian man who had gotten water before me stopped me and gave me his, while the Germans swore at the ground. "Take it, daughter," he said sympathetically. "God will punish them, the animals."

I had only one thought: to escape. But how? Where? Now women also were being taken to perform forced labor: to clean toilets and military barracks while being cursed at, humiliated, and subjected to every obscenity. Walking on the street meant danger. Young girls and women only left the house when it was absolutely necessary. Worse than the soldiers were the "Swabians," the fifth column of the Yugoslav Germans, who made a sport of harassing old Jews. They would hit them because they were walking on the right side of the street, or because they were walking on the left side. It didn't matter why—the Swabians always found a reason. Our despair was great. Every day there were new regulations, and we lived in fear of the next hour, or the next piece of news. We were like mice in a trap, searching desperately for an exit.

Bobby had a good friend, a Yugoslav named Mr. N., who visited us one day and spoke alone with Bobby for a long time. Mr. N. had a girlfriend who worked in the German commander's office. Two days later we had in our hands two blank travel tickets bearing the stamp of the German commander. I typed them out with the typewriter: "Permission for a round trip to Skopje," I wrote. Bobby's brother Marko lived with his family in Skopje, and we wanted to go there. Skopje is a city in a part of Macedonia that had belonged to Yugoslavia up until this time. But after a victorious land campaign it was awarded to the loyal Axis allies, the Bulgarians.[5]

We made our way to the train station early in the morning accompanied by the tears and good wishes of my sister-in-law and her family, who wouldn't dare risk such a dangerous escape. We separated; Bobby walked down a different street, afraid that [if we were together] someone would stop us and ask us where we were going. We met at the train station but pretended that we didn't know each other. We kept track of each other from a distance.

We weren't wearing the yellow armbands, which would have given us away. Finally it happened. The train arrived and we boarded it. We were alone in our compartment. During the journey our papers were checked. The conductor, a Yugoslav, took the papers in his hand, checked them, looked at our gray, fearful faces, checked the papers again, gave them back, and said, "Have a good journey, and watch out. Near Niš the rails are broken, so you will need to walk a little way. The best thing would be to walk on the left side of the train so that you can transfer more quickly from one train to the next. Besides, it is a better way, much better. Have a good trip, and be quick so you don't miss the connection with the other train."

We understood. We succeeded in getting quickly to the other train without being stopped by someone. Late that night we arrived in Skopje, Macedonia, and breathed a sigh of relief. Were we safe? Had we escaped the monster? I couldn't believe it, I was so afraid. I looked around while Bobby hastily urged me to get out of the street quickly. We looked for our relatives Marko and Viola and hid at their house.[6]

My sister-in-law Viola and her family took us in warmly. There were other refugees there from Belgrade, Viola's sisters and their husbands and children. The city was already full of Jewish refugees from the Serbian capital. The next day we met friends and wished each other well, and two days later we met in the park and had a chat. It was as if we were all relaxing at a spa. Unfortunately, the happiness didn't last long.

The Jewish community in Skopje sent officials from house to house to register the newcomers, and after a few days were politely but very firmly ordered to leave Skopje and return to Belgrade. The Bulgarians gave us no visas. Most of the unlucky ones had no choice but to return to Belgrade. They returned to their deaths. Many years before, Bobby had owned a small shop in Skopje, on which he had paid taxes. Because of this, as well as some money and kind words, we were allowed to become citizens of Skopje and thus to stay. We heaved a sigh of relief.

A relatively calm period began, although there were still all sorts of restrictions for Jews. One wasn't allowed to own a business or work, but one could still help oneself. The women sewed in secret, and the men learned how to make shoes out of straw, thread, and similar products because of the dearth of supplies. It worked, although it was often a bit difficult. One sold this or that to Aryan neighbors and stayed alive.

Viola and I shared the housework. Most of the time I was busy with the two children, seven-year-old Nina and the young, not yet two-year-old Mile, who was my favorite. He was so smart, beautiful, and affectionate, my little Mile. Often we had to spend nights in the basement when the bombs fell over Skopje. We snatched the children from their bed, wrapped blankets around them, and sat for hours, terrified of the attack and worried that the sleepy, whiny children would become ill in the damp basement. At such moments Mile was usually in my arms. I spoke softly to calm him. Fear often paralyzed his tongue, but he neither cried nor talked. He just stared at me with his big blue eyes and pressed close to me. Then I forgot my own fear and felt such love and sympathy for the children that my heart broke. My poor, precious little Mile, whose life was so short. He would never live to remember those terrible nights. He left me with only this memory of him and his small brave heart. I shall never forget him.

In July 1941 a new group of refugees arrived from Belgrade, bringing us novel tales of terror. One hundred twenty Jews had been shot. Horrified, we listened to the details. The men had been ordered to appear again at the Tasmajdan. They had to organize themselves into groups: businessmen, craftsmen, and intellectuals. Armed German soldiers organized and counted every group: one, two, three, four, five—the sixth man had to go out. There weren't enough men to make an even one hundred twenty. Then the voice of a German supervisor boomed: "Men with good handwriting can step forward." Many came forward hoping to be assigned to an easier job in an office instead of strenuous work on the street. No one knew what awaited him.

The rest of the group were sent home. When the men didn't return in the evening, the women made their way to the Tasmajdan with food, blankets, and coats. The wives assumed that their husbands would be transported to perform labor at another place. They certainly *were* transported to another place, a place from which they could never return.

The women, who were still hopeful, demanded that their husbands be released or that the things they had brought be given to them. The guard wouldn't allow it. "They don't need anything else. Take those things home, you Jew wives. Where they're going they won't need any winter coats." The women looked at one another, not yet comprehending what had been said. They began to beg and cry, and only when the machine guns were pointed at them ready to fire did they go home anxious, their hearts full of foreboding.

On the next day came a sad revelation. The "Jewish Commissar," a young German student who had lived with Jewish families in Belgrade for years under a false identity, passing as a Pole, came to the Jewish community to read off the names of those to be shot. The screams of the mothers, sisters, and wives of the innocent victims filled the city. It was too much for the "Jewish Commissar": crying hysterically, he went to one of his earlier "friends," a Dr. M., and begged him to leave the country as quickly as possible. Dr. M. followed his advice, and he is still living with his family in Jerusalem, as far as I know.

Depressed, we pursued our work quietly, and a short time later we were hit a second time. One morning at seven o'clock we saw a Bulgarian secret agent with a list going into Jewish homes. Forty-five men were taken. They spent the day in the police building, and in the evening they set out in the direction of Belgrade, under guard.

We shivered with impatience and waited for signs of life. Never again was anything heard from these men. Only after the war did we learn that they had been shot in Belgrade.[7] The women clung fast to the hope that their husbands were still alive until the very last day, the day of their own agonizing deaths.

I was among the lucky ones. Bobby was with me. All of his brothers except the youngest were with their families. We were almost ashamed of our happiness in the presence of the others who, quiet and pale, sometimes visited us. They barely managed to stay alive. The time passed. We worked, listened to the foreign radio station in secret, politicized, thought the war almost at an end, dreamed of freedom, peace, and happiness. The dreams were beautiful, but unfortunately they weren't realized.

Blockades went up unexpectedly every two to three weeks. The streets of the city would be closed off, which meant that soldiers with machine guns were standing on every corner, ready to shoot. Walking in the street or even looking out the window was forbidden. Most of the time police officers were in civilian clothes and went into this or that house, making arrests among the pro-Serbian populace or communists. They also looked for the Jews' unregistered valuables and confiscated them.

Many things were found, but this stopped, because the Jews became cunning and careful. Those who had a basement or a garden house buried their belongings at night. Others hid their valuables in pictures or in curtains. Each thought that he was cleverer than the next and that his hiding place was more secure.

It was the same with us. I had some jewelry buried in the garden. Vida had some small things hidden in the garden as well as in the basement and other places. It was the last emergency money, with which we hoped to rebuild our lives and livelihood again. In the worst case, if the war lasted longer than expected, we could use it to escape again and again without a destination, like the wandering Jew.

KATJA AND NATASHA

One day I made an acquaintance on the street while I was looking for a room with a girlfriend who had arrived from Belgrade. It was difficult because the Jewish homes were already full. Everyone had friends or relatives living with them. The Yugoslavs weren't renting, because they feared for their own lives and couldn't afford to have such dangerous elements as Jews living with them. One couldn't live with the Bulgarians, because they were enemies.

While looking for a place we heard a young woman on the street speaking German with her child. I turned around and talked to her and asked her if she knew of a room for my girlfriend. She said no and then looked at me for a while, said she was sorry, and walked away. I did not yet realize what this woman would mean to me and what role she would play in my fate.

A few weeks later I met her for the second time at Katja's boutique. Katja was a Bulgarian who had married a Jew and remained faithful to him. She had "connections." She knew people from the police and government and was afraid of nothing. When it suited her, she would pound on the table at police headquarters, scream, and win. Tall, red-headed, with beautiful teeth, Katja was a woman every man liked, and she knew how to use this to her advantage.

I visited her sometimes. It was amusing to chat with her and observe her face, which was so full of life, with its large mouth and wide nose. I especially liked it when she cursed the war and the Germans in a rather inelegant way. We were discussing the sentencing of a very well-known, rich man to six months at hard labor. He was a former mayor acknowledged as a Serbophile.

Then a woman entered. She greeted Katja and then told her something. She was very upset. I didn't understand what it was about. Then she turned around and said to me, "I'm Mrs. Rustenbeg. We've met." I had no idea who she was. When she left, Katja explained that she was the wife of the man who had just been sentenced to hard labor. She wanted Katja to make use of her "connections" in order to set her husband free. Soon after that he was indeed set free.

One day I ran into Mrs. Rustenbeg on the street but didn't recognize her at first. She walked up to me and asked if I would like to come visit her sometime. I went the next day. She lived in the most beautiful house in the center of Skopje, built in the Moorish style with a square tower. She welcomed me with great affection, and I was excited and fascinated by her charm and elegance.

Mrs. Rustenbeg had a large library with books in different languages, which she left at my disposal. I eagerly plunged into them. For the first time in a long while I felt happy, and an unusual friendship began to develop between the two of us. Natasha Rustenbeg was generous and helpful, but I was too proud and too shy, inhibited by my yellow armband. Afraid that I would cause problems for an Aryan friend, I only entered her home when she expressly asked me to.

She understood me without any kind of explanation, and with her inherent tactfulness she wrote short letters almost daily requesting that I help her spend a lonely afternoon. At other times she would invite me over ostensibly to ask me something she had not understood. An old Turkish servant in a fez brought me the invitations, which were often accompanied by small presents such as soap and cotton gauze, things that were difficult to acquire at this time. The servant was my friend, whom I always greeted with a few dinars.

Natasha and I spoke about many things. We spoke about literature, about the war, and about the persecution of the Jews. One time she told me that she had a brother who was living in São Paulo, Brazil. He was called Dr. N. and had been living there for many years with his wife. "You know," she said, "when all else fails we'll go to Brazil. We have relatives there." At this time I had no idea that I would eventually emigrate to Brazil and meet Dr. N. Only in 1947 would I be able to bring him the tragic news about his relatives in Skopje.

During the winter of 1942 not much changed. There were more food shortages, as well as more regulations and laws regarding Jews. There were more frequent blockades, and there was hope that an end to the war was forthcoming. Despite this hope, we feared that it would last longer than we could endure. There were rumors about work camps for Jews, and people said that barracks had been built in the interior of Bulgaria where Jews would be interned until the end of the war.

The news about the camps was confirmed and we began to prepare ourselves for the eventuality that the men would be imprisoned. Those who had money bought warm clothes for the men. We conserved tobacco and canned food when possible so that if the men were confined, they would be well supplied for a few months.

The women were sad. We were afraid of being alone, afraid of the air attacks that would be so much worse if we had to endure them without the protection of our husbands. Then came the spring of 1943. Bobby and I were still lying in bed when we heard the excited voices of my sisters-in-law in the room next to ours. I got up because I wanted to complain about the noise, but when I went into the room and heard why they were all speaking so loudly, I quickly changed my mind. Mathilde, Bobby's sister, had already run errands and come home with some news. "A big, new blockade is being planned," she explained. "This time they're rounding up Jews." A Bulgarian civil servant who had a brother in a key position had told his Jewish wife to warn her. It was not the first time Mathilde had brought home alarming news such as this. We didn't believe her, and scolded her. Everyone's nerves were on edge.[1]

I became pensive and nervous and went out. I wanted to know if there was any more news to confirm what I had heard. I met many friends and spoke with each one, but still no one seemed to know anything about it and everything was as usual.

Monday morning at six o'clock someone knocked at the door. Vida called me. "Irene, here is a little girl who will only speak to you." It was Katja's little seamstress, who looked around shyly and told me quietly that Katja wanted to talk to me and that I should come to see her. "Good," I answered. "I'll come immediately." But first I went to the Turkish bath to treat my cold, and when I returned at 10:00 A.M., Vida was already waiting nervously at the door. "Katja was here! You must go see her immediately. She has to tell you something very important. Hurry up! Go! I'm scared!" She began to cry, then took her children and went inside the house.

When I arrived at Katja's, she wasn't home. Her husband led me into his study and locked the door with a key. "What's the matter?" I asked. "What is this supposed to mean?" He was deathly pale and shaking. "You've got to escape," he said. "They're going to round up the Jews. Don't waste any time: it's happening this week." Horrified, I stared at him. "How do you know this?" I asked. "Katja heard it from a friend who told her in confidence. Leave! Don't ask so many questions! It's true!" How could anyone leave the city or the country? By escaping over the border into Albania? It was occupied by the Italians.

I returned home quickly and told Bobby and Vida what I had heard. Bobby left to get information from other sources, if possible, and Vida ran around, quite upset, packing the children's underwear and clothes into a bundle. We did not tell the others right away because we didn't want to cause a panic. But the terror came soon enough. Suddenly, I saw Jews everywhere on the street, going from one house to another with packages. The people tried to hide their possessions at the homes of good Serbian friends. No one thought of death; everyone believed the stories of "work camps."

Vida went to some good friends to hide the one thing that was more precious to her than anything else in the world, her children. Pleading and wailing, she went to Aryan friends. The women cried with her but would not help. Their fear of the Germans was greater than their compassion for the Jewish mother and her Jewish children.

Finally she found someone, the wife of a Serbian officer who was in a German prison. She wanted to take Nina but not little Mile. "Ninika," said Vida to her little daughter, "you are going to stay a couple of days with Aunt Maria. We have a lot of work to do here at home." The little girl refused. "No," she answered flatly. "I want to sleep at home with you, Mommy. Don't you love me any more?" We tried to change Nina's mind, and suddenly it occurred to me to promise her my wristwatch. "Does the watch really work, and will you really give it to me if I spend two nights at Aunt Maria's?" she asked, full of childish impatience and greed, staring at my wristwatch to make sure it really worked.

"Give me your word of honor that you'll be good, and I'll give you my watch right now." Our deal was finished. She ran off happily into the kitchen to show her treasure to our maid, a young gypsy, and to explain how she had acquired it. The gypsy laughed and said, "Oh, Nina, you're so stupid! Don't you know why you shouldn't sleep at home? Because your mother, your father, your brother Mile, and all of your aunts and uncles are going to be shot by the Germans, or perhaps hanged. That is why you shouldn't stay at home."

We heard a horrible shriek. Ninika lay on the floor beating it with her hands and fists and screamed, "I don't want my Mama to be hanged. I don't want Papa and Mile to be shot. I don't! I don't!" We were speechless. We didn't know how we could console the child. Vida took the girl in her arms and assured her that the gypsy had lied and that she wouldn't have to sleep at Aunt Maria's. "The child is going to stay with me," screamed Vida, almost as upset as her little daughter. "I'm not going to let the child go away. Whatever happens will happen to all of us together!"

Bobby's friends who had already heard the terrifying news came to the house. They wanted to talk Bobby into fleeing over the mountains into Albania. They had procured farmers' clothes and a guide who would show them the way across the border. I implored Bobby to leave, but he hesitated because he didn't want to leave me alone. The guide wouldn't take a woman along because it was too noticeable and too dangerous. That night we shut all the curtains and began to pack, every one of us deliberating escape, without knowing what to do with the children. But we packed anyway, for the uncertainty of our fate left us no peace from one hour to the next.

Early that morning I had gone to visit Natasha, this time without an invitation. I was carrying some clothes and some linens and was afraid of being seen by the Bulgarian agents on the street. Astonished because it was so early, Natasha and Kemal welcomed me. "What has happened to make you visit us at seven o'clock in the morning?" asked Kemal. I began to tell him what I knew. I begged him for help, and for a hideout in one of his Turkish houses, where no one would be looking for Jews. The men and women were separated in the Turkish homes. The women lived in a harem, or a house of women, where a strange man entered only under penalty of death. The husband, the father, or the brothers would refuse entry to a stranger.

Kemal promised to look for a hiding place among his tenants. I stayed with Natasha, fearfully awaiting Kemal's return. Finally he came back, but he hadn't found a hideout. Here again fear of the Germans was greater than sympathy for the Jews. The famous Muslim hospitality for those in need was not to be found. Kemal tried to console me. "Nothing will happen," he said. "It's only a false alarm. Calm yourself." I began to lose patience. "What kind of people are you?" I screamed. "Are you made of stone? Would you allow this shameful injustice? Are you so comfortable and indolent in your hearts that you won't lift a finger when innocent people are rounded up like cattle, carried off, and perhaps murdered? Doesn't anything touch you?" I cried loudly and uninhibitedly. I wanted to go. Natasha held me back. She spoke calmly and reasonably. "Irene," she said, "we really think that nothing will happen. Still, to calm you, you can sleep here in our house tonight. We'll be waiting for you early. But see to it that no one observes you coming here."

I went home to see what news there was and told Bobby about Natasha and Kemal's suggestion. "That's a good idea," he said. "You'll stay there tonight and I'll stay at the house of a friend, a Greek." The Greek lived in the neighborhood. Bobby had always planned to stay at his house in case of a blockade. He would get there by jumping from the roof of our house to the courtyard of the neighbors behind us, because they had promised to help and protect him. Therein lay our peace.

Each of us ran to our Aryan friends because we wanted to hear the news. We also asked for advice, for help, and for a hideout for ourselves and our loved ones. At night I would sleep at Natasha and Kemal's house, and in the mornings I would return home early. I became calmer and more hopeful that nothing terrible would happen. In contrast, Bobby, who was always even-tempered and in a good mood, was now nervous and anxious. He had had a mysterious visitor. One of his friends, a Bulgarian, had visited him, and Vida had observed that he was a German agent. At any rate, I saw Bobby give him money and his watch. What for? Had he gotten some important information? Had the man warned him, confirmed that this time the danger was to be taken seriously, that it wasn't empty rumor?

I don't know. Bobby stayed silent about the conversation, and today I know why. He saw no chance of escape, no way out of the trap, and he didn't want to put us in a worse state of despair than we were already in.

I ran to Katja again. She was beside herself. She wanted to help me as well as the others, and she talked of every possible way out. She suggested that I go to the interior of the country with false documents that she planned to steal from another female worker. But it was too dangerous because I didn't speak Bulgarian. Our only way out was an escape over the border to Albania. But it was easier said than done. Even if we had false documents, even if we had a guide who could lead us over the mountains, we would be arrested before we got out of the city, because the streets were teeming with secret agents.

I made a suggestion: Bobby should disguise himself as an Albanian farmer, and I should disguise myself as a Muslim woman. The predominantly Turkish and Muslim population of Skopje clung to its old ways. The women never went out without wearing a *feredža*. The *feredža* is a three-piece black garment that covers the body, the head, and even the face. No man can see behind the woman's veil, and no man would dare seize a veiled Turkish woman accompanied by a man and ask her for her papers unless he wanted to die quickly.

Katja took to the idea quickly and hastily sewed together a *feredža* for me. We still didn't have any clothes for Bobby, and it was difficult to get some. The farmers in the area wore white handwoven trousers, colorful jackets, and a white fez. At this time, Bobby still wasn't thinking of himself and his escape; rather, he tried to calm Vida, joked and played with the children, and deliberated where to hide. Didn't the basement have a thin wall that one could break through to reach the house next-door? Could the children escape via the roof with his and Marco's help? With me he remained firm. "You can't sleep at home, *duša moja* [my dear]. You have to leave. I can't stand thinking of you staying here." This evening I refused—I wanted to stay at home with my husband. But when he saw that I resisted, he lost his temper for the first time in our ten-year marriage. "Don't you see that you're making things difficult for me?" he screamed. "How can I take care of the children if I'm still worrying about you? How can I let you escape on the roof? Go to Natasha's! You'll help me that way!"

How well I know now what Bobby felt at that time. How well I know that he knew escape was hopeless, that all was lost, and that he wanted to give me the last chance, the very last chance. His love for me was greater than his love for himself, greater than his love for other people, even the children. Could I ever forget him? My husband Bobby? Silently I went to my room to get the *feredža*. Mile ran to me. "Auntie, why are you so sad? Do you want me to kiss you? I love you so much, and Uncle Bobby is mad," he said. I cried. I took the child and kissed him, and wanted to kiss the others I loved, when Bobby started again. "Go! Please go! Don't make a scene: we'll see each other early tomorrow morning. Don't come home too late." I left the house sick at heart. When I got to the street, Bobby called to me from the balcony. "*Duša moja*," he said, "take this picture of your father. There is money taped to the other side. You might need it." He leaned over and kissed me tenderly and lingered on the balcony to wave good-bye. I looked up at him, happy that our little disagreement was over, unaware that this was the last time I would ever see my dear Bobby in this lifetime.

BLOCKADE

The Rustenbeg family greeted me warmly, and it was a nice change. They tried to break the monotony of the evening and attempted, with good intentions, to improve my mood, but it was useless. I soon pleaded exhaustion because I wanted to be alone. These friends meant well, and I was ashamed of showing a sad face. Natasha led me into the small room in which Fräulein Hermine, the governess, usually slept. This room was outside of the apartment and was accessible from the back stairs of the house. She wished me good-night and then left. I went to bed and fell into a restless half-sleep, from which I awoke frightened. I turned on the light, it was one o'clock in the morning. I lay there and listened to the night. I couldn't sleep. What kind of noise was that? Was Alpi, my host's son, sick? I overheard footsteps and whispering quite clearly in the apartment. I was sitting in bed and straining my ears, when I heard someone come up and knock at my door.

I sprang out of bed, my heart racing, and threw the door open. Natasha stood there in her nightgown with a coat over her shoulders. "Come here," she said. "There's a blockade in the city." I had no strength to get dressed. I threw on a housedress Natasha had given me, grabbed her arm, and raced to the window. Blockade! We looked outside into the dark night and soon were able to see Bulgarian soldiers and agents with machine guns stationed on every corner. Kemal, Natasha, and I stood there, stunned. The coming dawn soon enabled us to see more details of this horrible spectacle.[1]

Vehicles of every kind stood before Jewish homes—horse- and ox-drawn carts, milk wagons. In the night the Bulgarians had confiscated any vehicles they could in order to transport the old and the sick. There were no exceptions. What lived and was Jewish, from unborn children to hundred-year-olds, from the blind to cripples drawing their last breath, from idiots to the learned, on this night they were all equal. They were masses of poor people thrown together, all subject to the same fate, contrived by an inhuman mind.

Next-door to Natasha and Kemal lived a Jewish family with a small girl, the playmate of little Alpi. The mother held the child in her arms, and the little girl cried. Natasha, forgetting about the danger, opened the window to throw the little girl a piece of chocolate. Kemal tore me back, closed the window hastily, and tried to calm his wife, who was crying. I didn't weep. I just stood there watching and observing the horrible tragedy. Was it reality? Were all these people standing in the street in the middle of the night with children in their arms real? These old and tired people who remained calm without grumbling or bothering to form a line, these men and women who remained next to their loved ones gravely aware of the pathetic situation—were they part of a play?

No one resisted. No one screamed. No one tried to save himself. No one tried to kill the torturer. What was it that made these thousands surrender completely? I didn't understand it then, and I don't understand it now. I will never understand it. I will only feel it till the day I die.

Now the procession marched past in a slow, ghostlike fashion under a soldier's command. How many did I see march by? As I write this today, I can still see them. I can see my friends. I can see them all with their silent, unforgettable faces and their tired, bowed backs.

The blockade lasted until six o'clock in the evening. We were still standing at the window when the last Jewish inhabitants of Skopje vanished before our very eyes. It was finished. German soldiers marched triumphantly through the streets of Skopje, and slowly the city came alive with curious, sympathetic citizens. They wanted to know what had happened to the homes and possessions of their neighbors. They wished to discuss with their friends the brutality and cruelty of the Germans—the Nazis, who showed no hesitancy about "interning" women and children. No one believed anything worse could happen. The horror stories about the gas ovens in Poland had not reached this tiny Macedonian city.

Kemal also went out. He wanted to reach Bobby. Strangely enough, at this time I didn't think that Bobby could have fallen victim to this demonic power. I trusted his great intelligence, his skill, his ability to get along in every situation, and his optimistic attitude, which he often characterized thus: "If I'm going to hang, I'm convinced that the rope will tear at the last moment." Unfortunately, my poor, dear husband was wrong. The rope didn't come undone because the hangman had tied it well, so well that six million people lost their lives before it finally did break.

Kemal came back without news about Bobby's whereabouts. However, he did tell us what he had seen outside. Everyone on the street had to prove their identity, and those without papers were suspected of being Jews and were incarcerated. Priests' clothes were pulled down, Islamic women's veils were torn off, and one looked and found here and there hapless souls who unfortunately had tried to save themselves by disguise. Posters were hung on the wall warning of severe punishment if the citizens of the city hid Jews in their homes.

What would happen to me? I suggested that I go to the Germans the next morning, but Kemal protested. "No, never! As long as you are in my house I will protect you. Only by force will someone be able to take you away from here. I would never allow it of my own free will and will try everything to save you. Be calm, and we will find a way out of this." At this point I finally started to cry. The tears flowed like a stream, and I lost all my strength. Natasha went with me to my room. No one could even think of sleeping, because we were sensitive to every noise, wondering if someone was coming for me.

The night went by, and the next day we learned where the eight thousand (?) people had been taken. They were in an abandoned factory outside of Skopje, and this was all we knew.[2] The days I spent in Natasha's house were filled with anxiety, especially whenever I heard someone climbing the stairs. I had thoughts of escape and plans for Bobby and me when things in Skopje returned to normal. I still held on to the idea that Bobby would soon appear and come and leave news of what I should do so that we could be together again.

Three days had gone by since the blockade, but still nothing. Every time I heard the front doorbell, I rushed to my room and locked the door. We had devised a knocking signal in case of danger, in which case I would immediately try to escape onto the roof of the house and hide myself in the tower. The tower was high, and I could only reach it with the help of a ladder, and even then only by swinging myself up with great physical effort. In the evening, under the protection of darkness, I tried to do it, and it proved to be difficult. I was unskilled and out of shape.

I was too fat, and it was torture, but still I managed, just as a person who has fallen into water and can't swim desperately manages to stay afloat. When I finally reached the top, I was so exhausted that I lay down on the floor. I would have preferred to stay there and not eat or drink anything, because I only wanted one thing: peace and quiet. I didn't want to constantly worry about staying alive. The resignation to which my friends had succumbed soon came over me. I began to believe that it was useless to try and defend myself and that the best thing I could do would be to present myself to the Germans so I could end this torture and free my friends of the burden and responsibility I was imposing on them. But again it was Kemal, with his strength, patience, goodness, and sense of justice, who kept me from taking these senseless steps.

On the fourth evening someone rang the doorbell, and I waited for the escape signal from Natasha, but she called immediately: "Don't worry, Irene, come out. Katja is here, and she wants to see you." I opened the door quickly, and Katja hugged me and cried. Again and again she thanked God that I was still alive. Kind, loving, brave Katja. If only there had been more people like her then, more of my comrades would still be alive. Katja not only helped me but also warned others and with her own money helped people escape when it was possible. She stood by every one of her friends in word and deed, and fear for her own life did not detract from her humanity.

Despite all Katja's efforts to stop it, a young seamstress who worked for Katja was seized and thrown into a camp. Katja had no peace and tried to find a way to save the girl. When one was as strong-willed as Katja, there was always a way. The little seamstress Berta had an admirer who was also Jewish but, luckily, a Spanish subject. The Spanish consul visited the camp in Skopje days after the blockade in order to energetically seek the release of his subjects, which was granted. Katja searched for the young Spanish Jew, found him, went with the prisoner to the consul, and implored him to conduct a marriage ceremony in the camp. The consul, who was not only an ambassador of Spain but also a person with heart, married the two young people in the camp. Berta was set free, and like many others, she had Katja to thank for her life.[3]

On this particular evening she had news for me. "I've seen Bobby!" she said. I responded happily, excitedly, and quickly. "Where? Where is he?" I asked impatiently. Finally I could see my husband again. How great the blow, how bitter the disappointment when she said: "I saw him in the camp, and he sends his love and implores you to stay strong, to endure, and to do everything in your power to stay free. He begged all of us to help you, and I promised we would."

My vocabulary is too sparse to express how I felt at the time. Today I still think it is a good idea not to reopen old wounds. I was living in Albania when I heard that the camp in Skopje had been cleared out and all the inmates transported to Poland, where only a few months later, in all probability without exception, all suffered a painful death in the gas chambers of Auschwitz.[4]

One morning, six days after the tragic night, Kemal returned unexpectedly soon from a walk outside the city. First he spoke alone with his wife in another room, and then he called me in. "Irene," he said, "we now know finally that Bobby is not free. Your only hope is to go your way alone. You've got to leave the country. You've got to flee over the border into Albania. Are you prepared? There is great risk, but there is no other way."[5]

I was ready for anything and didn't ponder it for a minute. Come what may, it was time to free my friends of the heavy burden that my stay in their home was imposing on them. "Good," said Kemal. "You'll have to go away today. I found a man who can lead you over the mountains to the Albanian border. Get ready. You have to leave around noon."

Natasha brought me a tablecloth to wrap my belongings in. I packed underwear, a few dresses, and, most importantly, a few photos of my loved ones: my parents, Bobby, Vida, the children, and other unforgettable friends. But I couldn't take the bundle with me, because it was too conspicuous and therefore too dangerous to carry on the street. The roads were swarming with secret agents who would gladly capture a Jew to earn a word of praise from their superiors, so I gave my last possessions to my guide's brother, who was supposed to return it to me shortly before I reached the border. However, I never saw him or my belongings again. His wife probably got the dresses and the underwear, and he probably threw away the pictures of my loved ones. I only hope that he didn't find the gold pieces sewn in to the shoulder pads of my coat, the shameless robber.

I left Natasha's house at about noon dressed in a *feredža*. My baggage consisted of a piece of bread and a piece of cheese wrapped in a handkerchief, a comb, and my glasses. The farewell to my friends was difficult. Kemal and Natasha cried, but I was calm. It was the calmness that I would often feel in the face of great danger, a danger that had only two sides: life or death, win all or lose all.

NAFI

We went down the back stairs of the house. Rifat, the servant of the Rusten-beg family, had to accompany me to the place where I was to meet my guide. Our path led us past the homes of many of my friends. The apartments looked strange, with the closed windows and the doors nailed shut. Only a few days earlier I had seen people living there, people who dreamed and hoped, whose children were laughing and playing. But today? It was all so unbelievable, so like a nightmare. I turned my eyes away and walked and walked. My heart was so full of pain that I couldn't, and didn't want to, think. We said nothing to one another on the way; Rifat kept the pace ten feet in front of me, as was the custom in Albania. Even the slightest suspicion could hurt us. Men and women didn't walk together on the street, because the position of a man was so superior to that of a woman that it would have been absolutely beneath his dignity to be seen with her. The woman followed the man submissively and meekly, as a slave follows her master.

Rifat stopped suddenly and pointed to a man who was walking near us without showing the slightest interest in our presence. "Do you see the farmer over there in the white trousers?" he asked me. "Walk behind him, talk, and don't ask any questions. He will show you the way." Then he bowed to me with tears in his eyes and said: "May Allah protect you and in his goodness make your path easier."

My last friend said good-bye, leaving me with my unknown guide and my fate. I felt so lonely, shut off from every human contact, an outlaw. Every person, every living being, was my enemy. Even a dog that barked loudly could mean mortal danger for me. The owner of the hound, be he the mayor of the village or a policeman, could ask me or my guide to show our papers.

My *feredža* protected me from curious glances, but was my guide to be trusted? We had been on the road for three hours, and still the man walking in front of me had not turned around. I continued to follow him in the brightness of the noonday sun, but for how long? My feet hurt, the heels of my shoes were not suited for the rugged and stony highway, dust burned my throat, and fear and pain were in my heart. Finally the man in front of me let me come close to him. This was the first time I could look at his face. He was young, perhaps thirty-five years old, a rakish, sly-looking person with dark eyes and a black mustache above his strong red mouth.

"Remove the veil from your face!" he commanded. "I want to see if you are young or old, white or black. Perhaps you are cross-eyed or you have a lop-sided mouth. Now, why are you hesitating?" Instinctively I held the veil firmly with my hand, but he grabbed the opaque cloth roughly from underneath my chin, pulled it up, and placed it on top of my head. Then he took a step back and observed me with half-closed eyes, as he would have looked at a cow or a horse before deciding on the right deal. "Ah," he said finally, "you are pretty, much prettier than I expected. Your skin is white, and I like you. With you it will be a pleasure to hike over the mountains at night."

I was shocked and pulled the veil down over my face, but the man spoke coarsely and forcefully. "Leave your face unveiled! Didn't you hear me say that I like the way you look? No man will see you on this road except me, and if someone should come by, you still have time to put the veil down again." I obeyed because I felt that in this situation any defiance on my part wouldn't help. We walked side by side, my guide looking at me out of the corner of his eye, and he began to woo me in his own way. "You know," he smiled, "a few days ago I also led two women over the border, a mother and daughter. The mother was too old, and the daughter was as skinny and ugly as a lame cat, so ugly that I still feel ill when I think of them. I can't stand these emaciated goats, and I noticed instantly that you were pretty and plump."

Although his words left no doubt about his true intentions, this man didn't seem like he could be a lecher or a murderer. I had the feeling, rather, that standing in front of me was a big farmer's boy who wanted to have great fun at least once in his life. Trying to turn his thoughts in another direction, I asked: "Do you have the money already?" "What money?" he retorted quickly. "Why, the gold pieces that you will get when you show me the way into Albania." "Yes," he confided, "I kept the ten gold pieces." "Then it's all right," I said. "You'll get the other ten when I'm across the border." "You're going to give me another ten gold pieces?" he asked, surprised. "Me? No, not me,"

I confessed. "I don't have that much money with me. But Kemal Bey, my brother-in-law, will give you the money when you give him a note written by me stating that you brought me safely to my destination."[1]

He was silent for a moment. I watched nervously out of the corner of my eye to see how my words had affected him. It didn't take long. "Why did you say that your brother-in-law will give me the money? Are you related to Kemal Rustenbeg?" "Certainly," I answered. "Didn't you know that Kemal Bey's wife is a foreigner? His wife and I are sisters," I lied for the third time, hoping to make a big impression on him. I wasn't mistaken. Bey was such an important person to the farmers there, a person of such high social and financial standing, that the mere mention of a distant kinship with him gave me the hope of winning the young man's respect.

Becoming more confident, I embellished my story by making a close kinship even closer, and I kept repeating that the ten gold pieces would be his upon delivery of the news of my safe arrival in Albania. It was beginning to get dark, and my companion suggested we rest. We sat on the edge of the country road, and I gave him my little bundle containing bread and cheese. He ate silently, while I held myself up with effort, because I was so exhausted from the unusual physical and mental strain.

My shoes were lying next to me on the edge of the road. I had thought that my feet might hurt less if I took off the thin shoes, but I soon regretted this, because when we got up to walk further, I couldn't get my feet back into the shoes, even with the greatest effort. They were so swollen, it looked as if all the blood in my body had collected there. Nothing helped and I had to carry my shoes. Limping, groaning, and soon bleeding, I dragged myself further.

The path was difficult. It was already so dark that I couldn't see the street in front of me. My guide took my hand and pulled me along behind him. Nevertheless, I stumbled, fell down, and got up again. We had to keep going, for we had no time. We wanted to get to the next village as soon as possible so we could spend the night at his friend's house. It seemed like we had been on the road for a long time, and we still weren't there. Was there no end to this journey?

We had already stopped talking to each other for a while, and I wasn't afraid anymore, because I was too tired to have any thoughts other than about rest-ing. My eyes still hadn't gotten used to the jet-black night, so I didn't see the huts until we were in front of them and my escort was knocking at the door. An old farmer opened it and let us in by the light of a small, primitive oil lamp. I looked around. We were in a tiny hut with a dirt floor, and there was no furniture, not a chair or a bed. I saw two women, an old one and one a little younger, about the same age as the man who opened the door. He spoke Serbian. "Sit down," he said, pointing to the floor, "and take off your veil. You're at home here." Obediently, I took off the black, concealing robe and sat down. Both women and the man carried on a lively conversation with my escort in a foreign tongue while they stood around me and gaped.

One of the women went to a corner and stirred a large kettle that was hanging above an open fire. Then she brought a big wooden bowl and placed it on the floor, and everyone sat around it. Everyone put their hand in the cornmeal mush and helped themselves. I overcame my disgust and ate with the others. Indeed, it was the first time I ate like this but certainly not the last. After the meal the men smoked and conversed excitedly. I thought they were talking about me. "Listen," said my guide in Serbian, "we want to sleep now. You, me, and my cousin will sleep in the next room, and the two other women will stay here." I was horrified. "How dare you talk to me that way!" I screamed anxiously. "Have you forgotten that I am Kemal Bey's sister-in-law? How dare you insult me like this! Is it customary in Albania to offend a guest who seeks refuge in your home? I should sleep with both of you because the women normally stay with strange men in one room? Go to sleep. I will stay here with the two women, as it should be."

The effect of my harsh words was even greater than I had anticipated. "Now, now," said my guide, "you don't have to scream. No one is forcing you to sleep with us if you don't want to. Lie down in the corner. Tomorrow morning you have to be ready because we're leaving early." Both of the men left, and the women lay down on the floor, using dirty rags as a bed. I withdrew into the farthest corner of the small, stuffy room. I didn't sleep a wink. I lay there wide awake, listening carefully to every sound and ready to scream if the men entered, knowing full well how futile it would be. I was seized by fear of rape and murder. But the night went by without incident, and I greeted the dawn with relief and a prayer.

When my escort entered shortly afterward, I welcomed him as an old friend, looking up at him confidently and full of trust, putting my continued protection in his hands. "What is your name?" I asked him. "I have to know the name of the good person who is my companion on this dangerous journey." "Nafi is my name, lady, Nafi, and I'm also called Veseljak, the funny one." I was both amused and consoled when I heard the name of my new friend. Veseljak—could a person who was called "the funny one" be bad? Could he kill a defenseless woman seeking escape? The two women and the other man had awakened, and we set ourselves down around the large wooden bowl and ate cornmeal mush for breakfast, just as at dinner the evening before. Then a guest appeared. He was a small boy around ten years old who hastily uttered something to the two men of the house and then disappeared. What followed was a lively debate in Albanian between my hosts. I understood nothing, but Nafi soon explained what was going on.

In the village, they had already heard that Nafi was here with his "commodity," and they warned him not to go with me to the next village because there was a wedding there and all the rural police were on the streets. The business of smuggling people and wares bloomed in these border towns. Residents attempted to protect the useful and often dangerous *kačak* [smuggler, renegade] just so they could put one over on the unpopular and arrogant rural police and border officials. Nafi was a man who decided quickly. "You stay here," he ordered. "I'll proceed by myself, and around noon the old lady from the next village will lead you to my home."

With a heavy heart I watched him leave. I had no choice—I had to obey. I tried to amuse myself while I waited by massaging my wounded feet. The old woman brought me a bowl of water and looked at my feet with sympathy. When I showed her my shoes and made clear that it was impossible to walk in them, she disappeared and came back with a pair of huge shoes made from straw and twine and a pair of red and yellow striped wool socks. I was delighted to accept this magnificent gift. The young woman had already seized my elegant blue shoes with the high heels and tried in vain to squeeze her large feet into them even though she was unaccustomed to such footwear. Nevertheless, she pointed to herself and to my shoes with a questioning and greedy look on her face, and I quickly nodded my assent. I happily pressed to her chest the splendid shoes that had caused me so much suffering.

Finally the old woman asked me to get up. I put on the veil, but it wasn't enough, and she brought me a large, dingy cloth that looked like a bed sheet, with which I covered myself. She wrapped herself in a similar dirty rag. I stared at her for want of a mirror, and in spite of the tragedy of the hour, I began to laugh. We looked like two ghosts out of a trashy novel, the wise women or apparitions near the cloister wall. Twice along the way we ran into farmers coming from the other direction. Each time my companion turned her head to the side to pull the dirty cloth tighter around her face and quickly held her arm in front of her eyes. I really don't know why she did it, because I couldn't imagine that these men would even think of giving these two grotesque and dirty figures a second look.

Nafi's village wasn't very far, and the house she led me to was nicer and bigger than the one I had slept in the previous night. Nafi greeted me and led me upstairs on a kind of chicken ladder. We were in the parlor, apparently the pride of the house. In the middle of the room I saw a small metal oven and marveled at clean, folded, thick handwoven blankets lying on the floor in the corner. In another corner I saw a large box painted primitively in garish colors. Nafi smiled and led me to the place where I would sleep.

I lay myself down, relieved and exhausted, on the blanket in the corner. Many men, women, and children came in and stood gazing at me in wonder as if I were a white elephant or some other fantastic animal. Nafi sat on the floor next to me, smoked, and explained the different levels of kinship: "She is my sister-in-law, and this one is my sister, that one is my sister's sister-in-law, and this one here is my sister-in-law's daughter." The small, half-naked, red-nosed children introduced themselves individually, and I understood that this one was the son of the niece of the sister-in-law and that one was a grandchild of the sister or aunt.

One young woman observed me curiously. She came up to me, felt my hair, stroked my cheeks, and touched the material of my dress. Nafi screamed at her coarsely, and she retreated, smiling shyly. "Why are you screaming at that woman, Nafi?" I asked him. "She is my wife," he confided ingenuously, "and she is jealous of you because you are pretty." "But why should she be jealous?" I questioned. "She is so young and pretty." "Yes," he acknowledged full of the pride of ownership, "she was the loveliest girl in the village, and I seduced her so that I could marry her. My sister told me how beautiful she was, and once I observed her secretly from the wall of her house." This was a heroic feat that was dangerous for young suitors. If her father or brother had caught him, he probably would have returned from his adventure quite unhealthy, and his family would have had reason for blood revenge.

I looked at the young woman. She had a pretty, fresh face with big, good-natured cow eyes, but she had a very noticeable disability: she limped. "What is wrong with your wife's leg?" I asked curiously. "Was she born with it, or did she fall as a child and injure her leg?" "None of those," he retorted casually. "She has been limping for a year. I shot her in the leg, and even though I took her to a doctor in the city, the damage was irreversible." "Why did you shoot her in the leg?" I asked, shocked. "Well, I called her, and she didn't come immediately, so I shot her so that she would come quickly when I called," he answered modestly with a guiltless expression on his face. Astounded, I gazed at my new friend nicknamed "the funny one" and found nothing amusing in his story.

"Nafi," I said then, "I'm hungry. Could you please get me something to eat? If possible, not cornmeal mush." My stomach had already started to rebel from eating this unusually heavy food. "Yes," he chirped eagerly, "I'll get you an egg." At that time I didn't understand the honor being bestowed on me; eggs, milk, and meat were treasures for the poor farm people. These items were the equivalent of cash and were not consumed thoughtlessly. Such a luxury was allowed only on important holidays. But unfortunately, the ungrateful guest couldn't appreciate the expensive gift.

The egg was fried in about a half-kilo of hot mutton fat, and I vomited after the first bite, to the horror of the family members assembled there. Despite the well-meant encouragement, I didn't want to eat any more of the unusual treat. Finally, Nafi happily ate the rest of the egg while the others watched enviously.

I returned to my corner mentally and physically exhausted and fell asleep. Late in the afternoon I awoke, and I immediately felt that I was being watched. Nafi was sitting next to me on the floor. When I saw his face, I was seized anew with fear. This man was young and hot-blooded, and I was convinced that in spite of his good nature, nothing was a joke for him. His wife's leg was proof of that. I was afraid of being alone with him and of going through the mountains with him at night. It seemed impossible to me. How could I dare fight against this strong and certainly dangerous man?

I was paling under his stare when a wonderful idea passed through my head. "When the war is over, Nafi, you can send your wife to visit me, and I'll show her the big city, and she'll live in my house as a guest," I said. "That is impossible," answered Nafi. "How can my wife visit you? Your husband would see her, and you know that it is forbidden for a woman to show her face to any man except her own." "Yes, you're right," I replied. "It wouldn't work. In my religion too it is forbidden for a strange man to see the wife of another man. If my husband knew that I was here in your house, with you sitting next to me looking at me like a man looks at a woman, he would kill both of us!" I watched him to see if what I said had had any effect. Nafi automatically moved away from me a little.

"Do you believe in God, Nafi?" I questioned. "Of course," he answered, surprised that I would ask. "I'm a Muslim and follow what Allah has commanded." "You see, even I believe in God, Nafi," I retorted, "and I know that *he* sent you to me as my rescuer. Because, you see, Nafi, I don't have a father or a brother, and my natural protector, my husband, is far away. How shall I, weak and useless woman that I am, finish such a difficult journey alone? My protectors are now God the Almighty and you, Nafi. Don't you feel certain that God has chosen you to protect me?"

Nafi sat there quietly with a serious look on his face and stared at me. "Tonight," I continued, "you and I will hike through the mountains together and enter another country. You know that I want to save my life and that God in his mercy has chosen you to show me the right way. If *he* wanted something evil to happen to me, then he would have chosen a bad person and sent him to me, not Veseljak, the funny, the good. I'm so happy that you're with me, Nafi, and I feel that, in spite of all danger, you will get me to my destination safe and sound. Will you promise me that? Will you do all in your power to get me safely to Albania? To please Allah? Promise me this, Nafi," I pressed. "Be my brother, my savior, and leader sent by God for this difficult journey." I spoke to him for a long time about this. Hours passed. Sometimes I begged, and sometimes I threatened that Allah would punish him and his family if he abused a defenseless woman. Finally, Nafi broke his persistent silence; taking the pipe out of his mouth, he said, "Right, sister, you're right. Don't be afraid, nothing bad will happen to you as long as Nafi, the Veseljak, is able to protect you. I give you my word, my *Bess*," he proclaimed fervently.

Relieved, I cried. I knew what it meant when an Albanian gave his *Bess.* The word of honor, or *Bess,* is holy for an Albanian in all circumstances. Nothing can lead him astray, nothing can make him break a promise, once he has given it. Neither danger, nor temptation, nor combat, nor money can make him break his word. He will keep it even if it costs him his life. Nafi looked at me silently, let me cry, and then tried awkwardly and touchingly to console me. "Don't cry, sister, don't be afraid. Nafi is here, and nobody can harm you. What is there to be afraid of? Didn't you say that God sent me as your protector? Whatever happens, even if death threatens us, they will first have to kill me before you die. Please don't cry anymore, dear sister, don't cry." In the absence of a handkerchief, he gave me the veil of my *feredža,* and I swallowed, sniffed, sighed, and dried my eyes. Beaming, Nafi smiled at me.

My guide explained that we wanted to set out late in the evening, in total darkness, and that I should rest now, not think, and keep my strength. I tried to, in vain. In spite of Nafi's protection and promises, as well as his goodness, I was not at peace. Where were my loved ones now? Had they been sent away to do forced labor? Did the children, Mile and Ninka, and all the others at home have enough warm clothes? Did they have enough to eat? Did Bobby have enough money eventually to bribe the guards and buy his freedom? When would I see him again? How could I get in touch with him? These thoughts and a thousand others overwhelmed me, making my fear for my own life seem less important.

Did I feel then the pain that the others still had ahead of them? To have envisioned what would actually happen would have been beyond any normal thought process. Only much much later, in Rome, did I see the pictures of the death camps, the pictures that would put anyone's imagination or idea of horror to shame.

It was late in the night before Nafi told me to put on my *feredža*. He was already dressed and ready. He pointed proudly to his revolver, which he hid under his wide belt; he also carried two hand grenades and a knife. Seeing these things didn't make me feel any better, and this strange, incomprehensible person once again terrified me. "Nafi, why do you need all these weapons?" I asked. "Won't our being armed make things worse if someone catches us?" "Don't worry," he assured me once again, "didn't I give you my *Bess* that I would protect you? Do you know the mountains and their dangers? What else can I do besides shoot if the border patrols catch us. What else can I do besides use my knife if the *kačaks* run into us, and how else can I get rid of wolves if they try to attack?" Defeated by his words but in no way consoled, I remained silent. Border patrols, thieves, wolves—what would happen on this journey?

Nafi's wife and all the other assorted relatives stood there ready for our departure. Each woman hugged me, and the men bowed quietly. An old man, ostensibly the family patriarch, laid his hand on my head and asked Allah's blessing. Then we left. A misty, ice-cold rain started to fall. I couldn't see the path in front of me, so Nafi took me by the hand and pulled me behind him. Softly, softly—we dared not step too firmly or the village dogs and police would hear us.

The path through the city was endless. Finally we were on the country road. I thought that I would be able to breathe easier then, when all of the sudden Nafi broke into a run, pulling me behind him. I gasped, but Nafi didn't slow his pace. Finally he stopped for a second, then ducked and threw himself on the ground, pulling me down with him. We lay at the foot of a mountain. "Lie still," he whispered. "There are often patrols here because the border station isn't far away. We have to get over to the other side of the mountain—that's Albania. We'll wait until the guards leave."

I tried to be calm but couldn't. Wouldn't they hear my heart racing and my loud breathing? Nothing happened—no one came up to us—and slowly the panic subsided. We got up, soaked to the skin and covered in mud from the wet, loose dirt. We were on our way! We climbed up the mountain that stood between me and freedom. How beautiful and how simple it sounds: "we climbed up the mountain." It's possible that *Nafi,* child of the mountains, climbed it. *I* was not accustomed to such physical exertion. I fought it. Sweat poured out of every pore, and I felt like my lungs were going to burst, I was so out of breath. I couldn't see the path in front of me, and Nafi pulled and dragged me. I tripped over stones, fell down. My hands were bleeding, and my feet felt like clumps of lifeless flesh, but I still didn't let myself or Nafi rest. Farther and farther I pushed, and eventually Nafi started to slow down. Fear drove me on. Now and then I snatched up a little snow from the brush to quench my agonizing thirst. The mountain was high, and it went higher and higher. Were we ever going to go down?

Morning was already dawning, and the sky hung heavy and low on the mountains as we arrived at the top. "Look, down there you can see the village. There is Albania and freedom," Nafi exclaimed, pointing his hand toward a gray, foggy area. I didn't see anything, but his words kindled new hope and courage in me.

"Come, Nafi, come quickly, the path can't be far away," I pleaded. "No," he replied, "we should be there in three hours." But still the longed-for descent was not easy. Now that we were no longer climbing, Nafi pulled me along, and I began to slide. I couldn't walk a single step, and slipped on the steep, wet terrain. I hit my head on a rock and was bleeding. Nafi was so upset that he wanted to carry me. But I pulled myself up and we walked, or rather slid, farther. Now I could see the village and happily pointed it out to Nafi. It was quite near us, and we could even hear dogs barking. Nafi didn't share my joy. He put a finger over his mouth and whispered hoarsely in my ear, "Stay very still. We have to wait till the dogs are far away, because they have caught our scent." We squatted down behind a branch, and I held tightly onto Nafi's shoulder. We hardly breathed.

Would luck abandon us now, at the last minute? What would happen if the border patrols noticed us because of the barking dogs and arrested us? Would they send us back? Would they lock us up? The dogs were very close by, running back and forth. We heard their sniffing and panting quite clearly and sat there for a long time. Suddenly I realized how nervous Nafi was getting and saw that he was slowly sliding his hand to the place under his belt where he carried his gun. "Nafi, no! Don't shoot!" I whispered, agitated, trying to hold back his hand. "If they hear the shot we're lost. Nafi, be calm!

Think of your *Bess*." Nafi lowered the hand holding the revolver and impulsively jumped up, pulling me with him. We ran down the slope. I fell, and he dragged me for a short time. Then he pulled me up, put his hand on my back, and we ran further.

Finally we were at the bottom. A hut stood at the foot of the mountain; Nafi pushed open the door with his foot, let me go, wiped the sweat from his brow, and proclaimed, "Now we're safe. This is my friend's home." Totally exhausted, I leaned against the wall. I don't know what happened after that. I'm not sure whether it was sleep or unconsciousness that encircled me with a pleasant darkness. When I opened my eyes, I was confused. The first thing I noticed was a small insect crawling close to my face on the mattress. I watched it with interest for a few seconds. Oh, there were other small insects of this kind. Was it fleas, I wondered, as my fingers became busy scratching. Later I learned more about these creatures and became quite good at distinguishing fleas from lice, having had a lot of experience with them over the years.

The second thing I saw was Nafi's friendly smiling face. He bent over me and exclaimed: "How are you, sister? Do you want something to eat?" He gave me a pot of milk and a big piece of cornmeal bread. I ate and drank greedily. I looked around for the first time, and saw unbelievable filth and became aware of an awful stench. The woman, who came closer to me, was still young, but she was dirty and unkempt. A few half-naked children were standing around her. She was not veiled and spoke coquettishly with Nafi in an unfamiliar language. Turning to me, Nafi said in Serbian: "Look how repulsive she is! But I have to be friendly to her because if she gets angry, she could tell the police that she has unwanted guests in her home." Laughing, he got up, tightened his belt, and walked outside with her.

I had time to think about my situation. Nafi's mission had been to bring me across the border. But now that I was across the border, what next? Tetovo, the nearest city, was three hours away. Kemal Rustenbeg had given me a tiny piece of paper when I left and told me to give it to a Turkish friend who lived in Tetovo. The note, which was in Turkish, read: "Protect what I am sending you and if necessary send farther." Apart from his name, I didn't even know the address of the man I was supposed to find. Should I dare risk going to Tetovo veiled and alone and asking someone on the street for the address of Hussein Effendi's home?[2] I had no choice, and I wanted to get away from this place as fast as I could. The stench, the vermin, and the filth made me nauseous. All of the sudden I got up, ran outside into the fresh air, and vomited. I washed myself at a well behind the house and felt better afterward.

Nafi came back, and I told him my worries. Trustworthy Nafi looked at me and stated simply: "I'll bring you to Tetovo. I'm not going to let you go until I know where you're going to spend the night." Thankful and calm, I put my trust in his guidance and dependability. "Wait a little bit, sister. Rest, and I'll see what is going on in the village," he said, and then he left once again.

He returned over an hour later. "I've got good news for you, sister," he shouted as soon as he walked into the house. I looked at him anxiously. "Come here," he said mysteriously, "Nafi has a surprise for you." Not far from the house stood a farmer's wagon loaded with sacks and pots. Nafi pulled out a big, dirty felt blanket from the sacks, wrapped me up in it, and lifted me up into the wagon. Protected by my *feredža* and wrapped warmly in the blanket, I sat, amorphous, turned toward the back of the vehicle. Nafi walked alongside the horse and carried on a lively conversation with the owner of the wagon. On the way, we ran into policemen on bicycles, Italian soldiers, and farmers. As we entered the city, nobody seemed interested in the totally unsuspicious-looking wagon.

When we arrived in Tetovo, Nafi thanked his friend, and I peeled off the thick, foul-smelling blanket. Then Nafi and I went on our way together. A man in city dress came up and greeted us. "I know him," Nafi whispered consolingly, "he's a *kačak,* a smuggler from Tetovo." The men greeted one another. I stood calmly, a few feet behind Nafi. Then the stranger suddenly spoke to me in Serbian. "Listen, lady," he said, "Nafi tells me that you're a sister-in-law who has to go to the doctor, but I don't believe him. I mean well, and I'm a friend, so don't be afraid to tell me the truth. Yesterday there were people here in Tetovo who had fled from the Germans in Skopje, but they were arrested and sent back there. Two of them had slept in my house, but I still couldn't hide them from the police." He then named two of Bobby's good friends and my heart sank. I believed what he said.

"Thank you, friend, for helping me," I stated. "Lead us to Hussein Effendi's home, because I don't want to stay on the street too long!" The men walked in front of me, and I thought of the fate of the fourteen unlucky ones who were almost safe when an evil star led them to tragedy. Would I meet with the same destiny? When we reached Hussein's house the men stopped, and Nafi said: "Sister, I'm leaving you now, but I have one request. Show this man your face and swear to Allah that I've treated you like a brother."

I pulled up the veil of my *feredža,* turned to the stranger, and said, "God is my witness that I'm telling you the truth. Nafi protected me with all his strength: he carried me when I could no longer walk, he gave me something to eat when I was hungry, he treated me only as the best brother would treat his only sister. I wish with all my heart that God in his goodness will reward him." Crying, I hugged Nafi and kissed him on both cheeks in Albanian fashion, thanking him again and again for his care and great generosity. Nafi stood there smiling and exclaimed to the other man, a bit embarrassed: "Do you see? She kisses me like a sister. I didn't lie!" Then this loyal and unforgettable friend Nafi, the devoted and brave "Veseljak," took leave of me.

Albania

DJEMILA

I stood alone at the entrance of Hussein Effendi's home and knocked. An old man opened a small window in the door and asked something in Albanian. I finally answered that I wished to speak with Hussein Effendi. He looked at me suspiciously, then slipped away, returning with a woman. Then he opened the door and let me enter. The lady spoke a little Serbian, and I explained to her that I absolutely had to speak with the man of the house and that it was important. The woman explained, "My brother is now in Tirana[1] because of an operation and will return in ten days. His wife and I are alone in the house with the servants. What do you want with Hussein Bey? Couldn't I or his wife help you in any way?"

Hesitatingly, I told her what had come to pass in Skopje, described the protection and concealment I had been given in Rustenbeg's house, showed her the message from Kemal on a small piece of paper, and asked for help and shelter until Hussein Effendi's return. The woman scrutinized me carefully while I spoke to her; no detail of my dirty *feredža* or my facial expression escaped her. I could feel her compassion but also her mistrust. She left me standing in the doorway and disappeared, then returned with a younger woman. "Follow me," she said. "First, you need to wash yourself in the back before you can enter the parlor." I followed the two women obediently.

They led me to a small room, and a servant girl brought me a bucket of hot water, whereupon I began to wash away the dirt of the last few days. But after that, of course, I put on the same clothes, because they were the only things I had. The servant girl led me into the parlor, and I could see from the ambience that I was in the home of a well-to-do man. Around the corners lay pretty cushions and pillows, rugs were hung on the walls, and a copper coal brazier sat in the middle of the room. A pleasant warmness encircled me.

A servant girl brought me a bowl of meat and rice, and I sat on the floor to eat, as was the custom in Albania. Each person had a cushion to sit on, and we sat at a round table that stood about twenty centimeters off the ground. We served ourselves from the big bowl with a spoon. Famished, I ate. After the meal, we drank a strong Turkish coffee heated above the coal pan in a large copper pot with a long handle. The woman of the house prepared and served the coffee, and I began once again to tell my sad story.

The women deliberated whether they dare shelter me in their home without the consent of the man of the house. "I'll assume the responsibility for this action," Hussein's sister finally said. "We can't send a homeless woman out into the street. Even my brother's anger can't be worse than the sin I would commit if I didn't take action." So it was decided that I would stay. They offered me one of the mattresses on the floor, and no sooner had I lain down than I fell fast asleep. I slumbered deeply for a long time. When I awoke, it was already dark and they were preparing dinner.

I wanted to get up, but what kept me from doing it? With a cry of pain, I let myself sink back into the mattress. I couldn't get up. All of my joints ached, and I had muscle pain from the great exertion; my feet were swollen and my head was on fire. I pulled myself together with great effort. I couldn't get sick now in addition to everything else. I was causing enough trouble for my hosts as it was.

News of a strange female guest in the home of Hussein Effendi was spreading like wildfire. Already the nosy neighbor women were coming over so they wouldn't miss this unusual diversion. Both of the women of the house had said that I was a relative from Skopje on my way to my husband in Tirana and that I had to stay here for a day or two to rest because I had caught cold on the way. Hungry for a scandal, the friends and acquaintances started to interrogate me.

"What is your name?" asked a woman, and before I could answer, Hussein Effendi's wife interrupted. "Her name is Fatima, Fatima Nova. Her husband works in the ministry in Tirana. She doesn't speak a word of Albanian, but she is a good Muslim and comes from the Serbian-speaking region. My cousin, Ali Nova, fell in love with her when she was a teacher in the girls' school. He is a modern man. He wanted to see his fiancée even though his parents were very much against this modern custom. But as you can see, she even travels alone. Oh well, that's modern youth for you." She chatted and lied many times, and the neighbors delighted in hearing this scandal that had taken place in the very respectable Nova family.

When the last woman had finally left, the three of us deliberated about what should be done with me now. To stay in Tetovo was impossible because the city was too small and too close to the border. It was too dangerous not only for Hussein Effendi's family but also for me. Tirana, the capital, was the only place where I could go underground. But how could I manage it? I didn't own a single document, there was a war going on, the country was occupied by the Italians, it was teeming with suspicious individuals, and travelers could be subjected to a rigorous search. There were no trains in Albania; one traveled by car, bus, horse, or on foot, according to one's class and resources.

As much as I wanted to take the trip, I absolutely had to obtain the proper travel documents. Nafi, who certainly would have been able to give me good advice, was not there. Djemila, Hussein Effendi's wife, reminded her sister-in-law that her nephew, the young Hassan, would probably have to travel to Tirana in the next few days with his ten-year-old sister. Hassan was from the capital but as a postal worker had been transferred to Tetovo. His little sister had spent her vacation with her aunt and now had to return to her mother in Tirana.

Djemila's sister-in-law questioned what he could do for me. "At least he is a man and knows the laws and how to travel better than we women," argued Djemila. "Let's get in touch with him and ask him to give us some advice." The servant was sent to fetch Hassan Effendi, and soon the handsome young man of perhaps twenty years arrived. Hassan spoke Serbian well. He felt honored and was flattered that his aunts would ask him for advice in such an important and delicate matter. He exclaimed boastfully that with all his connections, taking me to Tirana with him would be child's play. Quite interested, I asked him what kind of connections he had. "Oh, I know a lot of influential people in the ministry in Tirana," he chirped, "and if you were arrested, it would be very easy for me to get you out. You can certainly risk traveling with me without documents. I'll be leaving here in a few days."

My confidence in his connections was not very high. "Then you don't know anyone here in Tetovo who could help me?" I asked. "Perhaps someone from the police or the town council, or any other public authority?" "Yes, I do know someone who works with the local government," he hesitated. "We were schoolmates, but over the years we've gone our separate ways. We don't have the same political views. He is stupid: he thinks that the Russians can save the world," he stated thoughtfully, "but everyone knows that the Axis powers are going to win."

"Please, let me talk to him," I pleaded. "Call him, Hassan Effendi. Maybe he can help me." I saw a sudden glimmer of hope. It wasn't easy to convince Hassan to introduce me to a former school friend who, according to him, had no connections and knew neither an Italian nor an Albanian of great importance. Finally he gave in to my pressure and promised to look for the young man that evening and, if possible, to bring him to his aunts' house. The two women became very agitated. What would Hussein Effendi say when he returned and discovered that a strange man had been in the house? What would the servants think?

In this situation, Hussein Effendi's sister won the argument once again: "Hassan is our nephew," she said, "and both of us will stay in the room and remain veiled when the stranger comes with him. I'll take sole responsibility for this as well," she added bravely. Hassan arrived around an hour later with his friend, a short, shy young man. What could this unimpressive, quiet man do here? Hassan was right: this person definitely did not have any "connections."

I sighed and looked at him. I saw a pair of warm intelligent eyes that immediately touched my heart. When he spoke, I realized that the bashful man could articulate, and more importantly, he was able and willing to help me! He told me to remain calm and wait. He would talk the matter over with a friend of his who was absolutely trustworthy. He was convinced that this person would help me. "Now put on your *feredža!* You'll have to walk a short way with me, and you'll be back here in half an hour," he said politely. I forgot my aches and pains and went out with the young man, while the others waited, full of hope and curiosity. My new acquaintance led me to a photographer and let him take six pictures of his "aunt," who wanted to go to Tirana.

The following day he returned with an identity card and picture but no name. We decided that I should take the name Fatima Nova, the one that Djemila had so impulsively chosen for me the day before. The card was authorized on the same day with every possible stamp and signature. I was no longer a suspicious, outlawed individual. I was now categorized as a registered and entirely respectable person, or so I thought. Luckily, I had no idea that my identity card was not registered. But at that moment it probably wouldn't have made much difference to me. I was happy to be Fatima Nova, born in Tetovo, the daughter of Suleiman Fekri and the wife of Ali Nova. Who at this point would dare bother me? Unfortunately, I never learned the name of my helpful friend. He was one of the many unacknowledged people who expected no reward but helped when it was needed without making a big fuss. If he should ever read this book, then he should know at least that his quick assistance saved my life at one point. I went by the name of Fatima Nova until 1945.

I had been in the Hussein home for two days and now felt rested. I had gathered new strength and conversed with the neighbors, giving them new information about each member of the Nova family, defending the modern Muslim youth, inventing reasons why I traveled alone and why I didn't have any children. Other than that, I waited impatiently for my departure to Tirana, which was supposed to take place a few days later. But we left the next day, unexpectedly.

The reasons were urgent enough: in the afternoon, Djemila and her sister-in-law had a visit from a woman who was not veiled. She spoke Serbian and after a very formal introduction turned to me instead of to the women of the house and said: "What I have to say now concerns you above all. I hope that you have enough sense to advise these two women, and particularly their nephew Hassan, to reach an amicable agreement with me. I have found out that Hassan's request to go to Tirana will be granted and that he wants to travel there with you in the next few days. He has already packed his bags in the utmost secrecy, the cad! He really thinks that he can disappear from Tetovo without a word. Even if we are Catholic, this is hardly a good reason for not marrying my daughter, especially since all of Tetovo knows that he took a walk alone with you last night. No! He's going to marry her. And if he refuses, then the distinguished family of Hussein Effendi will have to pay for it handsomely. I'll send the police to this house so they can get a good look at this guest of the ladies, this teacher from Skopje, the wife of Ali Nova." And she screamed mockingly, "No, you can't fool me! This woman is no teacher and is not Frau Nova. She's one of these damn Jews who suck our blood! She's one of the beasts who has to be exterminated! The Germans will finish you off, finish off the subhumans who nailed our savior to the cross!"

The two Muslim women sat there deeply shocked and stared at the woman whose mouth emitted such filth. She continued to swear obscenely at Hussein, at all Muslim families, at Jews, at men, and at the entire world. They didn't understand everything the woman was carping about. It was better that way. It was probably the first time in their sheltered lives that these two well-bred, modest women had stood in the presence of such a torrent of hate and vulgarity. I was better able to cope with this kind of situation.

At least I tried very calmly to convince the woman that it would be better to discuss this matter with Hassan himself and that, by the way, her story didn't concern me. Regarding her threat to go to the police, she could be my guest and go there, because she was making a big mistake about me: I wasn't one of those damn Jews. The fact was that I was Fatima Nova. My husband, a high government official in Tirana, would sue her for slander. I advised her to choose her words and actions more prudently. Finally she left.

Distraught and afraid, we all considered what should be done. Enough was evident: I had to leave their home, not only for my safety but also for the safety of my well-intentioned but inexperienced hostesses, who had never had to fight for their lives. I, the Jew, knew how to save my skin and had it in my blood from many generations back: shrewdness, diplomacy, quick thinking and decision making were the weapons my ancestors had handed down to me. But even the quickest decision making didn't help me much in my present situation. I knew no one in Tetovo who could house me secretly until I left for Tirana.

Hassan's two aunts called for him and, crying, reproached him for his sins.

He listened unrepentantly, but fearing a scandal, he suggested that we leave Tetovo as soon as possible. He ran home nervously, packed his suitcase, and rented a car, which would be waiting for us at five o'clock the next morning outside the city. Hassan, his sister, and I were going to spend that night at the house of a friend who didn't live far from where we were supposed to meet the car. I said good-bye to the two women and thanked them and then left the house with Hassan under cover of darkness.

We spent a restless night in the small room of a young man. The two youths entertained themselves with card games, and Hassan's little sister and I stretched out on the small bed in our street clothes. She slept quietly and sweetly, whereas I was full of anxiety, thinking about the next day. Early in the morning we washed ourselves out of necessity, with Hassan rushing us. His guilty conscience was written on his face, and he wanted to get out of town as quickly as possible.

I ruminated about how strange life was. As many reasons for escaping as there were, I smiled when I thought of the tragicomic situation. Essentially this was a religious struggle between Muslims and Catholics and Jews. Each felt hate and contempt for the other, and the results of these feelings were infamy, war, persecution, and death!

TIRANA

We traveled to Tirana without further incident. Hassan showed his request for a transfer to Tirana and said that I was his aunt, who was traveling with him and his little sister. We said almost nothing on the trip so as not to make the driver suspicious.

Once we were in Tirana, Hassan led me to his mother's house and explained my predicament to her. She took me in without further ado, made some fresh coffee, and often shook her head in disbelief as she listened to my story, which Hassan translated into Albanian. She was a widow and lived in a tiny, modest house just outside the city. It had one bedroom and a kitchen, with running water in the courtyard, and was surrounded by a high wall. His mother pulled four cushions from a closet and laid them next to each other on the floor. We lay down and went to sleep.

Very early the next morning someone knocked at the door. Hassan opened the door to find two Jewish men from Skopje who had heard of the arrival of a stranger in town. Despite our caution, the distrustful driver had told these two men, whom he knew, that it looked like one of their compatriots was in the city. After they gave him some money, he showed them where I was. The two men were rich businessmen from Skopje, good friends of Bobby's who had "emigrated" to Albania long before the blockade had taken place. When I saw them, I jumped up happily. Finally I could talk with people I knew, people who could give me advice and help.

"Where is Bobby?" I asked impatiently. "Where are Marko, Vida and all the others?" I told them what had happened to me, what a horrible fate had befallen the Jews in Skopje, and also that my loved ones had not escaped the ghastly events. "What shall I do?" I inquired. "I've been saved by the grace of God, and I'm alone here in Tirana without money, without shoes, without even a coat. Everything that I own, I'm wearing now." They stared at me, embarrassed. "Yes," replied one, "it's difficult to give you advice. The best thing would be to register yourself at an internment camp. What can you do here alone without money?" Quickly the other one interjected, "We also have financial problems, and we can't help you!"

I was overcome with rage, and the blood rushed to my head. But just as I was about to blurt out angry words, I was overcome with another emotion. All of a sudden I began to cry. My anger blew over, and I was full of shame for the two men. It was a great disappointment to me, because I had expected help from these people who could not help me for a good reason. I had expected them to react with their hearts, but instead they had reacted with their heads, thinking only of money and their fear of poverty. It was in those moments that I first fully realized how totally alone I was—alone with my thoughts, my decisions, and actions. I was all alone, without Bobby.

I had been living with Hassan's mother for a few days, and I began to reproach myself for it. The room was too small for the family as it was; at night we slept on the floor right next to one another, like sardines packed in a can. I couldn't expect this poor woman to feed yet another mouth. The situation was becoming unbearable. Rifat, a young relative, was also sleeping there. He always showed up at night, when it was dark, because he too was seeking refuge. He was a communist, and the police were on his trail. His wife, who had already fled, was fighting in the mountains with the partisans against the Italians. In a few days Rifat was supposed to join her. Highly intelligent, he came from a rich and respectable family in Tirana, had studied in Belgrade, and spoke an almost flawless Serbian. He was fascinating to talk to, but his presence didn't minimize the danger for any of us.

Full of impatience and anxiety, we waited for him every night. When he finally did show up, we knew that another day was over in which nothing bad had happened, another day of liberty. Would there be no end to this madness? When would people live peacefully again? When would they go to work and spend the evenings with their loved ones? When would one person stop hunting down another? When would this game of hide-and-seek with death come to an end?

One evening Rifat didn't return. What had happened? Had he been arrested? Had he escaped? Had he been able to get away to his comrades? The doubt tormented us, but it was impossible to make any inquiries. We had no choice but to wait and hope and pray that he had saved himself. The next day Hassan's mother told me that there was a small bedroom nearby owned by a single woman that could be rented relatively inexpensively. I moved into it. My good friend had given me a straw sack, a small washbowl, and two empty boxes as a farewell gift. In spite of the language barrier, we had gotten along quite well.

"Fatima, Fatima," screamed my new hostess the entire day, "help me pull some water from the well!" She would use gestures to tell me what she wanted. "Start the fire," she would say, blowing with her cheeks full of air. She wanted me to understand from her extreme gestures that she was old and frail and that I was young and strong.

So I had had enough to keep me busy, but it didn't help me to buy bread. Of course, I couldn't even think of buying shoes or a coat, which I so desperately needed in the ice-cold rain. I racked my brain to think of something I could do. I spoke no Albanian and had false papers and no money. Would someone give me a job just because of my honest face? Who could I turn to? There weren't any factories here, and being a salesgirl was impossible. Working as a maid was a possibility, but where and how could one find such a position?

I often lay awake for hours at night thinking about even greater worries than job opportunities. I had other lodgers in my room. Fleas, bedbugs, and other parasites didn't upset me anymore, but there were rats! At first I just heard their rustling. In the thin ceiling over my head, they ran back and forth. I tried to convince myself that it was only cats playing, but soon they were running around in my room, jumping powerfully over my bed while I lay there almost paralyzed with fear.

When I complained to my hostess about my problems, she just smiled at me, meaning that she too had rats in her room and I shouldn't be afraid of them. But her encouragement was in vain; even today I am afraid of and repulsed by the hideous creatures. I'm ashamed to admit that I tried to escape the rats more often than they did me. I visited Hassan's mother almost every day. Friendly and generous, she always fed me. I always had to "try" something, whether it was soup, a cornmeal mush, or, sometimes, even a piece of meat, whatever she could afford on her small income. She certainly had to do without to feed me, but she did it in such a way as not to make me feel ashamed. On one of these visits I met a lady who was dressed in European clothes and, wonder of wonders, spoke French!

Sukriye Hanim[1] was the wife of a well-to-do Turkish industrialist and lived with her spouse in the Daiti, Tirana's elegant Italian hotel. She had known Hassan's mother since she was a young girl and was now making a friendly visit. No sooner had she learned of my situation than she promised me that she would do everything in her power to help me. Two days later she had good news: she had found me a position as a baby-sitter in a distinguished Turkish home. My responsibility was a pretty, fat, well-cared-for baby, and my job consisted in just being there. When the mother needed help bathing the child, I would hand her the soap, hold the towel, and give her the talcum powder. No other work was required. I couldn't even sit alone with the baby, because the mother wouldn't move a foot away from the child.

The father was an old gentleman of about seventy, and his wife was twenty-seven years old, plump, beautiful, uneducated, and uncomplicated. The husband insisted that his wife be with the child all the time and would not allow either of us to walk past the garden gate alone. He refused invitations and announced guests with the excuse that his wife wasn't feeling well that day, or that the baby was teething, or that he had a headache. So the mother and I were bored together. Even listening to the radio was forbidden by the tyrant; only when he approved could we listen to the news, something that interested me greatly.

At any rate, I was thankful that I had a roof over my head and didn't have to worry about getting enough to eat or drink. This bliss lasted for two months. Then the family moved back to Ankara, and I was on the street again. By this time, however, I had some money and could move into a better room, but a new period of hunger began. I bought enough bread and peppers so I wouldn't go hungry, but the final result was the slender figure I had been struggling in vain to achieve for the past twenty years. I had lost eighteen kilos!

My new hosts were pleasant. The wife was Yugoslav, and both she and her husband spoke Serbian. I also met some neighbors who were very interesting to me: an Albanian engineer, Gafur Brangu, and his wife Frau Frieda, a Czech Jew. In spite of his Jewish wife, Gafur was pro-German, and in the evening we would sit together on the dark patio and discuss the possibility of an invasion by the Allies. I was full of hope, my hosts were full of doubt, and Gafur Brangu was confident that the Axis powers would soon win the war.

In the meantime, the war raged on throughout the world. Cities were bombed and railroads mined, munition depots exploded into the air, people were killed, and no one knew whether he would live through the next day. The small wars of opposing parties were bathed in blood. Albania had enough of those. The king's loyalists, partisans, conservatives, and communists fought one another. Even the partisans couldn't agree with each other. But on one matter everyone agreed: they wanted the Italians out of the country, they wanted to govern their country freely and independently, and they hated their oppressors with a profound passion.[2]

The Italians were well aware of this hatred because the partisans constantly waged battles and surprise attacks against the Italian soldiers. The Italians would avenge themselves by continually implementing new regulations and laws, which usually were not obeyed. The newest of these regulations threatened with a large fine any resident who let unregistered persons live in his home. This made things worse for me. My hosts insisted that I register myself immediately or pack my bags as quickly as possible. Both the first and the second option were crushing blows for me. Once again I had sleepless nights, and I was at my wit's end.

Then I got a lucky break. One day I ran into an acquaintance from Belgrade on the street. Engineer Asriel was interned with his family in Cavaia and told me that the Jews there lived well and peacefully under the Italian occupation. On this day, for example, he had obtained a special pass to travel to Tirana to buy something. I quickly thought of a plan. "Could you take me back with you and let me pose as your wife?" I asked, promptly explaining my latest troubles to him. "We can try," he answered, "if you're ready right now. The bus leaves at three o'clock." My bag was always packed and ready. It contained a raincoat, a toothbrush, a comb, and soap. Soon we were on our way.

CAVAIA

We arrived safely. In this small village I met many old friends from Belgrade, each happy to find the other alive.[1] For the time being I lived with the Asriel family in the "red house." Five families had rented it, and each had one small room to itself; there was only one kitchen. I slept on the floor, covered with my greatest treasure, my raincoat. Old newspapers functioned as both mattress and pillow. After three days I was "exchanged," whereupon the pattern was repeated and I slept in another room. I went happily from one family to the next until I had stayed with all five. Then the impulse for independence stirred me to search for a room, and I ended up in the "white house."

Things there were loud and merry. With the exception of a young married couple who had a small child, only very young men lived there, the oldest being twenty-two. The whole day was devoted to making noise, screaming, singing, chopping wood, and cleaning the stairs, and in the evening there were reports. Everyone was helpful. One loaned me a stinking horse blanket, and another filled an old sack with straw for me to sleep on. I lived like a princess!

My nutrition had also changed. I didn't eat bread and green peppers here, because they had much better fare: fresh, sweet figs. They were cheaper than everything else, and I stuffed myself as if I were eating all the figs of a lifetime at once. Unfortunately, my stomach rebelled against this wonderful, cheap fruit, and the consequence was that I lost five more kilos. Now I looked like a skeleton; there was no trace of my former fullness. But this didn't bother me, because life here was so peaceful. I had so much time that whenever I felt weak I could lie down on my straw sack and sleep. Nothing disturbed me, neither children's screams nor singing.

The people of Cavaia slowly got used to the peculiar foreigners. They looked on in amazement as men helped their wives carry water across the street. The men were usually with their own spouses, but sometimes they even took walks with other women on the dirt road. These male foreigners helped with the housework and even washed clothes and floors. It was just unbelievable! The veiled Muslim women regarded their sisters with much distrust, but the Muslim men stared at the foreign women with great interest and goodwill, provided, of course, that they were young and beautiful.

One night a young single woman was taken away forcibly by a young man who fancied her. Nobody got very excited about it, because Frau Erna's reputation had long been disreputable. But it was a different story when an old, respectable, and very wealthy townsman went to a Jewish home and told a couple in confidence that the Italians wanted to hand the Jews over to the Germans and then immediately asked for the hand of their barely fifteen-year-old daughter Miriam to "save" her. The parents of the young girl could do nothing but say no. They said that their daughter was too young to get married and that the suitor was too old for her. They didn't dare say that it was blackmail, although they suspected that it was. How were they to know?

That night the Jews of Cavaia were carried off, or at least that was the story that went around like wildfire. An hour later the first pessimists were already on their way to save themselves. Some fled to the next village, and others hid in a nearby forest, whereas the optimists wanted to wait till the next morning to see what news awaited them. Anyway, I don't believe that even the bravest among us slept very well that night.

It turned out to be a false alarm. Miriam wasn't allowed to go out of the house, and her excited mother calmed down a bit. But the incident had other consequences. Solitary women whose husbands were in concentration camps began to befriend men whose wives and children had been taken away. A considerable demoralization began. There were women who began to do "housekeeping" for a few young men; brother-in-law and sister-in-law began to live in the same room with one straw mattress, the one wanting the warmth, protection, and advice of the other. The feeling of loneliness was worse than ever. Around this time I was offered a position as housekeeper for two brothers, a doctor and an attorney, and many were astounded that I didn't take the offer gleefully. I preferred loneliness. I was waiting for Bobby. The war had to end sometime. One day the people would return from the work camps. Perhaps they would be sick, weak, and in need of physical and spiritual help. Wasn't it my duty? It was nothing to be proud of, to wait for Bobby. But at least I would be able to look him in the eye.

It was not always easy for me. Life was so difficult, and I understood the other women who wanted to capture a moment of happiness in their miserable lives. Today was today. In those times who could think about tomorrow? And still good things blossomed from the unions. I knew many women who had found a father for their already orphaned children, others became good companions and mothers for children whom they had not brought into the world, and still others had become true marriage partners, because their suffering and fear had united them for the rest of their lives.

In the "red house" they were diligently working on a list of all the Jews in Cavaia, and I was writing all the names down. A request was supposed to be sent to the Pope. Perhaps he would have pity on the handful of people here in Cavaia and we would be "transferred" to Italy. Maybe we could stay in the Vatican and wait there until the end of the war. These and other audacious dreams and plans made the time go by more quickly and fanned the flame of our faint hope. An inhabitant of the "red house" went to Albanian friends daily and heard the latest news of the Allies behind tightly locked doors. He made short notes of the most important events in order to relate them later to an anxious audience.

So one day we heard that in Greece another transport of Jews had left for Poland, and indeed a few days later four Greek Jews arrived in Cavaia—a married couple, a young girl, and a man.[2] They registered with us in the "red house" in order to be put on the "Pope's list." I wrote down the names of Ernst Alger, his wife Katarina, Hilde Luft, and Egon Kreiser. Herr Alger told us that he was able to save himself and the others only with great effort and the help of his purely Aryan German wife. He said that Egon Kreiser was a chauffeur by profession and had brought them out of the country by car.

However, soon there were surprising and interesting rumors going around the little town. At first it only seemed like a plot of a complicated love story: Egon was Hilde's fiancé, but it appeared that Herr Alger could boast of being Hilde's lover. So the neighbors had a nice diversion. The scenes between Frau Katarina and her spouse were loud enough to add substance to the amusement. Because there was neither a theater nor a movie house in Cavaia, the arguments became a source of merriment for the ones not involved. But not for Herr Alger.

After a violent fight between these two men interested in one woman, Egon Kreiser told the following pretty story, under the seal of secrecy, to anyone who wanted to hear it. He, Hilde, and Ernst Alger had actually been in a Greek camp together. Through negotiations by his wife (Katarina), Alger became a kind of "senior soldier" of the camp and was an intermediary between the prisoners and their supervisors, the German guards. Then began the filthiest business that the vilest scoundrel could ever think up: the betrayal and sale of pathetic creatures who had long ago been betrayed and sold. They were the poor souls who waited in Greece for the deadly transport to Poland.

The German guards needed money. Alger knew what to do. An evil plan was devised, and for his collaboration they promised Herr Alger his freedom, along with freedom for his girlfriend Hilde and Egon Kreiser, if it proved successful. It is very difficult for me to write down this story, but this book shall conform to the truth even if, God forbid, it might give rise to anti-Semitism once again. Alger went to a well-known rich man and told him in confidence that his relations with the Germans were such that he could set one or another unlucky person free and help him flee to a foreign country. But the Germans demanded an enormous sum for such a job. The poor, tortured individual promised to pay everything as soon as he was set free, but Herr Alger insisted on payment in advance. "Tell me where you have hidden your money and your valuables, and I will show you that I can set you free within twenty-four hours," he promised. The man accepted all the conditions, thinking that he had nothing to lose, that perhaps he could pay dearly for his own life as well as those of his loved ones.

With a document from his victim, Alger procured the money and told the Germans. As a matter of fact, the Jew was led out of the camp the next day. It looked as if endless horizons were opening up for a new kind of business. The game was played more and more often, and now the poorest came to Alger and offered him their last shirt, but Herr Alger was unyielding. He didn't need any shirts; he needed money, gold, and jewels—that was the price. Those who had it paid it. Again and again people were secretly led out the big iron gate at night. What happened to them? Egon said that they were led to another camp. Who had seen them?

The Germans kept their word. A day before the transport to Poland, Ernst Alger, Hilde Luft, and Egon Kreiser were set free. They unfortunately "escaped" to Albania, to the shame of our poor tortured people, to the shame of humanity, and in case they had these kinds of emotions, to the shame of themselves. We never had time to find out more about Alger and his friends.[3]

On 5 September 1943 our small community was thrown into panic once again. Italy had capitulated![4] At first we didn't believe it, and listened to the distressful news skeptically. But three days later we were panic-stricken and terrified when we heard that the first Italians from the nearby port in Durazzo had fled by night and fog to Bari and that the Germans had begun to occupy Albania. Wild confusion began. People sought escape everywhere and anywhere. The clever and cautious knew farmers in the next village or the village after that and tried as quickly as possible to secure their help. Each person concealed from the others where he intended to go. One couldn't worry about saving the others, because no one knew if he would be able to save himself.

Strangely enough, this time things were the most placid in the "white house." Ruben, one of the young guys, stood at the top of the steps and called out in a loud voice, "Brothers and sisters, don't lose heart, we won't fall into the hands of the Germans. Enough innocent victims have surrendered without a fight. I have connections with the partisans, and today they will come down from the mountains and show us where to go. Remain calm, and those who have something to pack, bring your things here to the hall. Take only the most important articles—don't burden yourselves with old straw sacks. Pack your clothes. Don't be afraid. We will fight, and we will win!" A deathly silence reigned as he spoke. Then an excited murmur rose, as more and more people continued to gather inside the "white house" during the speech. People exchanged ideas: what would happen to the children, to the older ones, to the pregnant women?

But Ruben reassured us even about that. "Children, the old, and the sick will hide out in the partisan villages. Decide among yourselves who wants to go with me. Those who do should meet me here in a half-hour in the 'white house.' To the others, may God be with you, as well as with us!" A few old people murmured "Amen." The room emptied quickly, but only a few minutes later it was full again. Almost all of the people had decided to flee across the mountains. Ruben tried to organize everyone. Families stood together, young men and women were on one side, and the old and sick sat on the steps. Those who had bundles or knapsacks sat on them. It was a sad group that gathered there: the faces were pale and thin; mothers' eyes were red from tears. The young men were tough and defiant, and the older people were resigned to their fate.

I stood near the door. I didn't have anything to carry. I was wearing everything I owned. Then Bella, my young neighbor, came up to me with her not yet three-year-old son. "Farewell, Irene," she told me, "May God protect you." I looked at her, astounded. "Why are you saying good-bye to me?" I asked. "Where are you going? Aren't you going into the mountains with the rest of us?"

"No," she replied. "I can't. My little Bernie is sick. He is coughing, and I'll kill him if I don't take better care of him. I'm going to Tirana; one can always find a hiding place there. The Albanian baker is driving there, and he promised to be here in a few minutes. He has become attached to Bernie, and he's going to take me to his mother." She hugged me and then walked toward the road holding her small son's hand. I watched her. The baker was already there in his truck. The child ran happily toward him. "Drive the truck, drive the truck!" he crowed. The man smiled and put him on his lap. Bella got in, and slowly the vehicle started to move. "Wait! Wait!" I cried suddenly. "Bella, wait! I'm going with you to Tirana!" The truck stopped, and I climbed in with Bella holding on to my hand. We left.

What was I thinking? What impulse drove me to go to Tirana, where I had no friends and I didn't know where I would spend the night? On the way there we saw the first German vehicles with officers, and the closer we came to Tirana, the more Germans we saw. They were in vehicles and on motorbikes, and a few were walking. But was I mistaken or was I seeing straight? These Germans didn't look as happy, as sure of victory, as fat and rosy-cheeked as I remembered them being in Belgrade. These were very young boys, kids even, that we were running into.

Bella and I parted ways in Tirana. I walked quickly across the empty square in the center of town, which was full of noisy soldiers, and headed in the direction of New Tirana. Maybe I could spend the night in the house of my former hostess. In the morning very early I could look for Hassan's mother and ask for shelter. My heart raced as I walked up to the home of the Benga family. I knew by the look on their faces that I was an unwanted guest. They left me in no doubt about whether I could stay there. I stood there, despondent. It was too far to walk to Hassan's home, it was already starting to get dark, and it was forbidden to be on the street after six o'clock. Suddenly the woman took pity on me. "You can sleep in the Brangus' home. Only the maid is there. Frieda is with the children in a cloister near Dibra. The children have whooping cough, and they need some fresh air," she explained. "Gafur himself is in Dibra. He's becoming an important man to the Germans," the neighbor bragged. "The Germans appreciate help and cooperation." He then continued to talk about Gafur's and his views of the Germans, which I only half-listened to. My thoughts were elsewhere.

Frieda was in a convent near Dibra. Where was Dibra?[5] Was it possible to get there? I worked my brain feverishly trying to come up with a plan. "Please," I pleaded with Mrs. Benga, "don't you want to tell Gafur's maid personally that I have your permission to spend the night there?" "She wouldn't dare question your authority," I coaxed bluntly. "Please lead me there; in your presence I feel protected."

I don't know whether it was my power of persuasion or Mrs. Benga's soft heart that caused her to get mixed up in matters that her husband forbade.

She decided to accompany me to Gafur's house. After she told the maid to let me stay there for the night, I asked her to wait a moment. I wanted to ask such an intelligent and noble-minded person for advice. "Would it be possible to travel to Dibra and eventually to reach the cloister where Frieda is? How far away is Dibra? Could one get there on foot?" I tried to find out as precisely as possible, and Mrs. Benga gave me the information willingly. "Yes, it is possible to get to Dibra," she told me, "and I will try to get you as far as the camion you take to get there, without my husband knowing. Many workers who up until now have worked with the Italians in Durazzo and Tirana want to go back to their families. Many are from Dibra and the surrounding area. Leave here tomorrow morning at 6:00 A.M., and I'll meet you at the next corner. I'll tell my husband that I'm going to buy flour from a farmer's wife. Then he won't be suspicious when I leave the house so early."

As planned, we met the next morning. The streets were still empty, and we were the only people in New Tirana who didn't think it was too early to go to the center of town, most certainly teeming with soldiers. Near the marketplace there was a lot of traffic. But it wasn't full of farmers selling butter, cheese, and vegetables; it was full of frightened people, mostly Albanians from the interior of the country, who were looking for ways to get home. Besides the two of us, we saw no women.

On a side street we found an open camion. Men with bundles, luggage, and cardboard boxes stood around. One man, presumably the owner of the vehicle, was standing on a small box, and the passengers were paying him for the trip. Someone told us that the vehicle was going to Dibra. We pressed into the line, but when I gave the man some money he blurted out: "A woman? What are you looking for in Dibra? What kind of woman travels alone in these circumstances? Can I see your papers?" He snapped gruffly. Shaking, I gave him my identification. "Fatima Nova," he said, "you're from Tetovo, what do you want in Dibra? Or is this a pleasure trip?" he sneered. I didn't understand what he was saying, and Mrs. Benga quickly translated into Serbian for me. Then she spoke for me as she opened her purse and gave him another bill on my behalf.

ROAD TO DIBRA

The man became friendlier. I received my ticket and climbed into the vehicle with the others. There were no seats. We stood, crushed against one another, and when we went around a corner, I was pressed against my neighbor. Because the men stood firmly on their feet, it was difficult to fall. To my great astonishment, my neighbor asked me in Serbian, "Are you Jewish, miss?" "No!" I retorted, shocked. "How could you think such a thing?" "I heard you speaking Serbian with a woman before you got on; the Jewish people always speak a few languages," he replied calmly. "I'm Czech," I lied, "but I lived in Belgrade, and that is where I learned Serbian."

"So you're Czech!" he replied, astounded. "What brings you to Tirana?" "My cousin was married in Tirana. She is the wife of Gafur Brangu, the Albanian engineer. I spent some time with her before the war began, and then I couldn't return home. Now my cousin is with her children in a cloister near Dibra, and I want to stay with her, because I don't want to be alone in the city in these troubled times. And I'm afraid of the English bombs," I ornamented my story further, in order to make it more believable. "Well, well," mumbled my fellow passenger. "I see, miss. I'll watch out for you a little bit on this trip, if it is okay. You need not be afraid of me, but it is always better when a woman has some protection on such a difficult journey as yours. I too have a young wife at home, and I wouldn't like to see her in a vehicle with over fifty men. We don't know whether we'll reach Dibra today or not."

I gratefully accepted his offer after I had observed his candid demeanor. My new acquaintance was a house painter who had worked a few months in Tirana and wanted to return to his village, not far from Dibra. "Why do you think that we won't reach Dibra today?" I inquired. "It is only six hours away; we can surely get there before nightfall." "Yes," he replied, "if everything goes well. But now so many unexpected things happen on the road. For example, we could get mixed up in a battle between the Italians and the Germans, or the partisans could launch a surprise attack on the German troops during our journey, or planes could bombard the place where we are right now. After all, we are at war."

Embarrassed, I remained silent. He was right: we were in the middle of a war. It turned out that my neighbor had foreseen correctly. Our six-hour journey lasted somewhat longer. I arrived in Dibra three days later, late in the evening. When and if my other traveling companions made it, I do not know. My adventurous destiny led me down other paths than those I had originally intended for myself. When I look back now, it seems almost unbelievable, and so strange, that I could have experienced all that I did in a single journey. The events followed each other in rapid succession. Had I seen this adventure in a film, I probably would have smiled at the director's vivid imagination.

We had been on the road for two hours now, but I wasn't bored, because the men laughed and joked so loudly and merrily. My neighbor told me about his wife and his small farm. If my feet had not hurt from standing for such a long time in the vehicle, I would have imagined this journey to be an excursion of unruly schoolchildren. The soldiers whom we ran into on the way blurted out funny curses in either Albanian or Serbian, and the men who did not understand them smiled back cheerfully and viewed it as a spontaneous tribute to the people. But why did the vehicle stop suddenly? Curious, I leaned forward to see what was going on.

In the middle of the road in front of us stood two men with machine guns. We had been stopped by the Germans. The driver showed his papers, but he couldn't make himself understood to the man in uniform. The German pointed questioningly to the men in the bus. "They're workers going home," the driver tried to explain in Italian. But the German was at a loss. Now I could see that we were in front of a large gate, ostensibly the gate to a farmstead, since we were in the middle of a country road. On the gate itself I saw a primitive-looking placard with various German abbreviations. It seemed that a particular agency had established control here for the present. The German whistled shrilly, and the gate was opened from the inside. Our vehicle drove in, and we found ourselves in the courtyard of an administrative unit.

What I saw then made my blood run cold. We were the only ones there. We waited while the German official went into a house. What had happened to my unruly traveling companions? They were all now very busy. One hurriedly opened a cardboard box and hid something in the corner of the vehicle; another opened his shirt and pulled something out from under it; and a third wanted to hide something under the driver's seat. I looked a bit closer and recognized what it was: weapons—bombs, hand grenades, revolvers, and ammunition. I saw death before my eyes. If the Germans caught sight of the weapons, we would all be shot on the spot. I would probably be viewed as the leader of the band, because I was the only woman in a vehicle full of mostly illiterate men. My neighbor also understood the situation we were in. "Can't you speak with the Germans?" he whispered to me. "Surely you speak their language. Try to save us!" What could I tell him? And how could I explain that my intercession would get us nowhere?

Quietly, I began to pray fervently. I pleaded to the powers above, in whose hands alone our rescue or destruction lay. The German soldier, now accompanied by another, went into the yard again. The two were carrying on a conversation about a "stupid blockhead" who would arrive shortly and then settle the matter. The one was saying: "Just look at the idiotic faces of some of these guys! They're certainly simple people, workers and farmers, you know. I really have no desire to do that." Trying to make myself invisible, I pulled my scarf down over my face, and my sense of hearing became keener in these moments. I took great care not to miss a word of the conversation between these two Germans.

"You're right," said the one. "The story of Niš still leaves a bad taste in my mouth. I get sick just thinking about the damned mess." Both of them walked back and forth in the yard, looking over at us now and then. They no longer tried to explain anything to us. We sat still in the vehicle; each person was busy with his own thoughts, and no one felt like talking. "Goddamn son-of-a-bitch, shit!" swore the first soldier. "What are we supposed to do now?" It looked like he was thinking something over for a few moments. "What would you think," he asked his comrade, "if we let the entire brigade go before 'the old man' returns? At least we would spare ourselves the mess." The other readily agreed. I couldn't believe my eyes: the gate was opened, the driver put his foot on the gas pedal, and we were outside!

Are there words to describe how I felt at this moment? The men started conversing wildly with one another. My neighbor laid his hand on my shoulder: I was shaking from head to foot. I broke out in a cold sweat and vomited. What sinister power was inherent in German uniforms! There were about fifty men with weapons in our vehicle, and there had been only two German soldiers, yet all fifty had acted as if they were paralyzed. Not one had taken the initiative to rescue us. If the two soldiers had fired on all of us with machine guns, I don't believe that one of the men would have thrown a single bomb.

We were traveling at a quick pace now, in a hurry to reach our destination before nightfall. Our vehicle was stopped once again at a crossroads, this
time by an Italian who waved us down. He had a long black beard and wore a uniform shirt that was unbuttoned and had no insignia. The Italian stood on the street near a small wooden barrack and made desperate gestures in order to get our attention because he wanted to hear news about Tirana. He asked what had happened to the Italians there, whether ships with Italian soldiers and private citizens were leaving Durazzo, and whether help had been sent from Bari. It seemed that the high spirits of my comrades had developed into a cynical kind of humor. They told the Italian tales of horror about noses and ears being cut off, about Italian women and children crawling on their knees, of German troops raping, murdering, robbing, and pillaging. And all of it was done only in Italian homes. According to their description, there wasn't one single Italian citizen still living in Tirana.

I hardly spoke Italian and at first didn't get into the conversation, but when it became too colorful for me, I asked the Italian if he spoke French. "Yes, madame," he said, pleasantly surprised. "Good," I said. "Let's just say that they're telling you gross lies here. The Italian soldiers were disarmed in Tirana, and I heard nothing about these atrocities." He looked at me with relief and gratitude.

"Where are you going?" he inquired. "We're heading for Dibra," I said. "Presumably Dibra and the surrounding area are in the hands of the partisans. Maybe we can reach our destination safely before nightfall." "Oh," he said, "you're traveling into the partisan territory? I'm going to ask you, and perhaps the partisans, to do a big favor for me." Moving his hand in a circle around him, he said, "Here, in this very place, is an underground Italian ammunition depot. I was the commander here. My subordinates fled. I'm here alone, and I don't know whom to turn to. More important, I don't know to whom I should hand over this ammunition. There is enough to blow up the road from here to Tirana. If you would, as soon as you have the chance, send people here. I'll wait as long as possible and hope that neither I nor the ammunition will fall into the hands of the Germans."[1]

He then gave me more accurate information about precisely where he was located and wished me a pleasant journey. We traveled on, and two days later I had the chance to convey this valuable information to the right person. But I want to relate the events in the order in which they took place. Late that afternoon we arrived in a small town. Our driver explained to us that he couldn't drive any further: it was too dangerous to travel on the country road at night. We were going to spend the night here. We climbed out of the vehicle, walked on legs that had become stiff, and the men went into a small pub to get a sip of *rakija* or something hot to eat.

It seemed to have quickly gotten around the little town that strangers had arrived who needed a place to sleep. Soon women were there offering accommodations for money. In this town almost everyone, with few exceptions, spoke Serbian. I conversed with a fat woman who appeared good-natured; she said that she had an extra bed for me and that I should go with her. My new friend, the traveling companion, accompanied me to this woman's house. He wanted to know how and where I was going to spend the night. She led us to a large, pretty home, let us go in, and showed me my "room." We went up a steep flight of stairs and found four beds in a kind of anteroom. From there one could climb a ladder to an attic, where there was another bed. "You can sleep here, ma'am," she said to me. "Be so kind as to pay ahead of time. You never know if you're going to get your money in the morning," she added slyly, "so let's play this safe."

I was ready to pay her, but then something occurred to me. "Who is sleeping down here?" I asked my hostess. "There? Oh, sleeping there are four men, for whom I have made the beds tonight. But you need not worry: if something should happen, you can always scream. I'm a light sleeper and I'll hear you, little daughter," she consoled. I sighed. "Auntie," I said to her, "would you allow me to sleep in your room? I don't need a bed," I added quickly, "and it is enough if you would allow me to be near you. I'm afraid of strange men. Please, Auntie, let me do it." The old woman looked me over for a moment, then said: "All right, you can sleep in my room, but you still have to pay." I quickly reassured her that I would even give her more money and that she could rent the bed upstairs to someone else.

I went downstairs with her. My new friend followed, eyeing the woman and the entire house suspiciously. He was getting ready to say good-bye to me and look for a place to sleep when a young man entered the house. "Good evening, mother," he said and then looked at me. "Who is this?" he asked, astounded. His mother told him, "A woman from Tirana who is traveling to Dibra and wants to spend the night here." "Spend the night here . . . ," he said, repeating his mother's words, and came up very close to me. "What is your name and who are you?" he addressed me gruffly. "Can you prove your identity? What do you want in our house? Perhaps you're a spy?" His face became purple, he screamed more and more, and his voice cracked. "I'll report you! I'll go to the next German commander! Now there is order in our country, you communist, you Jewish seductress! Don't you think that I can tell by your face that that is what you are? So you want to go to Dibra, to the other comrades that stir up our people. You aren't from Tirana. You're from Moscow! But just you wait, the Germans will stop you!" he howled.

His face was purple. He pointed toward the door and screamed: "Out with you or I'll call the Germans for help!" I was shocked to death and just stood there, incapable of answering. My traveling companion took charge, grabbed my hand, and pulled me quickly through the door. Outside we began to run, still hearing the voice of the angry man. We ran to the other end of the small town.

There my comrade looked for and found another room for me and promised to pick me up the following morning at six o'clock. He didn't lie. When I told the two women with whom I had found shelter that I felt sick, I went to my little room, lay down on the tiny bed fully clothed, and fell asleep. I woke up when I heard a knock at my door. Terrified, I jumped up. They were already there to pick me up! I had dreamed that the Germans wanted to shoot me; it had come to that. But when I opened the door hastily and saw the good-natured face of my traveling companion, I realized where I was. "Let's go," he said. "Our vehicle is waiting at the marketplace, and I hope we'll leave soon. We could be in Dibra in two hours." He gave me a piece of bread and a few figs. I ate greedily.

A new surprise awaited us at the marketplace. The men stood around the driver and spoke excitedly, gesticulating with their hands. We pressed closer. What had happened? One of the people there told us. "We can't travel any farther; we're stuck," he related. "Last night the partisans blew up the bridge that led to Dibra in order to obstruct the Germans." He added, laughing: "Some crazy person wanted to cross the river on a horse, but no one knows this region better than I. The Drina is treacherous and torrential, and to drown in it would not be a nice way to die." He finally said, "No, it is better to wait until the Germans fix it. It won't take them very long; they're good at that sort of thing. Perhaps it will be ready again in ten days."

I faced a difficult problem. What was better—to stay here in this small town, where in just a few hours every person would know who I was and ask nosy questions; where I was in constant danger of a frightened populace's handing me over to the rural police; where my fear of the Germans left me no peace; and where death constantly lay in wait? Or was it better to try to cross a torrential river on a horse? I had never in my life sat on a horse, nor was I a good swimmer. And still I decided to take the second way out of this dilemma. Without exception, all of the men advised against this hazardous undertaking. "Lady, you'll drown," they admonished. "Be reasonable. It's too dangerous even for the men who have been riding horses since they were children, even for those who know the river and its malice. Only six of us have decided to risk it." I stood by my decision and added myself to the six men who wanted to try to borrow horses.

My traveling companion looked at me and shook his head. "Poor woman," he said sympathetically, "what have you had to live through that makes you fear drowning less than you fear the Germans?" He took me by the hand and pulled me away from the circle of men. "Go back to your room," he ordered. "I'll try the best I can to take care of everything for you. Lay down and go to sleep. You'll need all of your strength."

I was so tired. I was profoundly tired of everything. But it wasn't sleep that I needed. I needed peace, security, no more fleeing from enemies, I needed to be able to live with nice people near me, I needed a corner for myself alone. But was there still such a place in the world for a Jewish woman? I lay on the strange bed and tried to focus my attention on my situation and to think about it. But my thoughts always wandered. Why did people hunt each other down? Hadn't God created the world for all creatures? Had he forgotten something? Why were there persecutors and persecuted? Where was God's justice, his love, his omnipotence? Where were the miracles that we had learned about in school?

Yet on this day a miracle occurred! Without knocking, my new friend stormed into my little room. I jumped up, startled. What had happened now? "Come quickly," he said to me, "I've got a nice surprise for you!" "Have you found a horse, or has the bridge been fixed in two hours?" I asked, looking at him skeptically. "No, it is not a horse that I've found, but your cousin!" he reported, beaming. "My cousin?" I asked full of curiosity. "Which cousin?" "Well, the cousin whom you're going to visit: Gafur Brangu from Tirana."

I stared at him, speechless. Then slowly my mind started to work again. "Tell me," I pressed. "Where have you seen him? How do you know him? Tell me quickly!" "You know," he said. "I've been worrying about you. I sat in a small inn in the marketplace and thought about how I could help you. I saw a man there with a nice new machine gun strapped across his shoulder talking with the other men about the war. You know, he was almost making a speech, and many people were listening to him. I went closer, and he was saying how good it was that the Italians were finally out of the country and that Albania was now free thanks to the help of the Germans. I asked one of the men there who this man was, and he said that his name was Gafur Brangu and that he was from Tirana. He also added that he would become a great man with the help of the Germans. When I heard his name, I went right up to him and said, 'Gafur Brangu, your cousin is here, and she will definitely be happy to see you.' At first, he didn't understand me. He said that he didn't have a cousin, but when I wasn't frightened away by his words and explained to him what you look like, he hit himself on the forehead and said: 'Of course! My wife's cousin! The Czech woman! Who also speaks Serbian! Bring her to me quickly. I want to speak with her.'"[2]

We went to the inn. Gafur was standing in front of the door. I ran up to him. Crying, I hugged him in front of all the strange men gathered there. It seemed as if an angel from heaven had descended to earth to save me. Embarrassed, the big, strong man stood there. Then he bent over and whispered in my ear: "Calm down, don't make a scene. I will definitely help you if it is in my power to do so." I pulled myself together.

Really, it was high time I started controlling my nerves a bit better, I thought to myself. After I calmed down a little, I told him how and why I was there and that I saw no other way of escape than to flee to his wife, whom I had hoped was in a cloister. I anticipated finding a hiding place there, perhaps doing some kind of work and staying there until the war was over. He let me talk until I finished and listened to me earnestly. Then he told me that Frieda was not in a cloister, but lived presently with his brother in Dibra. "The cloister was attacked by gangs of robbers, and staying there would not be safe. I'll send you to my brother, and you can stay with him and with Frieda and the children until I have a better idea what to do with you. For the time being you will be in safe keeping."

What a comfort it was to have another person make a decision for me. I didn't want to think, and I didn't want to bargain. I felt weak and helpless. Gafur took care of everything else for me. When I told him about the destroyed bridge, he laughed and said that he could even find a way to help me go across but that I didn't need to ride a horse over the river. I didn't stray one foot from Gafur's side. He talked with many people, and I noticed that he was treated with great courtesy most of the time, but I also noticed the dirty looks some were giving him. His new position seemed to bring him more enemies than friends. Unconcerned and laughing, he remarked about it. "The fools want to make war against Germany," he said. "It's too bad for them and their pretty little town. They'll have to pay bitterly for their stupidity. It is my duty as a patriot to warn them and to try and arrange an amicable settlement between the partisans and the German troops. The blockheads don't know what a great favor I'm doing them."

I said nothing. Earlier in Tirana I had had vehement discussions with Gafur, but today I didn't respond. Perhaps it was fatigue or indifference about everything. Perhaps it was cowardice or fear that he wouldn't offer to help me escape if I said to him now what I had said to him so many times before. Who knows? Gafur went into a garage. A pretty new Italian omnibus was parked there. He showed a man there a paper: "The vehicle is requisitioned," he informed him. "I need it in half an hour with enough gas and a reliable driver to take my cousin to Dibra. Because the bridge is damaged, the driver has to take a long detour. I will give him the required information and instructions for the German authorities. If he should meet partisans on the way, then he will probably know how to defend himself."

The man dared not object. Gafur's imposing personality, paired with the German identification and a machine gun, nipped every possible protest in the bud. The driver was young and attractive. Gafur explained to him exactly how he had to drive and once again attached great importance to my well-being. I gladly would have had my traveling companion with me again, but he would have energetically refused a trip under Gafur's protection. He knew that in another situation a bullet from one of his countrymen could hit him. He belonged in the other camp.[3]

So I departed alone. I sat next to the driver, and we hardly spoke; mostly I just looked out the window. Many people were in transit. Alone and in groups, they filled the road: farmers and workers who wanted to get home to their families as soon as possible and hadn't found transportation. Some of them tried to wave down the driver so they could ride with us a few kilometers. However, he was totally unsympathetic toward their plight and merely drove on.

A group of about ten men tried another method. All of them stood in the middle of the road with outstretched arms, and like it or not, the bus had to stop. After a short negotiation and obvious payment, the driver explained that he would take them to their point of destination. During the trip the men chatted with the driver. "There is a lot of riffraff on the road," they said. "One's life is no longer safe. It is better to sit in a bus than to walk, even though the gangs of robbers are so well armed that they could easily hold up a bus. If something happens now, we will defend ourselves. We've got weapons." They proudly showed us their various weapons. One had a rifle, another a gun, a third had grenades, and everyone had a knife. I shuddered, thinking of what would probably happen if we fell into the hands of the Germans this time. Would these Germans "avoid the mess" as their comrades had done yesterday?

Nevertheless, a little while later our bus was stopped. We didn't see soldiers in German uniform standing in front of us, but two young men in English uniform. We had arrived at a partisan patrol. All of us had to get out, show our papers, and state where we were coming from and where we were going. Then, not only the men but the vehicle was thoroughly searched. Five minutes later the two partisans had possession of rifles, revolvers, knives, and hand grenades. Each of my fellow passengers received a paper with verification and a signature to show that he put the weapons at the partisans' disposal of his own free will. We could leave. The two soldiers politely wished us a nice journey, and we climbed back into the bus with mixed feelings.

The men were furious, but secretly I was relieved. Our only weapons were two umbrellas that they left in the hands of their owners. Or at least so I thought. We were barely out of sight of the two soldiers when the driver asked me to stand up next to him for a few moments. I stood up. He lifted up the seat on which I had sat so peacefully the whole time, and I almost fainted from fright when I saw what a powder keg I had literally been sitting on. Full of joy, the men slapped the driver and one another on the shoulders. They surpassed each other in describing how they would defend all of us in case of a battle, thanks to the cleverness of the driver. These harmless family men seemed to desire nothing more than to take part in a small engagement: blood should flow and heads roll, according to the well-known model. This time fate had pity on me—luckily, up until the departure of my traveling companions no opportunity presented itself. One of the men gave us a magnificent farewell gift: a large piece of ham and an entire loaf of bread. In spite of all the danger, the driver and I ate with a hearty appetite.

"I think we'll reach Dibra by nightfall," said the driver, and he calculated how late it would probably be when we arrived. We continued our journey. It was already starting to get dark, and I became drowsy. I was awakened by the sharp jolt of the brakes. The vehicle came to a halt. It was yet another partisan demanding our papers. The man who stopped us this time wore an elegant English uniform, carried a machine gun on his shoulder, and held a dagger in his hand. The partisan, who had an extraordinarily intelligent-looking face and spoke Italian with a strong Serbian accent, scrutinized us.

I trusted him immediately. "We're heading for Dibra," I blurted out spontaneously. "I'm a Jew from Belgrade fleeing from the Germans. Is it true that Dibra is now in the hands of the partisans?" "Yes," he confirmed, "you're correct. Dibra and the entire surrounding area are in our hands. You can't get there today at least. Gangs of robbers have made this region unsafe. I wouldn't advise traveling any further tonight, because the gangs are well armed. Today they attacked a camion that was traveling down this road carrying more than fifty armed partisan fighters. Our people escaped the fight unscathed, but how can the two of you defend yourselves against such riffraff? Drive back to the nearest town. Early tomorrow morning my people are traveling back to Dibra; you can drive behind their vehicle and have protection in case of an attack." The driver was hesitant about stopping the journey. "I know most of the bandits," he confided. "They're from my region, and they certainly won't harm me."

I was skeptical; my peace of mind vanished. The forest stretched darkly before us, and I was frightened. I brought all my powers of persuasion into play. Finally, both the strange soldier and I succeeded with pleas and sensible argument in talking my traveling companion into spending the night in the nearby town. Before we went further, we chatted a while longer with the partisan. I told him about the Italian ammunition depot and gave him as exact information as I could about where the place was. He made notes, saying that he hoped to be in possession of the expensive goods as quickly as possible. Then he gave us the address of a home where we could spend the night with his introduction.

At the house, my companion was given a mattress spread out in the kitchen, and I was given a small room above a dump. If the tiny countless bedbugs had left me in peace, I most certainly would have slept well. When the first rooster crowed, I was already downstairs in the warm kitchen. I had travel fever. Every minute we stayed here seemed to me like lost time. I wanted to get to Dibra, to Frieda; I wanted to be safe. The driver wasn't in as much of a hurry as I was. He went away and promised to pick me up in an hour. I was to wait here, because he had something to do. I sat impatiently. Hours went by and he still hadn't returned. Had he abandoned me at the last minute? The people in the house tried to calm me down. "The bus is parked in the marketplace," said a young man we had sent to look for the driver. "Shall I take you there, miss?"

We went to the marketplace. The bus was there, and not far from it stood the driver, who was talking to a few people. When he saw me, he came up and said, "We're going to leave around noon. I have a few people here to take along." A good businessman, he was taking advantage of the opportunity and looking for moneyed travelers who were happy to find a ride in these troubled times. When we were finally ready to leave, at two o'clock, I looked in astonishment at my fellow passengers.

What a curious party had assembled here! It was a family. The first person I saw was a young woman in a soldier's uniform, armed from head to toe. She had a rifle on her shoulder and a gun in her pocket, and hand grenades hung from her leather belt, where a bag of ammunition was also attached. She was accompanied by four children. The oldest was probably six years old, and the youngest she held on her arm. An old man, ostensibly the grandfather of the children but perhaps the young woman's father, was also heavily armed. He led the two other small children. The family had lots of luggage: pillows, blankets, baskets, bedpans, and milk bottles. The grandfather and the woman only spoke Albanian. Many women, men, and children said good-bye to the strange group.

The driver enlightened me about our new passengers. We had the high honor of being accompanied by the wife and father of a great hero. This young woman's husband had accomplished a daring feat. One morning he had succeeded in leading a partisan group into the mountains right under the noses of the Italians and the entire youth of the small town. And ever since, not only the hero but also his family had been the pride of the local patriots. The woman gave me one of the red-nosed kids while she breast-fed the youngest. While this was going on, the two oldest played war. One blew into a horrible tin trumpet, while the other hit the bed pan with a wooden spoon. Entertainment was now provided; there was no longer any chance of boredom. When we arrived at a small, damaged bridge, the driver demanded that the woman, the children, and I get out. He didn't want any extra weight in the vehicle: he was afraid there might be an accident because of the difficult maneuvers he had to accomplish to steer the vehicle on the steep, curving, narrow road. So we took the children and walked up the forest path. Once in the forest, we found fresh green nuts; the children played happily with them, while the young mother and I sat on the damp earth and watched.

Suddenly the woman leaped up, pulled the gun out of her pocket, and shot three times in the air in rapid succession. I jumped up, startled. She laughed, gave me the revolver, and gestured to me to try. The Albanian woman couldn't understand that the shooting was no joy for me, that I had had enough of war and bombs, cannons and gunfire. Imploringly, I tried to keep her away from the nonsense. Had she no idea what danger she could cause us? We were alone in the forest; robbers, German soldiers, or partisans might hear the shots, and then woe to us and the children. My desperate pleas for her to stop shooting only excited her. She then took a hand grenade, walked away from us a bit, and threw it against a tree.

I was so horrified that I abruptly grabbed the baby lying in the grass, caught one of the others running around, and ran down the steep slope. Laughing, she followed us with the other two children. The vehicle was once again on a good road, so we could get in. My knees were still shaking. The woman was apparently describing the amusing story to the grandfather, because he soon broke out into peals of laughter. In jest, the woman pulled out the gun and pointed it at me: I closed my eyes. I have never been a heroine and never will be. On this day I had the opportunity to prove this twice. No sooner had I convinced myself that this dumb, childish woman was harmless than I stood before a stronger foe.

Our vehicle was halted once again: two young men in English uniform wanted to be taken along for a part of the journey. Courteously, the driver stopped. It wouldn't have been very clever of him to turn down partisans. The two young men got in, sat behind me, and conversed softly. I noticed that they spoke Serbian, but I couldn't make out what they were saying. I sat there quietly. The children slept. Only the baby cried, but that didn't bother me anymore; I was happy that the din of the oldest had stopped.

Suddenly one of the young men tapped me on the shoulder. "May I see your passport, signora?" he asked politely. I gave him the document. "Fatima Nova," he read out loud and gave the fatal document to his comrade. Then he said, "You're under arrest, signora. You will get out with us at the next command post." For a moment my heart pounded and I felt dizzy, then I became quite calm. "Brother," I implored him in Serbian, "please sit down next to me. I want to talk with you." He did as I requested. "This document is false, brother," I said. "My name is not Fatima Nova but Irene Eskenazi. I'm not from Tetovo, but from Belgrade; I'm a Jew fleeing from the Germans. My entire family has already fallen victim to them, and I'm trying to escape. I'm heading for partisan territory, to Dibra, to stay with a friend of mine who is also Jewish but married to an Albanian. At present she is living with her brother-in-law, and I hope that I'll be able to hide there. Do you, a freedom fighter, want to make trouble for me instead of trying to help? Am I to be hunted down on all sides? Have I robbed and murdered, so that no one will leave me in peace?" I pleaded.

"Prove your testimony to me," said the young man in a businesslike manner. "It is wartime, and the streets are full of suspicious individuals. It is our duty to look closely at travelers who don't have impeccable papers. Our country is teeming with spies and traitors. You don't speak the native language here; you say that you're from Belgrade, but you speak Serbian with a pronounced German accent; you say that you just came from Cavaia, but you have no proof that you were interned there. How can I believe you?"

Documents and proof on pieces of paper were things that I didn't have in my possession. I put all my energy into formulating what he now had to understand. I was without costly documents, true, but there were thousands of people who were able to show important identification and were, nevertheless, criminals. One could buy the most beautiful passports, even from neutral countries, with money and the right connections. He should well believe my words. I appealed to his intelligence, to the purity of his ideas, to his humaneness, and to his conscience. It was all in vain. He wanted proof.

"Who is the man whose wife you are going to stay with?" he asked. "Gafur Brangu," I replied. He laughed. "You have fine friends, but at least you are candid." I understood that I hadn't gained much by naming my rescuer. "Do you know more people from Tirana, and do you want to mention their names?" Desperate, I started to think very hard. I didn't understand enough of Albanian politics and its many political parties to know who was working against whom. It could too easily happen that by mentioning a name I would harm not only myself but also the person mentioned. I stayed silent. I looked at my adversary. How young he was! How passionately he loved his country! Suddenly I thought of Rifat, Hassan's cousin. Didn't he bear a certain resemblance to him? Didn't his eyes glow not unlike those of the person sitting next to me?

"Do you know Rifat from Tirana?" I inquired. "He is an old friend of mine. His wife has been with the partisans for two years now, and I hope that by now he is too. I saw him a few months ago for the last time, and I don't know if he has succeeded in escaping to the mountains as he planned."[4] Surprise was painted all over my neighbor's face. "Rifat B.?" he exclaimed. "Of course I know him! During the Italian occupation I sat in the same prison with him!" The man asked if I could give him further news of his whereabouts, so I summoned up my courage. Perhaps this would save me. I described how we had slept in Hassan's mother's house in the same room, how we had talked for hours and hours, always afraid that the police would knock on the door at any moment. We were afraid that they would force me, Rifat, and perhaps the entire family out of the house. I also described how Rifat simply did not return one evening, and never let us know what happened to him. "Rifat now has a responsible post," said my neighbor after I finished speaking. "I can call him from the next command post. If he can confirm what you have said, then of course you will be free to go."

We drove into a small town, and our vehicle stopped in front of a primitive building. "Wait here," said the partisan to the driver in a commanding tone, "perhaps I'll need you." We walked into the barracks, and the young man was cordially greeted by all of the men who went in and out. He seemed to hold a high office. The partisan thumbed through various papers, apparently looking for something, and gave orders, while I sat on my poor, wretched bench and waited. Then he whispered something to two uniformed men who sat at the nearest desk and afterwards left the room. I knew that I was being watched. He returned about thirty minutes later. "Come here, comrade," he said to me. "I want to write a letter of introduction for you to give to the appropriate man in Dibra so that you won't end up in the same situation you were in today. I congratulate you: your account was confirmed entirely by your friend Rifat. You can thank him when you have the chance. He has saved your life."

Confused, I listened to his last words. Saved my life? He had probably saved me from a lengthy interrogation and probably from going to prison, but he certainly had not saved my life. It was much more likely that Gafur had saved my life by not letting me ride across the river. I said this impulsively to the man sitting behind the desk. "Have a seat, comrade," he replied in a friendly manner to my frankness, and offered me a cigarette. We were now two acquaintances carrying on a conversation, and not prisoner and gendarme. "You are an intelligent woman," he said "and you will understand what I'm going to tell you. Rifat saved your life in the truest sense of the word. If his account of you had been bad, or if he had not remembered you at the right moment, then at this very minute you would not be able to smoke a cigarette because you would already be dead. You probably would have been shot as a spy. We're in the middle of a war, and we don't have the time to concern ourselves with suspicious people. Women like you shouldn't travel with false papers; you are too easily noticed. It would be better for you to fight with us or to look for a hiding place in a small town and remain as quiet and inconspicuous as you can. When you arrive in Dibra, stay off the street as much as possible. And as soon as you can, take this paper to the command post and register yourself. Tell the commander there that I send my greetings." "What is your name?" I asked. "Just say that you have spoken with 'Glavnik.' And now, my dear, I wish you the best. I'm glad that your fate has let you remain alive."

He pressed my hand firmly and accompanied me to the door. I staggered to the bus. Then he raised his fist in a gesture of farewell, and as we drove away he went back into the barracks. I didn't answer the excited driver's questions. I felt totally empty; I could neither think nor speak. After a while the driver said we would soon be in Dibra. I looked out the window: we were driving on a narrow road; to the right and left of us were high mountains, and the way was incredibly dark. This was a good place for the Germans and partisans to fight, I thought, as I looked at the narrow gorge between the mountains. I imagined how the bullets would whistle from one mountain to the other and how the Albanians, who knew their forest, would coax the enemy into the most dangerous places in order to attack them there.

Even before we had come out of the dark, romantic valley we were held up. Neither by Germans nor by partisans, but by a gang of robbers. Suddenly, as if by magic, thirty men were standing in front of us with guns pointed. I didn't notice them until our vehicle stopped. They looked fantastic! No pirate film could have realized better characters on the screen, not even if all of Hollywood were there. We saw dark, bearded figures who wore dingy white cloths over their small white fezes, like the Bedouins. "Get out! Put your hands up!" they commanded. Our traveling companion's children screamed piercingly.

What happened after that was a comedy worthy of a happy ending. While one of the highwaymen walked toward the driver pointing his gun at him, suddenly our grandfather put his hands down, joyfully blurted out some words that I didn't understand, ran away from our group, and rushed up to one of the robbers. The bandit in turn screamed out something, and the two hugged each other, kissed each other on both cheeks, and patted each other affectionately on the back. Members of both parties observed the two with great interest. After much explanation, the rest of the bandits abandoned their threatening stance and our old man was hugged again and again. Then the robbers bowed respectfully toward his daughter-in-law, and the children were cuddled. It was like a fairy tale. What had produced such a transformation in these wild characters? The old man's brother-in-law and the hero's uncle were members of the band. Not a hair on our heads was touched; it was a matter of honor to let us go our way.

After a splendid leave-taking, we drove on. Were we heading for new adventures? A half-hour later we arrived safe and sound in Dibra. Our small party dispersed, and each went his own way.

DIBRA

I looked for Gafur's brother's house until someone showed me where it was. A big gate stood in front of the premises. I knocked. A young man opened the gate, and I asked for Frieda, Gafur's wife. She came outside and looked at me in astonishment. After I had explained the most important things, she led me into her brother-in-law's home. That night I slept peacefully on my mattress. Tomorrow was another day, and I wanted to think things over. Things were quite lively in Dibra. From early in the morning till late at night

I heard gunfire and blasts from small and large bombs. It was a hellish din. "Don't be alarmed," Frieda consoled, "it's only the local folk having fun." They would hold "general practice." They shot into the air. Now and then it happened that someone was hit by mistake, but no one seemed to get excited about it. After three days I observed unhappy people around me. Gafur's relatives had had enough of unwanted guests, and Frieda had had an altercation with her brother-in-law. After that the two of us, each taking a child, went looking for a room.

Dibra had a very mixed populace: Albanians, Serbs, and Bulgarians made life just as difficult for one another there as anywhere else. There was great hatred between them, and every few years internal struggles arose. The Bulgarians would enter the homes of the Albanians by force, robbing and singing, or the Albanians would do the same thing to the Serbs. It depended on whose turn it was to avenge a given crime. There was always some cause for revenge. Thanks to Gafur's name, we found a small room with a tiny kitchen at the home of one of the richest Bulgarian families.

Mr. Stojanow thought he would be protected because of our presence. A wonderfully peaceful time began for me there. Frieda and I didn't have to do anything all day except delouse the children and knit. Mrs. Stojanow gave me some leftover wool. I would knit a shawl, and when the shawl was finished I would undo it and start again. It amused me, and I always hurried to finish it quickly. Sometimes I would knit until late into the night. We would also read newspapers from time to time. Some were from the year 1936, and some were even from 1939. Once someone loaned us a book, but unfortunately it was in Albanian.

Soon we knew all the neighbors, and visitors came to see us. The women were curious about Gafur's foreign wife and wanted to get to know her cousin. Most of the Albanian women who visited us were heavily veiled. Frieda spoke a little Albanian, and some of the women spoke a little Serbian, and over thin Turkish coffee we made ourselves understood to one another as well as one could. Once one of the visitors asked me where we came from. "From Prague," answered Frieda. "Prague?" the visitor asked. "Where is that?" "In Czechoslovakia," Frieda answered. "Aha! from Germany," said the woman. "No, in Czechoslovakia," answered Frieda patiently. "Oh, in France!"

Once again Frieda answered, "No, in Czechoslovakia!" "Oh, in England," replied the visitor. "No, in Czechoslovakia!" "Now I understand," said the visitor, looking at us full of awe. "It's in America. Well, well, my husband's nephew lives there." We gave up.

Another time an old woman visited us with her daughter-in-law, who was called "Nuse." *Nuse* is the Albanian word for "bride." A young woman is called by that name from the time she marries until another son brings a new bride into the family. Often she is called "Nuse" until her own son gets married. The *nuse* doesn't have an easy life. The mother-in-law and the older sisters-in-law look upon her as a kind of unpaid servant who must jump up and accommodate everyone. She does the most difficult housework, and she has to be quiet because she is the youngest, the *nuse*.

We regretfully observed the poor thing during our days in Dibra. She seemed to have a particularly demanding mother-in-law. "Open the window! Close the window! Give me my shawl! I'm cold! Take my shawl away, you stupid thing, it's hot here!" The old woman screamed continuously. This is what we heard the entire time. The young woman didn't say a thing. With great haste she fulfilled every wish of the old tyrant. I felt so sorry for her. "Please have a seat," I urged her. "Drink your coffee while it's warm." Shy and obedient, she sat down but didn't touch the coffee. When I urged her again to drink it, the old woman looked at me sternly and said: "She doesn't drink coffee, she is still a *nuse*."

I saw myself living tranquilly in Dibra for the rest of my days. One morning we were awakened by louder shooting than normal. It almost sounded like the thunder of cannons. We had become so used to shooting that we left the house anyway because it was market day and we wanted to see whether we could buy some vegetables or even a few eggs. Conspicuously few farmers were at the market this time. I was picking up green peppers, a major staple, when a wild confusion broke out at the marketplace. The roar of guns could now be heard clearly in the vicinity. Bombs flew, and we scattered in confusion; jumping over baskets filled with vegetables and apples, we ran home.

Two hours later the evil magic was over. It had only been a few Albanian guerrilla fighters who didn't agree with their Albanian communist comrades, in whose hands Dibra now lay. These guerrilla fighters belonged to Gafur's party and wanted to unite and work together with the Germans. They were quickly driven away, and all of Dibra was proud of the rash victory.

So when we heard the din of artillery a few weeks later, we didn't get too alarmed. We stayed inside, baked a huge loaf of cornbread in case the battle should last a little longer this time, and waited for whatever came to pass. But this time, the things that came to pass were grave. A fierce battle raged around us. The city was hit with heavy artillery. Neighbors whose homes were not as sturdily built as ours came to us seeking refuge. There were already victims to mourn: a dead child here, a casualty there, another with only half an arm. Frieda, Mrs. Stojanow, and I, along with other women, bandaged and helped temporarily where we could.

In the evening our home was full of people, because it was the only house in the entire area that was structurally sound. Perhaps it could withstand the bombs. At night, we slept pressed up against one another on the floor in the large parlor. Down blankets and bedcovers were hung at the windows for protection. No one knew who was attacking. Was it Albanian gangs? Was it the Germans? Around morning someone went up to the second floor and looked out onto the street. The man ran back down the steps crying loudly. "It's burning! It's burning! Our homes are in flames! All of Dibra will be destroyed!" he cried. Almost everyone ran up to the second floor. Yes, it was burning! It was ghastly. We saw huge fires everywhere; it looked as if not one single house was still standing. We stood there devastated. The noise of cannons had subsided; now, apparently, one used other methods to wage war.

In a small city like Dibra, fire wasn't the worst thing that could happen. I went downstairs to sit down, and an old woman whom I had heard about sat near me. She was clever and brave. Someone told us how she had been alone one day in her small home when she noticed armed men outside who probably wanted to rob the house. Her soup was sitting on a primitive brick oven. The fact was that arms were never lacking in Albanian homes, so she decided quickly to throw all the ammunition she owned into the open fire. The explosion was so powerful that from that time on all robbers and burglars avoided her house.

Now she was consoling the people there. "Is it the first time that people have lost their homes?" she asked. "Whom God gives life, he also gives the strength to endure it. Come here and help me barricade the door so we can protect this house from fire. It is difficult to ignite it from the outside, so the murderers certainly will try to break in and ignite it from within with flammable liquids and bombs. Come, don't be idle!" she urged. All the furniture in the house was put in front of the door. The house itself was situated in the middle of the courtyard, as in all Muslim homes, and the walls around the courtyard were high and sturdy.

Soon we heard heavy pounding on the door. "Open up!" commanded some Albanians. We didn't move. "Open up!" bawled the voice again, and they beat and kicked at the door. The old woman motioned to us to stay quiet and went alone to the entrance. "What do you want, sons?" she cried. "Open up! This god-damned Bulgarian has hidden gold in his house." "The Bulgarian left with his money long ago," she said. "In this house there are only women and children who were afraid of the fire. Go away, you brave sons of Albanian mothers! Don't break Allah's commandment and break into a house full of women!" Calmly, and without showing any signs of fear, she spoke with the men in the street. They knocked and kicked the door a little more, and then we heard the gang walk off into the distance. After a while I went up to the second floor again. Carefully I looked out of the window. I saw a few soldiers walking on the other side of the street; they were Germans. Dibra had fallen.

New troubles were brewing. Already that day there were more deaths, not including the ones from the previous night. The teacher and a few other respectable men of Dibra had been shot. If house searches uncovered weapons, the fathers and sons were given short shrift. Not opening the door quickly enough was seen as popular resistance and often led to execution by a firing squad.

Placards were posted exhorting the populace to surrender their weapons willingly, and every house had to post a paper on the door with the name, age, profession, and sex of each occupant. A large percentage of the population of Dibra was illiterate, so neighbors would come to us and ask us to fill out their forms. Frieda and I couldn't decide how we should fill out our own papers. Should we give Fatima Nova as my name? Already the young boys and men who could read were carefully studying the names listed on the doors. How easy it would be for one to become suspicious and report some-one to the enemy. Frieda and the children had been calling me Irene. We stuck to the story about my being a relative, but did anyone actually believe it?

Finally we decided on a new alternative and wrote down Irene Nova. I read mistrust on everyone's face. I thought that Mr. Stojanow observed me in a strange and nervous way. Finally, out of fear, I spoke to him. "I see that you suspect my secret," I said to him one day. "I don't want to deny it: I'm really a Jew. But why do you want to betray me? Could you give me a few days until I can find another hideout? Perhaps I can find a place to stay." Mr. Stojanow hadn't known a thing; I had only imagined his suspicious glances. My excited imagination caused me to see enemies everywhere. He promised me that he would keep my secret and tell no one, not even his wife.

We no longer had any peace, slept totally clothed, and every footstep we heard on the street made our blood run cold. Our fear grew daily, while we feverishly awaited news of Gafur. His wife and children were here—wasn't he going to come and rescue us? Would he arrive before it was too late? Many tears flowed in Dibra. There were more and more executed to mourn. Finally, after fourteen days of waiting, Gafur arrived one morning. We heard him before he stepped into the house. Noisy and boisterous, he joked with a few people. He was not alone; armed men accompanied him. The small city in which he had spent his youth hid many enemies. It could easily happen that one of his childhood friends could catch him off guard and punish him for his friendship with the Germans.

He walked into the house and kissed his wife and children. Gafur exuded life, strength, and security. "Tomorrow morning we're traveling back to Tirana," he said. "At least, Frieda and me and the children." With a twinkle in his eye he teased, "There is no room for Irene in the vehicle; I'll pick her up next week." That night was the first night in a long time that everyone in the house slept peacefully, even me.

TIRANA REVISITED

The trip back to Tirana took place without incident. Neither robbers nor communists nor Germans harassed us. Now and then German guards inspected Gafur's papers. The documents had been issued by such high officials and were covered with so many stamps and signatures that no one demanded to see the papers of the two women traveling with him. "My wife and my sister," interjected Gafur when they looked through his documents and then at us. "Heil Hitler!" they replied.

Nothing stood in our way for the remainder of the journey. After we arrived in Tirana, I spent three nights in Gafur's house. As soon as I arrived, I knew that I couldn't stay there very long. Gafur had taken it upon himself to be the savior of Jewish women: a young woman was living in his home as a housekeeper, and a mother and two sisters aged seventeen to twenty were daily guests at his table. I observed the women's hostile stares and knew that I was disturbing things. Frieda said nothing. Gafur and the housekeeper asked me at least three times a day if I had found a place to stay yet. I went to Hassan's mother, but unfortunately she couldn't take me in. Her house had been searched and she was suspected, rightly so, of having given refuge to people who were being persecuted. It was impossible to find a room.

Durazzo had been evacuated, and every house in Tirana was filled with relatives and friends. People I had known in Cavaia were there as well, and I asked all of them for shelter. Again and again I heard refusals—no one had room for me. But finally I got lucky. Uncle Mika, an elegant, wealthy old gentleman who had been a well-known person in Belgrade, took me in. The owner of a large business, for years he had been the man older unmarried women and widows dreamed of marrying. Cleverly, again and again he had managed to pull himself out of love affairs and maintain his precious freedom. Now he regretted his former sins and complained bitterly about how sad and difficult his life was without female companionship, how much he disliked the people who shared his house, and how wonderful the good old days had been. "Not once have the two asses been able to cook a simple soup, nor have they been able to sew a button or start a fire; I have to do everything. No woman wants to take over our household; the women want either money or youth, and neither can be found here," he complained sadly.

I looked pensively at his old, haggard face. "Uncle Mika," I said. "If you have an extra bedroom for me, then for the time being I could come to see you, cook a soup, and start a fire as well." His face lit up. "That would be wonderful! We have an extra bedroom for you. Do you want to look at it?" I thought of Gafur and the four women in his home and answered quickly. "What is there to see? If it is an extra room, then I agree. Wait for me a little: I have to go to the people with whom I'm currently residing and tell them I'm moving out." Gafur's family and guests didn't make the departure very difficult. They watched me leave without tears.

Uncle Mika lived somewhere outside Tirana in a tiny, dilapidated house. My bedroom was a dump: it was full of coal, old boards, various tools, and other such junk. We put a few boards across two boxes, and my bed was ready. Unfortunately, however, there were neither pillows nor blankets. But even if I had had down blankets there, I wouldn't have been able to sleep. Rats were everywhere, the coal dust was so bad that I couldn't breathe, there were no windows, and I had blocked the small door. I only stayed three days there as well.

Then once again I had some luck. Mrs. Benga came up to me on the street, and I told her all my troubles. "Come to visit me tomorrow morning when my husband isn't at home. Perhaps I can help you," she told me. I gratefully remembered how helpful she had been to me before the trip to Dibra, and I went to her the next day. She was not alone. She was chatting with an unusually thin woman who had a beautiful face with a small, disturbing mouth. It was obvious that she was from a good family, because she sat there looking elegant and sure of herself. "I've heard that you are having problems finding a place to stay," the elegant woman said to me in a friendly tone. "Perhaps I can help you."

The woman explained many things about herself and her current situation. "I own a large house in New Tirana, and in these dangerous times it is not advisable to keep employees in the house. My husband is a high official, and he doesn't like it when servants leave and tell everyone what they have seen and heard where they work. For this reason I'm doing all the work myself. I would gladly offer you room and board if you would help me with the housekeeping. We could live together like sisters," she added in a friendly manner. I enthusiastically seized the opportunity.

There were no rats in my new living quarters; everything gleamed and sparkled. I observed spacious rooms on the ground floor, as well as large terraces and stone staircases. The kitchen was white, the pots shone like mirrors, and the floor was almost as immaculate. Because there was no water in the house, it had to be pumped from the well in the courtyard outside, which was part of the large extant reservoir.

My duties were not insignificant. Every morning I got up at five o'clock so that I would be able to finish my daily chores: the steps had to be scrubbed, the parquet shined, the windows cleaned, and most important of all, the water had to be pumped. I had to move the pump handle up and down twelve hundred times to fill the reservoir. To make things easier, I discovered a system for myself: I pumped a hundred times without stopping, took a short break, and then pumped another hundred times. Sweat streamed down my body, my heart pounded wildly, my hands became blistered, and soon the blisters popped. Everyday I had to wash clothes, and soda was not spared. My hands were open wounds.

Madame Neyre had shed much of her initial kindness. Her manner was cool and malevolent when she questioned why the wash wasn't as white as normal or whether I thought the stairs were clean. Because we lived like "two sisters," I was allowed to eat with her at the table. She filled up my plate, and her hand shook as she served me. I felt like the stepsister from a fairy tale. The worse she behaved toward me, the nicer, one could almost say more loving, her husband was to me. He followed my every step and roguishly tried to pinch me or to steal a kiss. It was disgusting. One time he tried to give me a secret present on the stairs: cough drops. I think my hour-long coughing fits disturbed him at night. The excessive work, malnutrition, and vexation had so weakened me that I was only a shadow of my former self. My nerves were also in a bad state. I cried easily, lost control, and told Madame Neyre to go to hell along with her husband and her house.

We now argued often. Once during a bombing raid when we were all in the basement and the house was shaking at the hinges, she demanded: "Irene, go upstairs quickly and fetch my coat. It's cold here." "Get it yourself," I retorted. "My life is too precious to me, just as yours is to you." "Be quiet!" she snapped back. "You seem to have forgotten that you're an unregistered person staying in my home." I noticed an evil wind blowing.

I felt worst when visitors came to the house. As dirty as I was, wearing

Madame Neyre's old nightshirt and her husband's slippers, she would call me from a task to display me like a dancing bear. She proudly exhibited me to her friends as if I were her own piece of property. "She speaks several languages and reads novels," she whispered to them while I angrily executed the work I had allegedly been ordered to do.

At this time, someone offered me a similar position. The only difference was that in the other job I wouldn't be treated as a sister, but as an "only child." One of our emigrants, Mr. Melanow, had become a widow. His wife had died of typhus, and three children between the ages of seven and thirteen remained. He lived in Scutari and had come to Tirana in order to find a housewife, a governess, a female companion, in short, a "girl for everything."[1] Now on the lookout for the daughters of the land, Mr. Melanow chose me. After deliberating briefly, I decided not to accept his offer, whereupon he drove back to Scutari.

About two weeks later, however, he returned and asked me for an interview. Mr. Melanow painted a most enticing picture of what kind of life I would live in his house, and when I stood by my decision, he played his best card. "You don't know what you are turning down," he said, "or you wouldn't be so proud; you would beg me to take you into my home." I became curious and I tried to discover what was behind his puzzling comments. Mr. Melanow was not stupid. Since he spoke in this manner, there had to be something interesting. "Don't you want to tell me what you're trying to say? There is a possibility that I would change my mind," I added falsely.

He confided his secret to me, and his bait was not insignificant. Mr. Melanow was not living in Scutari for nothing. He had succeeded, with a lot of money, in finding a man who would take him and a few others to Italy on a barge. Everything had to be done very quietly in order not to attract the attention of the Germans. The barge was to be ready for the escape in about six weeks. Now what could I say? I didn't say a thing—I was speechless in the truest sense of the word. The great dream of us all: Italy, Bari, where the Allies were, was so near and yet so unattainable and far away. Only a few hours on a boat, and then one was in the land of milk and honey. We thought with envy of those who were already there. Italy meant freedom, refuge, and food; to those of us who went to bed in fear and woke up in fear, it was a paradise on earth. My sense of balance had been disturbed. Upon mature considera-tion, I once again decided to reject his offer.

I kept on pumping water, scrubbed, swept, and swore at my own stupid-ity or whatever one could call it. Madame Neyre harassed me intentionally now. She was jealous. In all likelihood, she had probably noticed the tender glances her husband gave me during our communal meals. Nothing was clean enough any more. When I washed the windows, she stood behind me and pointed out remaining bits of dust in the most impossible places. She made me chop wood for storage and was constantly amazed at my voracious appetite.

One day when I was scrubbing the large stone steps in front of the house, Ronny came by. Ronny was Bella's husband; we had been neighbors in the "white house" in Cavaia.[2] Astounded, he halted. "Is that you, Irene?" he in-quired. "You look a sight!" Well, I probably didn't look that pretty in my tat-tered blue nightgown. I was thin, haggard, and sick with fever and a cough.

He took the brush from my hand and scrubbed powerfully. Now it looked really clean. At that moment I realized that Madame Neyre was probably right: I really wasn't a perfect worker; my efforts left a lot to be desired. Ronny put down the brush and then said: "Irene, when things become too miserable and discouraging for you, come stay with Bella, Bernie, and me. We would be happy to have you. It is a little crowded in our house, but you'll find it just as good as you have here. We have a small bedroom and a closet. Bella's three brothers and four cousins are living with us as well. Altogether there are nine adults and one child." He gave me his address. I hid the little slip of paper in my shoe in order not to lose it and thanked him warmly.

I made use of his invitation sooner than I thought I would. A few days after my encounter with Ronny, I had a fight with Madame Neyre. It was laundry day, and she was already in the kitchen early in the morning. I was in the process of scooping hot water out of a large container with a bucket so that I could pour the water over the laundry. She came right up to me, jerked the bucket from my hand, and screamed in my face: "How dare you use this bucket for pouring hot water! Will you never learn how things should be done in my house? But today I'm going to punish you!" And be-fore I understood what she wanted, she began to pour out all the hot water sitting on the stove and turned on the water faucet over the sink. "There!" she exclaimed, satisfied. "Today you'll pump fresh water, and quickly! I want to get the bath water ready for my husband!"

I was overcome with a cold rage. I put down the article of clothing I had been scrubbing and said, "If you want to take a bath, then pump the water yourself! Likewise, if you want your clothes washed, or if you want to drink some water, you'll have to do it yourself!" The effect of my outburst wasn't long in coming. "How dare you speak to me like that!" she screamed. "That is the thanks I get for having treated you like a sister in my own home? That is the thanks I get for having left cupboards and closets unlocked? You don't appreciate any of it?"

I laughed and then replied. "You're right. You did leave all the cupboards open, except for the one that contained bread and cheese. That one was always locked tight." Then I turned around, dried my hands, and went out of the kitchen. Ten minutes later I was standing in front of Madame Neyre holding my raincoat. "Where are you going now?" she asked calmly, having regained her composure. "Don't you want to finish your washing?" "No," I said, "you'll have to do it yourself, or your husband will have to do it, if he should have the urge. I'm staying with friends tonight. Because I have lived like a sister in your home, I have received no wages for my work and I don't need to give notice of termination." I said good-bye quickly and had the satisfaction of knowing that I had left a dumbfounded Madame Neyre standing alone in front of the washing vat.

I spent the entire day looking for accommodations in friends' homes. By six o'clock I was tired, hungry, and depressed after such a long day. I stood in front of the Cafe Berlin thinking that perhaps I would meet someone who would let me sleep in their home that evening. The Cafe Berlin was where emigrants met their friends and exchanged the latest gossip. I spotted Ronny, and he saw me immediately. "What are you doing on the street at this time of night?" he asked me. "Ronny, I don't have a place to sleep tonight," I replied. "I'd like to take you up on your invitation now." Had he really meant what he said?

Without further ado, he took me by the arm and led me to his house. Bella and the young men took me in without any pretense of kindness. It was natural for me to be there: I was with friends. Again, I had no bed to sleep on, but one of the young men loaned me his jacket, which I used as a pillow, and another loaned me his coat; everyone contributed something to make my rest as comfortable as possible. We lived together like a family. Bella and I cooked, washed, and mended for the young men. In the evening we sat around the glowing brazier and talked.

What plans and what hope were hidden in these half-children! They wanted to build up their home and their homeland; they wanted to help those who returned from the war. They longed for freedom, peace, and work after the war ended. Only one of these young men perhaps fulfilled his dreams; the others are dead. One day when I was no longer living with them, they were arrested and thrown into prison. A few days later they were shot in the forest. They haven't been forgotten. My thoughts become entangled, rushing back and forth, as I remember the people I once knew and loved who no longer exist. They are around me as I write. I feel their presence, I see their faces, I talk to them. Why did they have to die? Who can answer me?

One day as I was walking by the Cafe Berlin in Tirana, where I often went, I noticed a small group of friends whispering about something. Curious, I walked up to them. I was greeted with the false amiability of someone whose interesting discussion has been interrupted, a conversation about which I should know nothing. The first time this happened I lost patience and asked one of them, "Do you think it is right to keep news from me that has perhaps as much importance for me as it does for you and your family? Does it hurt your pride that a woman wants to take part in your men's discussion? Have you forgotten that Bobby is not with me and that I have to think for myself?"

An old man turned around and said to me, "You're right. Come closer, my child, the discussion is just as important to you as it is to us. It's about a Mr. Melanow from Scutari." His secret had leaked out. The owners of the barge were looking for rich travelers because the price was high and few could afford it. They thought that they could perhaps save their lives. But still, some didn't want to risk the trip, because it was just too dangerous. The barge could fall into the hands of the Germans, which would mean sudden death for sure. Or it could run into a sea mine, and they could all drown. Excitedly they discussed the pros and cons of the undertaking. I went back home to talk the matter over with my small "family." Because I knew Mr. Melanow, it was decided that I would travel to Scutari the next day in order to speak with him. In Scutari I met even more emigrants from Tirana. All of them wanted to talk to Mr. Melanow, but they all tried to hide it from one another. They pretended that they had come because they suddenly wanted to see the picturesque city of Scutari or because they had friends there whom they were simply dying to visit.

The house where Mr. Melanow lived was far from the city. It stood isolated, and I saw no neighbors. A very young girl opened the door for me. "Why do you wish to see Mr. Melanow?" she asked. "He usually gets home around evening, but you can safely tell me what it is about. I'm Mr. Melanow's housekeeper." Then she said shyly, "My name is Ana R. Don't you recognize me? We were neighbors in Skopje!" I looked at the girl more closely. Yes, of course, it was Ana, the oldest daughter of a poor family with many children from Skopje. Things must have been bad at home for her parents to let this child become a widow's housekeeper. She told me in confidence that her parents were happy to have one less mouth to feed. "Mr. Melanow is rich," she said. "Maybe he'll marry me after the war, although he is a little old for me. I'm only one year older than his son, and he doesn't respect me at all. Even though I'm in the same position as his deceased mother," she added in her naive, childish way.

"Where do you sleep?" I asked her bluntly. She pointed to the double beds in the next room. "How do you expect a fifteen-year-old to respect you?" I asked her. "You are too young yourself to be able to see your situation clearly. And Mr. Melanow is pretty irresponsible to put you in this delicate position, with three boys in the house, one of whom is almost old enough to be a man." I felt sorry for the young girl, especially the way she looked standing in front of me. I regretted my words and said reassuringly, "Well, I also believe that Mr. Melanow will marry you after the war is over."

A little later the man of the house returned home. Pleasantly surprised, he greeted me, then ordered the young girl to leave. "I want to speak with her alone," he said in a commanding tone. "Don't come back before an hour is up." She left obediently. "So, you did find me!" he began our conversation. "I can send the girl back to her parents in Tirana. Do you want to stay here?" I corrected his mistake, informing him why I had come. "My friends and I would like to travel to Bari with you. Ronny has money and will pay for our portion," I explained. "Please, give us the chance to escape. Don't let your personal feelings affect your decision. Grant us the opportunity of saving ourselves," I pleaded angelically for everyone.

"The barge is big," he said. "It can hold about a hundred people. Why shouldn't I give you the chance? We're leaving in about three weeks; I don't know the exact date yet. Don't worry about it, just drive back to Tirana and be ready. I'll send my son to you a few days before departure, so you and your friends can spend the last few days here in Scutari." He gave me his word. Relieved, I returned to Tirana to tell Bella, Ronny, and the others the good news.

Two days later there was great agitation among the emigrants in Tirana because the barge had left port. All the Jews in Scutari on that day had left. There was still enough room for thirty people, and a few friends in Tirana were informed by Melanow's son at the last minute. Regrettably, the son forgot to pick up little Ana R., whom he had left at her parents' home, and it seemed that he had also lost my address. Would my fate lead me to cross paths with Mr. Melanow once again? I hoped so, if only to prove to him that when it is God's will, people can find their way out of the lion's den even if the one who threw them in was their brother.

Life in Bella's house continued as usual. I was once again looking for work, and I knew that I couldn't stay as a guest in the new accommodations forever. Almost at the same time, I found both a job and housing. I had worked my way to the top, advancing from maid to teacher. My pupil's father had a large fabric store on the market square. One day I walked there to get something for Bella's little Bernie, and we got into a conversation. The father stuttered a few words of German, which he was quite proud of. "Don't you want to take some German lessons?" I asked him. "I'm a great teacher and would gladly teach you for a good price," I added. "I'm too old for that," he replied, "but could you perhaps teach my children?" Excited, I took him up on it. "When can I begin?" I inquired. We had come to an agreement so quickly. "Do you speak a little Albanian?" When I said no, he asked, "How will you be able to teach the children German? Won't it be too difficult?" I didn't give in. "I guarantee you that the children will speak German. Please give me four weeks, and you'll see the successful results!" He probably noticed by looking at me how desperately I needed the job, because he took me up on my offer and, wonder of wonders, paid for the first two weeks in advance!

The next day I went to his house. My surprise was great when I saw my pupils: nine children sat there on the floor. All except one got up when I entered. My pupils were between the ages of three and sixteen. The youngest, a little boy about two years old, didn't pay the least attention to me. "Guten Morgen, Kinder," I said slowly and clearly. "Bitte, setzt euch" [Good morning, children. Please sit down]. I made the corresponding hand gestures, but all eight stared at me with open mouths until I pressed one firmly into his place on the floor and sat down myself.

Now the others laughed. The ice was broken, and the first communication had taken place. As time went by, we got to know each other better and better. I pointed to everything one could see in the room and articulated the name for it in German. No success. I began to sing. General laughter. So we sang "Ich bin, du bist, er ist, wir sind, ihr seid, sie sind" [I am, you are, he is, we are, you are, they are]. Or "Das ist das Fenster und dies dort Papier, hier ist ein Bleistift und dort ist die Tür" [That is the window and here is paper, here is a pencil and there is the door].[3] The month went by and my new employer was satisfied. Although the children didn't speak German, they sang in German and it was fun for them. Not only my pupils but all the little girls and boys on the street greeted me in song: "Ich bin groß und du bist klein, er ist schmutzig, sie ist rein" [I am big and you are small, he is dirty and she is clean] or similar folk songs.

I became a well-known person, and my fame spread. New pupils wanted to take the entertaining German lessons, and I earned enough to be able to rent my own room. I ran into a friend from Skopje who explained to me joyfully that he had rented an entire "house" for himself and his family. "It has two rooms," he said. "The rent isn't much, but nevertheless I can give up one room. My mother can sleep with us in the other." I rented it and moved in the next day, quite happy about it.

The new house was a magnificent building that stood in the middle of a courtyard. The owner of the house had built it with his own hands from loam and mortar. It stood on pillars, and just looking at it made it shake. It also had a staircase; the steps were perilously narrow, and we were always happy when we had once again been able to get upstairs without falling down. The rooms were nice, but they did have one small but insignificant disadvantage: my neighbor's room was situated over a horse's stable. The horse was temperamental and suffered from insomnia; at night it neighed loudly and reared up, and our house reared up with it. The neighbors thought that they would land in the horse stable at any moment, and they wanted to exchange rooms with me. But then they decided to stay where they were because at least it was warmer above the stable, even though the smell and the flies were annoying at times.

My room had been built over a spring. The boards of the floor had such large spaces between them that a small cat could easily slip through them. The dampness left much to be desired. Large worms that came from the spring found my walls and my floor much more pleasant than the wetter terrain below. It was not always dry in my abode. When it rained, I could just as easily take a walk there as on the street, because there was no dry place. But our landlord made up for all this. He had a heart of gold. Even when we moved in, he helped the Kajevic family carry the "furniture" upstairs. Half an hour later he visited us and brought a little sugar along as a gift—a rare and great kindness.

The landlord came from a small region near the Yugoslavian border and because of this spoke Serbian. He was perhaps forty years old, but because of his slight build and his comforting and shy personality, he seemed like an old man. Often his face would break out into a smile, and because he had no teeth, it didn't make him look any handsomer. But we learned to love him. On his first visit he asked me: "When are your things going to arrive, little miss?" "They've already arrived," I replied. "Didn't you see that I brought a coat and a small bundle? Those are my belongings." He looked at me in amazement. "Where do you want to sleep, little miss?" he asked further, thinking that I had been joking with him. "On the floor," I replied. "I'm used to it, and I sleep so well there." He was indeed startled when he realized that I wasn't joking. "Wait a moment," he said, "you will not sleep on the floor."

He went downstairs quickly, hammered together some boxes and boards, and ten minutes later had a splendid bed for me. He brought some straw and a horse blanket that stank and had vermin, but it was warm.

"Poor little miss," he said to me again and again. "I will help you out. Tomorrow I'll make the bed much nicer, and I'll find a nice blanket for you." I thanked him, touched. "You know," he continued, "I'm surprised that you haven't found a husband yet. You're so pretty! Are all the men in your country blind?" "It seems like it," I replied. "I had a husband, and he abandoned me. He went to America and left me here alone." It was the only thing that I could possibly say to him. This good person couldn't have understood what it was like to be a Jew, to be persecuted and always have to hide.

Soon he had related this interesting piece of news to his wife, and she related it to her girlfriend. Because of this our lives were in greater danger than before. That the story about the husband who went away was a lie was evident to him from the beginning, although he assured me that he couldn't understand how a man could leave such a pretty wife. If he had been in his place, he never could have done it, he had assured me candidly. In time he moved all sorts of things into my room to make it look nicer. Now I had, in addition to my bed, a beautiful glass wardrobe with elaborate legs decorated with lion's heads. Our landlord bought this and that from Italian households. He asked me to go with him and look at a musical instrument that an Italian wanted to sell and asked me to tell him if the man was demanding the right price. I went with him into the Italian's home. It was a piano. I opened it and started to play. Totally enraptured, he wanted to buy it so he could put it in my room. I dissuaded him with great effort.

His great attentiveness, in addition to the joking remarks, had not only attracted the attention of my neighbors but also provoked the jealous wrath of his wife. She cast evil glances my way whenever she saw me, and if she hadn't been afraid of her husband, she would probably have murdered me or at least scratched my eyes out or pulled out my hair. This state of affairs became very uncomfortable for me. I would gladly have moved out, but I didn't have the slightest capability of doing so. How could I make it clear to the woman that I didn't have the least intention of stealing her husband?

My professional possibilities had expanded considerably. Sukriye Hanim, who had found a position for me in the home of Turkish friends right after my [first] arrival in Tirana, let me teach her children.[4] Through her recommendation, I came into the house of Ekrem Bey Vlora. I can still remember what a vivid impression that first visit made on me. A strong-looking man opened the iron door after I had knocked several times. He left me in the courtyard in order to inform his employer about the stranger who had come to visit. I later learned that the man was Ekrem Bey's personal bodyguard. He never left the house without the company of this armed and devoted man, who had worked for the family for years.

I looked around timidly while I was waiting. What splendor and wealth were here inside these walls! How well kept the garden was! Servants in white jackets went in and out, while a fat old woman sitting on a stool under a shady tree did some sewing. She was looking after a pretty little three-year-old girl who was playing with a kitten. The little animal miaowed pitifully when the child pulled its tail, held up its hind legs, and let it run. Finally, after she had thrown it up into the air, it had had enough torture and escaped, whereby she ran after it screaming.

"Entrez, madame," I heard a voice say suddenly behind me. I turned around. A little, old, fat man stood on the top step of a large staircase that led into the house. I approached him, and he led me courteously into a large room that was sumptuously decorated with expensive silk rugs and antique furniture. A servant brought coffee in fine, thin porcelain cups. In a disjointed French I referred to Sukriye Hanim's recommendation.

Would this man hire me as a teacher for his children, despite my impoverished appearance, which was surely conspicuous in these surroundings? Unexpectedly, Ekrem Bey switched into German. With an almost unnoticeable accent, he spoke with great ease and carefully chosen words in my mother tongue. "I'll introduce my pupils to you, and I hope that they will make teaching a pleasure. Both are intelligent and well brought up," he said with a refined smile. Two young girls came in and, a little embarrassed, curtsied in front of me. Leila, the oldest, was about twelve years old. Sossi was ten or eleven. They were cousins, and the parents of both lived in the large house, since they had abandoned their property in Valona because of the war.[5]

We quickly became friends. The lessons really became a source of joy and serenity for me. The children were of well above average intelligence. I didn't need to sing here. I taught them with pictures and objects, and after a short time they were both speaking and writing a good German. The lessons were given in a large room. Our desk stood near a window that supplied plenty of teaching aids. When we were tired of grammar and writing, we had only to look into the garden and there was stimulation in abundance. The trees, the birds, the kitten, the gardener, the flowers—all of life outside lent itself to interesting topics with thousands of variations.

But this wasn't the only thing that made my stay in this household so pleasant. Ekrem Bey worked in the same room; usually he was already sitting at his desk and writing assiduously before we entered. For a long time I didn't realize that he would often put down his pen in order to listen to our lesson. One time he said to me suddenly, "When the time comes for me to emigrate, I hope that I will have your ability to earn my keep in a foreign country. But, unfortunately, I don't think I'll be capable of doing it," he said sadly. "All of my knowledge will be of no use to keep my family and me alive without my house, my sustenance, and my secure salary. How strong you Jews are! How all the suffering brings out the strength in you! No one will ever succeed in breaking you. You can only be bent. I admire and envy your strength, madam," he said. "And you can be sure that I will do everything in my power to save you. You will belong to that group who will perhaps one day, after many years, when the victims have decayed and the world has forgotten, recall the past. Remind the young mothers that children were taken away from other mothers to be gassed. Remind the older people that their husbands and sons were shot and hanged. Remind the men that their wives and mothers were degraded and murdered. Remind the people of all countries whom you meet of all the horrors of war. Perhaps the seeds of your words will grow. Perhaps they will fill their hearts with Christ's words: 'Peace on earth' and 'Love your neighbor as yourself.'"

From that day on, after Ekrem Bey first said those words to me, we would talk together for a little while every day after the lessons were over. These few minutes were sheer pleasure for me. I had never met a person of such high culture and profound learning. Ekrem Bey Vlora was one of the most distinguished men in his country. A diplomat by profession, he was erudite and a citizen of the world. He came from a home where wealth and art went hand in hand with science and politics. At the time when I met him, he was attempting to stop every intervention in the confused circumstances of his country. Unfortunately, he was not able to stick it out. Near the end of the war he allied himself with the Germans, and as he himself had predicted, the day came for his emigration. It was a pity that a man of such great intelligence and profound ability could not put his talents to better use than working with Hitler and his satellites.

The Germans now had a firm hold on Albania. Every day new orders and decrees rained from the "higher" and the "highest" positions above. A segment of the Albanian civil servants accommodated themselves to the new rulers; the others fled to the mountains or kept as quiet as possible and bided their time. The approximately three hundred Jews who were still in Albania searched for protection and a place to hide. Almost without exception, the populace of Albania, regardless of social status or political persuasion, gave them help. Their sense of justice wouldn't allow them to refuse the right of asylum to innocent men, women, and children.

We all had friends in Albania: one found a place to hide at a cobbler's, another at a teacher's, a third at a minister's.[6] It all depended on where one's destiny had led one. Whenever there was actual danger, Ekrem Bey let me know. He would say something like the following: "Madame Irene, would you like to be our guest here for a few days? Go right ahead with your lessons, and you can spend the night here. We will put up a bed for you in the big room." I gratefully accepted the invitation and went out and warned my friends. As long as I slept in the Vlora house, all the other Jews were fully aware of the danger that threatened us and did everything possible to avoid it.

Nevertheless, there were victims, for example, Bella's brother and cousins. They were arrested on trumped-up charges and disappeared. Ekrem Bey advised me to live closer to his house so that in emergencies his servants could reach me late at night. I found a room in a side street near the large house. My new landlords were a young Italian man and an Albanian woman of the lowest class. There were jealous scenes almost every day. The Italian hit his girlfriend mercilessly when he thought he had reason to. Plates and bowls were shattered, but all with little success. No sooner was the jealous lover out of the house than the young woman slipped out with her face made up as if she were going to a carnival. She was going to visit a friend at her sister's place, she confided to me with a twinkle in her eye.

The Albanian woman didn't know that I was Jewish. Whenever I spent the night at the Vloras', I would tell her about a secret affair with a distinguished married gentleman whose name I unfortunately could not mention. Such an explanation satisfied her curiosity. It was less dangerous to have her think that I was amusing myself at night with love affairs than to have her speculating that I was saving my life.

Once I found myself in the lion's den. Guerrilla fighters made life difficult for the Germans and their pro-German populace. Again and again individuals came down from the mountains and "liquidated" this or that person. It was almost impossible to catch one of the fighters. The latest measures against the dangerous foe were of a bureaucratic nature: the inhabitants of Tirana and the other towns were required to have their papers stamped by the German commander's office. Upon inspection of their papers, those who had ignored these instructions would be viewed as enemies and dealt with accordingly.

What followed was a massive flight of the young Albanian men to their brothers in the mountains. Jews didn't leave their abodes anymore, or they too fled to the outlying villages, where the risk was just as great. I spoke to Ekrem Bey about my situation. Because I had to work, I was forced to be on the street, and I was in constant danger of being stopped. Ekrem Bey advised me to register myself with my false papers, so one morning I went fearfully to the commander's office. I was the only Jew in Tirana who did this and consequently was viewed by the others as insane. I stood in a long line. When I finally reached the desk where the German officer sat in uniform, my heart beat so loudly that I was sure one could hear it. My knees shook, and I almost fainted. The officer asked me some questions in Italian, and I answered none of them verbally; I shook my head again and again, pointing to my identification papers, which were lying in front of him. He finally wrote in the date; Fatima Nova received a German stamp on her document with a nice signature. I quickly left the terrible room.

Again I had shown little heroic bravery. Why did people have to scare other people? Hadn't this occurred since the dawn of time, and would it never end? The fact that I wasn't the only one who was afraid was not much consolation to me. Fear was everywhere in this country: in the cities and villages, in the mansions and huts. Fear had crept into the farthest corners of the world. Fear was in every heart! And also in every heart was the victor, the oppressor, who today still held the power in his hands but tomorrow or in the next hour would be nothing more than a creature who feared death.

The Allies were bombing Tirana almost daily now. We usually heard them coming around ten o'clock in the morning. They didn't stay long, but long enough to prove that they were there and that they weren't sleeping. Bari, Italy, was close by. Almost every day we awaited the arrival of the Allies. We yearned for their appearance—maybe today would be the big day. Would they let the paratroopers jump? Were we close to liberation? Every day we were disappointed, and we waited for the next day full of anticipation.

Life went on. I taught my pupils and told further stories to my landlady about my secret love affairs. I spent the night in my room more often and Ekrem Bey called me to his house at the last minute more frequently. The chaos in Tirana increased, followed by secret assassination attempts. Political parties fought each other with greater hatred, and most of the leading politicians didn't dare go on the street without bodyguards. Nevertheless, people of the opposition party always found an opportunity to kill their foes. The government itself did not spare death sentences. At seven o'clock one morning I saw lying in front of a building the corpses of seven people who had been shot in the night.

I had yet another horrifying experience: When I went to Ekrem Bey's house early one morning to teach, I saw something white blowing in the wind far from me, in the city square. Because of my nearsightedness, I couldn't make out what it was. I walked closer, drawn magically by the white object billowing in the breeze. Only when I stood in front of it did I realize what it was. I beheld two men who had been hanged in the night. They had been dressed in white flowing garments before the execution and now swung horribly in the air. I turned away, shocked.

DR. K.

Uneasy weeks followed. Day and night, events took place that haunted me. I became obsessed with an incident of a personal nature: a good-looking gentleman about forty years old was trying to blackmail me. He stopped me on the street one day. "How are you, madam?" he asked politely in Serbian.

I was certain that a friend of Bobby's was standing in front of me, and I chatted amiably with him. Only after I had told him a little about my job did I ask him a question. "How are you getting on here? Do you have a job? Are you alone, or have you been able to save members of your family? And please excuse me, I've forgotten your name. What was it again?"

The man calmly let me finish talking before he replied, "I'm Dr. K. and I work with the political police. Could I meet you this evening at five o'clock in front of the Hotel Imperial? I have something to discuss with you." Police, false papers, raced through my mind. I pulled myself together—perhaps he hadn't noticed my horror—and I said as nonchalantly as possible, "This afternoon at five o'clock? I'm giving lessons, and six o'clock is curfew, so it's impossible. Could you tell me right now what it is you wish to discuss with me, Doctor?" "No!" He replied curtly. "I don't have time for that presently. I'll meet you at five o'clock sharp in front of the Imperial." He then gave me his hand and went away quickly. I stood still for a moment and thought about what this request could possibly mean. Should I be at the designated place at five o'clock? Would it not be better to flee Tirana immediately? I decided to meet him there.

I arrived punctually but saw no Dr. K. Impatiently, I looked at the clock again and again. Now it was 5:26, and I had to be at home before the six o'clock curfew. I set out in that direction, when I heard someone call out, "*Milostiwa* [dear lady]! Come up here!" I looked up and saw Dr. K. waving at me invitingly from a small hotel terrace. A light went on in my brain. Watch out, it flashed. "Come down here!" I yelled. And despite eager waving and shouting on his part, I shook my head again and again. He probably wanted to avoid being seen in front of the busy hotel. Finally he took the trouble to come down to the lounge below, although he didn't come outside to speak with me; he had me paged by one of the hotel employees. I sat down in a comfortable easy chair as though I had the upper hand. Before he could open his mouth, I began, "Herr Doctor, it is unfortunately later than you intended. Please tell me quickly what you wanted to talk about. I have to get home before the curfew."

"The curfew is not important," he parried, "because you are under my protection. That means under the protection of the police, mind you! You can walk the streets with me at any time without risk. I want to speak with you for a while," he said looking at his watch. "At eleven o'clock I have to be in my office. You can stay here till then, and we can discuss our business leisurely over dinner." Our business, I thought. Did I hear him correctly, or did it have something to do with information about the Vlora household? Or did he want news about other people whom I knew? And if so, why in a hotel and not in his office? He obviously reveled in my latest fright. Then he put his hand on my lower arm, leaned toward me a little, and murmured: "Don't be afraid, child. Nothing bad will happen to you. From now on you are under my protection. Write this down in your calendar. This is your lucky day!" he chirped eagerly.

Surprised, I looked at him. "Excuse me, what do you mean? Would you please give me an explanation?" I demanded. He leaned closer to me, looked into my eyes, and said: "You mean you honestly don't know? Do I really have to tell you that I've been watching you for weeks, that you're the only woman I like here among all the foreigners? I know that you live alone. I know that you have a job. But from now on things will be different. Because we've now become friends, you won't have to work anymore. You can live in the hotel, wear nice clothes, and live a life that befits a woman like you. And above all else, you won't have to be afraid of the police anymore," he added laughing. "I'll make sure that your papers are in order. Now take a look at me! Can you believe that you've had such good luck?" he asked vainly.

I smiled. So it was a "declaration of love." Now I would clear everything up and rob this absurd fellow of his illusions of a passionate affair. He thinks he's Don Juan in person, I thought scornfully. I was now in a good mood, and a nice dinner in this pretty hotel wouldn't hurt me. Besides, I felt so superior to my rival that it gave me pleasure to give the right answers to his melting sighs and his purring words. The game could commence. I played the first card and bluffed enticingly. "I feel so honored by your concern," I said. "And how flattering it is for me to know that I'm the only woman in Tirana whom you like. I don't know how to tell you how much I regret that we will not be able to form a 'friendship.' I'm no longer single, I'm married."

"That is nothing new to me," he retorted unruffled. "Your husband is in a German concentration camp." "Yes," I replied, "that's true, but I hope that he'll be released soon." "Do you really believe that?" he sneered. "Aren't you more afraid of following him there?" I would gladly have smacked his smirking, evil face, but I pulled myself together with all my strength and said calmly, "There is not the slightest reason why I should follow him there. I'm married to a Jew, but I myself am Czech, purely Aryan. Unfortunately, I lost all my papers when Belgrade was bombed. As you can see, I'm still free, while my poor husband ended up in the camp with all the other Jews of the city." It seemed too risky to bring up my "Fatima Nova document," so I tried my luck with the Czech story.

Dr. K. didn't interrupt me, but when I finally finished my narrative he said pensively, "How strange! All my information about you appears to be false!" He pulled a slip of paper from his pocket, smoothed it out carefully, and read out loud: "Irene Eskenazi, wife of Nissim Bobby Eskenazi, living in Belgrade, daughter of Seligman Levi and Elisabeth Levi, born in Darmstadt on 2 April 1909." Then he put the paper in his notebook and returned it to his pocket. "It's really unbelievable how poor my informants' work is. Normally one finds out everything for the police very quickly. Even people with false papers and authentic stamps are known to us. Amazing, amazing," he murmured and looked at me out of the corner of his eye. For a moment I gave up—this enemy was really dangerous.

I took a cigarette from his open case. I only wanted to gain some time, and maybe another tactic would help. I tried again with the helpless-little-woman, honest-batting-of-the-eye technique. "You're right," I said. "I lied to you because I was afraid. I thought you were my enemy because you're with the police. Since that horrible day my family was taken away from me, I can't trust anyone anymore. I question every offer of friendship. And certainly you're the first one who will not take advantage of my situation—you only want to help me. Should I come to your office tomorrow morning so that you can help me obtain legal residency and documents?" I asked childishly. "Of course, you will be able to do that, I am under your protection," I added naively.

Apparently moved by my confidence in him, Dr. K. took my hand into both of his and pressed it tenderly. With great effort, I was able to overcome my aversion to him and let my hand stay in his for a moment instead of pulling it away violently. "Yes, of course, I'll do everything in my power to help you; no sacrifice is too great provided that you will show me love and affection," he added, forgetting the noble role I was trying to force him into. "I love you, I desire you, I want to own you!" he blurted out. "Your pride and haughtiness excite me. I want to bend it; you shall become small and submissive, you shall appreciate the master in me!" Suddenly he changed tone. "Forgive me," he begged. "I don't know why I'm talking to you about love. I don't want to force you to do anything. You shall come to me of your own free will and offer me your heart. I know that a woman like you has to be conquered."

Gaining time was gaining everything, I thought. I tried hard to steer this conversation toward more tranquil topics. Now and then, Dr. K. cooed more words of love and tried to press my hand meaningfully, while I murmured something about a "great surprise" and remarked that "I have to get used to the idea." Finally it was 10:30. Dr. K. accompanied me through the strange and empty streets, and now and then I heard the pronounced footsteps of the patrols in an alley nearby. We didn't run into anyone. I went to bed full of worry, anticipating new complications and dangers. They weren't long in coming.

Dr. K. pursued me with his propositions. They wouldn't have been worth mentioning had my admirer not been a high police official and had it not been wartime. To be sure, the odds were not in my favor. Dr. K. became more and more importunate, and my excuses became lamer and lamer. Until now, neither his words of love nor his money had been able to change my mind. He realized that stronger ammunition was necessary. Worst of all, he threatened that he would arrest any Jew whom he saw me talking to on the street. So I kept clear of both my married as well as unmarried male friends. The consequence of this was that my acquaintances talked about a secret lover, and everyone believed that I had grounds for avoiding their nosy questions. The situation was embarrassing but not dangerous.

Herr Dr. K. resorted to more drastic measures. One day when he once again waited for me outside the home of one of my pupils, he surprised me with the following words: "The next time you come here you can tell your students good-bye; that is to say, you're going to be leaving Tirana." Startled, I asked him what he meant. "Well," he said, "I'll probably be transferred to P. in the next few days, and I've decided to take you with me." This was the first time I forgot my diplomacy toward him and expressed my rage uninhibitedly. "You will hardly manage that," I said. "Haven't you understood that I'm not thinking of becoming your girlfriend? You're losing your keen eye," I jeered. "If it continues, you'll ruin your career!"

Cold with rage, he answered: "Leave my career out of this. I'm used to getting what I want. You will be no exception. If I can't have you for better, I'll have you for worse. At any rate I'm the most powerful, so be warned! You will go to P. with me even if I have to arrest you and take you there in a police car." The idea that he had just articulated seemed to give him great pleasure. "Certainly, I'll have you arrested: you'll go to prison in P. And when I arrive, you'll beg me on your knees for freedom. I want to see you on your knees, you haughty, arrogant Jew whore!" he hissed, and he quickly crossed the street, leaving me alone with my thoughts.

An open deck! I knew that he was the most powerful, and I was afraid of him. I turned for counsel to Ekrem Bey, who told me I could spend the night in his home. Apparently, he couldn't and didn't want to get involved. I slept a few nights there, and when I found out from my landlady that no one had come by looking for me, I went back to my tiny room a little more composed. It was likely that Dr. K.'s ardent desire for me had subsided and he was leaving me alone. I neither saw nor heard from him. Totally unexpectedly, I learned from someone else that he hadn't given up his plans.

The Alger family had been living in Tirana since the Germans had invaded.[1] The Jewish community had been convinced for a long time that Ernst Alger was an informer for the Germans. We talked to him with great caution, secretly thinking about what would happen to him when the war was over. He knew we were mistrustful and tried to dispel our suspicions by providing a service to this or that person who needed protection. If someone had been arrested for possession of false papers, then Alger succeeded in setting him free, prudently not revealing his connections. The fact that his wife was a German Aryan seemed enough of an explanation for the visits he made to the German authorities.

I ran into Frau Katarina Alger on the street. For some inexplicable reason she had a soft spot for me. It often happened that she would warn me about immediate danger. I called it "Frau Alger's dreams," because she often told me that she had had such horrible nightmares the night before, that something was going to happen to the Jews, and that I should try to save myself. Because Frau Alger's "dreams" always coincided with Ekrem Bey's requests that I sleep in his home, I believed her. This time she hadn't had a dream but said to me openly, "I would like to discuss something with you and warn you about a grave danger that threatens you. Please, come inside the restaurant with me. I don't want anyone to see us."

We sat down in the farthest corner of the small inn, and Frau Alger began her story. "Do you know someone who works for the police?" she asked me bluntly. "No, I don't know anyone there," I replied without hesitation. "But why do you ask?" I inquired, truly worried. Frau Alger smiled and for a moment laid her hand on mine. "I know that you don't trust me because I'm German," she acknowledged, "but this has nothing to do with politics; it is a purely private matter. As a woman, I can't stand back and watch it. Just because a certain woman doesn't want to sleep with a particular man, I can't watch him hurt her. Which is what someone intends to do to you!"

"Please, tell me about it," I entreated. "I think I know what it is about." "Last night a high police official visited us in our home," she began. "I know his relatives in Germany," she added hastily, "and he asked me to say hello to them, if the opportunity arose.[2] While I made coffee in our small kitchen, I heard what he said to my husband: 'I've gotten it into my head that I want to see that woman diminished. Her resistance and impertinence toward me have to stop. I could have had her arrested today, but I want to see her come to me of her own free will and ask me to help her. It's enough if you tell a few Jews that you have heard that Frau Irene will be seized and arrested by the Albanian authorities as a Communist and, in addition, that the German authorities will seize and arrest her for being a spy. When this happens, I think that she will certainly remember my address.'"

"Do you know what this means?" Frau Alger asked sympathetically. Yes, I knew what it meant for me: more running away, perhaps arrest, perhaps death. Perhaps I would be arrested as a communist or shot as a spy. The enemy was right, he was stronger than I; by all accounts, he had won. It no longer had anything to do with a love affair; no, his vanity had been offended, his male ego had been wounded. He hated me and wanted to avenge himself. It was so easy for him to take revenge on a Jewish woman. These thoughts passed through my head quickly, and I was overcome with a profound depression.

I thanked Frau Alger for her warning and promised that I wouldn't reveal her name under any circumstances. I walked home to think about the matter. I had to be alone, but in my tiny room I couldn't think of any way out. I wanted to go discuss the matter with Ekrem Bey. He was older and wiser, and even if he couldn't help me directly, he could probably give me some advice. Perhaps he would send me to one of his villages near Valona, although the danger for a woman traveling alone was not minimal. Every village policeman could search me from head to toe. No, it was useless. I didn't even speak Albanian.

I was so preoccupied with my morbid thoughts that I almost bumped into someone as I was crossing the street. Jokingly, the other person had run into me when he saw that I wasn't paying attention. It was Dr. K. "Where are you going in such a hurry, pretty woman?" he asked as if we were the best of friends. I was momentarily so dumbfounded that I couldn't answer. Then I heard myself say against my own will: "I've been looking for you, Herr Doctor. I would like to talk to you."

He gallantly opened the door to the small bar nearby. We were the only customers. "May I know what changed your mind?" he asked affably. "You didn't really like talking to me that much before," he reminded me, beaming with self-satisfaction. I would gladly have slapped his smirking, confident face, but instead I spoke words that a guardian angel must have whispered to me. "I want to apologize for my hateful outburst the last time we met," I said. "I was in a bad mood that day and had to take it out on someone." Smiling in a conciliatory manner, I added, "Of course you know how women are." He fell for it immediately.

"So we're friends, then?" He asked, kissing my hand tenderly. "Will we stay together this evening? How happy you make me! I knew that you would be reasonable and see what is best for you," he added. I pulled my hand away but smiled at him warmly and said, "Yes, I realized that the best thing for me to do would be to go to P. with you. The only thing I ask of you is to have a little patience with me. I don't want to stay with you just yet. You know me well enough to know that I take life seriously, and it has taken me a long time to decide what I want to do. My decision is made, and I'm happy about it. I want to travel with you to P. and begin a new life with you there. Will you have enough patience with me to wait?" I spoke softly and meekly, playing the part of the shy young woman who has made up her mind to pursue bittersweet sins.

Dr. K. appeared touched. "Yes, sweetheart, I want to wait," he answered magnanimously, kissing my hand again and again. "You know," I began to talk childishly once more, "how happy I am to have you as a friend? You're one of the most influential men in all of Tirana, and people in such high positions don't usually bother with a small, insignificant emigrant." Beaming, I assured him, "I've been extremely fortunate." Then I continued speaking a little dreamily. "I believe that I'm really a lucky girl, because just think, only today I had the honor to speak to ——— Bey, the regent of Albania!"[3] My voice almost broke from awe when I told the lie. Dr. K. was more than a little amazed about my latest splendid acquaintance. "You've spoken to the regent?" he inquired, and his mouth remained open from amazement, while he stared at me with eyes like those of a young calf.

Dr. K. looked so ridiculous that I took heart and ornamented my story with dazzling colors. "Yes, just think, when I went to Ekrem Bey's house this morning to teach, his excellency asked me to accompany the children when they went to visit his wife's relatives. She didn't feel well yesterday, and the children were supposed to go there for a short visit," I said lying for the third time. "So we went there, and my pupils' aunt greeted us joyfully. What a fascinating woman! How warm and gracious she is," I raved enthusiastically, "I was totally charmed by her, but then—even more so by him!"

"That is to say, he came to his wife's room for a moment. He wanted to say hello to both young nieces, so I had the opportunity to meet and speak with this important man. He talked with me for fifteen minutes," I said proudly. "I looked furtively at my watch while we were conversing. The regent asked who I was, where I came from, and how I liked Albania. He spoke to me so naturally that I trusted him immediately and told him the story of my life. I explained that I was Jewish, that I was afraid because I have illegal papers, and that I hoped I would survive the war living in Albania.

"Do you know what happened after that?" I asked dramatically. "The regent held my hand and said, 'I promise that nothing unjust will happen to you here in our country. I will grant you protection and help at any time. Anyone who even tries to touch a hair on your head will pay for it bitterly. I do not tolerate injustice in my country. A week ago two policemen were hanged because they raped and imprisoned a girl on trumped-up charges that she was a communist. The punishment was severe, but it had to be so that no men will degrade our land and spread vice here. Albania has always been a country of high morals. Our women have always been sacred to us and will remain so. Therefore, again, don't be afraid, whoever and whatever threatens you. It is enough if you come to me personally or if you send word through Ekrem Bey Vlora,' he reassured me.[4]

"Isn't he a wonderful person?" I asked, ending my imaginative story enthusiastically. "Isn't it a glorious feeling to have two such friends? The regent of Albania and you, Herr Doctor?" Dr. K. looked at me silently for a long time before he said, "Too bad you're not a man." I didn't understand what he meant, and he gave no further explanations. He suddenly had to leave; he kissed my hand again and left. It was our last meeting. He disappeared from my sight but not from my thoughts.

How many countless women were blackmailed by men like him? Hate and loathing were the only things these men left us. It's always the same old story. Some women try to forget the horrible incident as if it were a bad dream; others, such as young girls who are not yet mature enough to resist the obscenity, are injured for their entire lives. That which should blossom into beauty and purity is soiled by coarse hands and base souls.

THE DREAM

It was now 1944. How long since I had been with Bobby and others dear to me? When was the last time I had shared my thoughts and worries, my joys and sorrows, with close friends? It seemed like an eternity. Loneliness oppressed me. When would the war finally end? When would my loved ones return home? I dreamed about them a lot: Nina, Mile, Vida, Marko, and others visited me at night. I would almost always wake up from these dreams covered in sweat, my heart racing. Again and again I tried to interpret the dreams and imagined it was because I would see them all soon.

I dreamed the last farewell, and I will never forget Bobby's good-bye. The dream went as follows: I was in an inn and I asked the waiter if he had seen my husband. "His name is Bobby," I said. "Three days ago he went on a trip together with many others, and he hasn't returned yet. I want to go look for him; can you help me?" A woman answered that she wanted to help me find him; the way was too difficult for me to go alone. The street was icy, and the hill was steep. The woman held me tightly by the shoulders and pushed me up the slippery slope. To the right and to the left yawned a black abyss. Suddenly I knew that the woman behind me was a man. I turned around and said, "I don't want to go together with a man. I want to wait for Bobby alone."

"But the way is difficult; you will fall. You can't go alone. Let me help you," the man said to me. "No, let me go by myself. I won't fall," I protested. Then he disappeared. But I walked and walked and came to a house. There I asked a woman where Bobby was. "I want to help you look for him," she said. "I'm his mother." We searched for him together but didn't find him. Then a large mass of people came up to us. We saw men, women, and children covered in filthy rags. They walked silently. I leaned against someone who stood in front of me so I could see better.

Many people were watching the noiseless procession. They too were silent. I asked someone in the crowd if he had seen Bobby. "No," he said. "We were all on an excursion and we're going home now." Then I heard Bobby's voice cry loudly, "Irene!" I spotted Bobby in the long line: he was pale and thin. He smiled, cried "Irene" once again, then collapsed. I turned around and wept. Bobby, I heard your last farewell, I saw your last smile.

THE PRINCESS

My greatest consolation during this time was my pupils. Leila and Sossi made astonishing progress. Both were sweet and trustful. The few hours I spent with them every day dispelled my fears and appeased my loneliness. They told me about their experiences. Sossi was maturing early and talked extravagantly about engagement and marriage and painted the most fantastic picture of her groom, her wedding dress, her honeymoon, and her children. Leila often made up fairy tales that were filled with princes and princesses. So I wasn't very surprised when one day they told me about a beautiful princess who had visited them the day before. As always, I played along with them and asked them to describe everything to me down to the last detail: what the princess looked like, what kind of a dress she wore, how big her house was, how many servants she had, and whether there were fountains and fireworks in the garden.

Leila, who had a great gift of observation, got up, shook her ebony curls affectedly, and limped around the room. "That's what she looks like," she affirmed. "But she is so sweet that one forgets immediately that she limps." "But why should she have to limp?" I asked her. "Simply let her be tall, blonde, strong, and healthy instead of dark-haired and frail." "But it's not my fault!" protested Leila. "She isn't a fairy-tale princess, but a real princess. Just ask father," she added sulking. "He was there when she visited."

Ekrem Bey had observed the little performance. "Yes, Madame Irene," he smiled, "it's true. The princess is beautiful, but she really does limp. Leila imitated her well." The children told me more and more about this unusual woman, and my curiosity to see her increased daily. She was the great-granddaughter of Sultan Abdul Hamid, the "Red Sultan."[1] The war had caught her in Tirana unawares and kept her there. She lived with her grandmother, the sultana, who was the oldest daughter of Sultan Abdul Hamid. They resided in a villa not far from the Vloras' house with a cousin of Ekrem Bey, Mukerem Bey Janina. He passed for the fiancé of the princess and the protector of both women. Soon I had the opportunity to meet her.

One morning Ekrem Bey stood in our communal workroom and tried awkwardly to make a manageable bouquet from a large bunch of unmanageable flowers. I offered him my assistance with this difficult endeavor, and the problem was solved immediately. "The flowers shall be sent to the princess," he said. "Leila and I will be her dinner guests today." The next day Ekrem Bey said to me, "Madame Irene, you now have a new pupil. The princess wants to learn German."

I didn't have a minute to spare, but I was so curious that I went with Leila and Sossi the next day just to see her. A gorgeous young man opened the door for us. I thought he was at least a prince or a film star, but Leila enlightened me, whispering that this beauty was the house cook. A few dogs and lots of cats jumped in our way. "The dogs belong to the princess, and the cats belong to the sultana," Sossi whispered. We were led into a large room, where a distinguished-looking gentleman about forty years old greeted us warmly in German. It was Mukerem Bey Janina. He accompanied us into the next room. "The princess is waiting for you," he stated, and disappeared. I beheld a gorgeous young woman sitting in an easy chair in the corner of the room. She was covered in a flaming-red gown, and a small white dog lay sleeping in her arms. My vocabulary is too meager to describe the beauty of the woman. She had blue-black hair that was parted in the middle and fell long and straight to her shoulders; her eyes were the deepest brown, vaulted with slender eyebrows; her eyelashes were so long that they looked as if they were glued on; her skin was the color of luminous ivory, her cheeks gently rounded; her mouth was full and beautiful. I stared at her, completely enchanted.

She appeared to be accustomed to such silent admiration. The princess smiled unembarrassedly and asked me to sit down. I took a seat opposite her. The film star masquerading as cook brought in a couple of pathetic cakes and poured the tea. Only then was I able to speak again: "I have never in my life seen such a breathtakingly beautiful woman as you, Princess, and I beg you to forgive my uninhibited staring. Please don't take my words as a dumb compliment, but you really look the way one imagines a princess out of a fairy tale." A slight smile crossed her lips when she heard me speak. Not saying anything, she let the small dog down onto the floor and got up. She walked, or rather limped, toward the door holding onto objects or leaning against the wall. In the process she held up her long garment a little, so I saw a foot with a clumsy shoe that contrasted sharply with her overall elegance.

I followed her with my eyes. Confusion and pity raged within me. What a horrible trick of nature! How unhappy this half-child must be to reveal this drama to me, a stranger. She turned around at the door and said: "Please excuse me for a moment. I want to change clothes." Seeing the consternation in my eyes, she added: "Perhaps in the meantime you'll change your mind and my beauty will impress you less."

A wave of compassion came over me. I wanted to rush up to her, caress her, and console her like a child that one has punished wrongly. Poor little girl that she was, I felt her isolation and her bitterness deep inside me. In a few minutes she returned wearing an elegant short dress with a low neckline, which made the sad contrast of great beauty and a terrible disease stand out even more. Without an introduction she explained, "As you can see, I'm a cripple. I have tuberculosis of the bone, and soon it will be so bad that I will no longer be able to walk. I'm now twenty-one years old, and more than half of my life has been spent lying down. I'll probably have to lie down a long time before I die. You'll have to come visit me often. I like you."

I got up spontaneously and kissed her on the cheek. I couldn't speak. The following day I walked over to give her her first German lesson. She patiently repeated back what I recited to her for about ten minutes, then threw the book in a corner and laughed: "It's stupid to waste time with this boring instruction. Instead let's talk before you have to go to another pupil." So we chatted. She told me about her strange and unhappy life. Her father and mother lived far away and didn't bother about her; the sultana, her grandmother, had raised her. The princess had spent years in sanatoriums in Switzerland, she loved Nice, she painted. She had been a model for famous artists countless times, and she admired Henri Matisse, whom she knew well. She laughed, she sang, she bubbled over with good cheer and youth. By the time I left her house, I already loved her as if I had taken care of her since her childhood. As time went on, I got to know her unusual charm a little better. Everyone who had come into her house, either as a guest or as a servant, was subject to her spell. She knew it only too well and playacted a little to fulfill their expectations. But when she was interested in someone, she stopped at nothing to win them over.

Her hunger for love was enormous. Because her disease kept her from going out, she collected people from various social strata in her home. Most of them were parasites of the worst kind: uninvited guests who always appeared at mealtime; women who borrowed clothes and coats without reservation and never returned them; men, painters, sculptors, singers, and poets who enjoyed free lunches and cigarettes. In addition, if they were in a tight spot, they could borrow money from Mukerem Bey. The servants obviously profited from such a lifestyle as well. The cook brought the princess a thin tea with a little toasted bread for breakfast, while kitchen staples such as milk, eggs, or butter disappeared.

The more frequently I visited, the more deterioration and thievery I witnessed. The cook often didn't prepare meals. Apparently no one had given him enough money to go shopping, and there was no food left. So he sat in the warm kitchen, read, and ordered eight to ten meals from the best restaurant in town. The bills that arrived at the beginning of the month were worthy of a prince's household. Mukerem Bey settled the accounts. One day I spoke openly with him about the mismanagement of the house. "What can I do, Madame Irene," he said, resigned. "It is not easy to be the boyfriend of a princess. The illness has spoiled her so much that the concept of money is foreign to her. She lives as if she were still in the home of the Red Sultan, where money problems didn't exist."

The sultana understood even less than the princess about the household, if that was possible. When I saw the old woman for the first time, I was just as impressed with her grotesqueness as I was with Nesy's beauty. She seemed ancient. The sultana was a small, frail, stooped figure with keen bird's eyes and a hooked nose. Her snow-white hair was cut short, and her cheeks, lips, and eyelids were made up garishly. She thanked me with her screeching parrot voice. "You can come often," she said dictatorially, after examining me from head to toe. "The princess needs company, and you seem to entertain her. I'll pay for your visits." Nesy smiled at me apologetically and took the old woman tenderly by the arm. "Come, Mommy," she said, "let's go for a walk in the garden. The sun is shining so beautifully now." The two limped outside supporting each other.

Mukerem Bey was the stabilizing influence in this house. Calm and composed, a gentleman from head to toe, he moved between the two peculiar women and their odd guests with aristocratic dignity. We soon became friends. He discussed his money problems with me and asked me my opinion about this or that parasite who became more impertinent each day. He shared his worries with me about Nesy's health or told me about the latest self-indulgence of the sultana. The mood of the old woman was simply too extravagant for the circumstances then. For example, the cats received canned meat daily, a luxury that Mukerem Bey acquired with great difficulty and paid for dearly. Sheets and tablecloths were cut into strips so that the cats could sleep better. If a cat had kittens, then blankets and pillows were taken from the bed and arranged for her. Mukerem Bey had to procure new ones, of course, because the sultana didn't want to sleep on a bare mattress.

The princess and the sultana would vanish, the servants stole, and the guests were as ravenous as predators. Mukerem Bey drove to his estate, got some money, and paid the bills. One time he went on one of his many journeys and asked me not to leave the princess alone, so I slept in the house for the first time. I stayed there for a few days, and it was then that I got a more profound insight into the dissipated household. I spoke with Nesy about all of it, and she asked me to live there and help fix the disarray. I refused. The noise and behavior were repugnant to me.

A short time after that I became ill. It had become a habit for me to see after my problem child every day, if only for a few minutes. When I hadn't come around for two days, Nesy rode over in a field wagon to see me then and there. When she entered my tiny room, I was lying on my old straw sack on the stone floor covered with a tattered blanket. Except for a wash bowl and a small box, the room had no furniture. Nesy rushed up to me as fast as she could drag her poor legs, crouched near me on the mattress, and swore that she would take me home immediately. Once again I declined.

She left and returned an hour later accompanied by Mukerem Bey and the cook. Nesy shouted at the door: "I have a surprise for you. Close your eyes! I've brought something beautiful!" I sensed her joyful agitation and obediently did as she asked. I heard her hobble back and forth as the two men put up the bed in the corner. There was hammering and nailing amid Nesy's excited commands. My heart opened up to this lovable creature. The metamorphosis of my room was so strange and moving that I laughed and cried when I saw it. In addition to the wonderful bed, the table, and two expensively carved chairs, there were pictures hanging on the walls, a red crepe paper lampshade, green paper curtains, a small threadbare rug, a beautiful old mirror, and a clothesline, on which my clothes were hanging. My washbowl and the box were modestly hidden behind another paper screen. It looked like a place where a little street girl might try to earn her keep.

Nesy was happy. I moved from my cold place on the floor to the large bed,

stretched out comfortably, and, since nothing else was expected of me, got well quickly. Our friendship deepened. Nesy followed me with all the intensity and egoism of an ill person. She would rather have seen me not work at all and live with her so that I could be at her disposal all day long.

Never in her life had she been offered friendship, except by Mukerem Bey, that wasn't out of self-interest. Everyone wanted something from the princess: money, entertainment, or her. Parental love was something she had never experienced. So I became, though she violently disagreed with me about this, a kind of motherly girlfriend for her. The difference in our ages wasn't large enough for her to see the relationship more clearly. I understood and felt responsible for her, for her health, for her stupidity. I loved her fondly with all her virtues and faults, just as a mother loves her sick, spoiled child.

I stayed overnight more and more often, thereby gradually getting involved in the household. To the horror of the cook and the housemaids, I would go into the kitchen and [other] rooms and check the cupboards and supplies. However, I didn't give up my rented room. Now I had three different places to sleep. When there was danger I stayed in Ekrem Bey Vlora's house, when I had a fever I stayed at Nesy's, and when everything was normal I slept in my own room.

There were many reasons why I couldn't agree to live in the princess's home. Apart from her moodiness and her domineering nature, I feared the riffraff that frequented her house. People of all political persuasions from every social strata entered through the front door. Mukerem Bey shared my dislike. I could drive away a small number of them with my icy attitude, but only those who still possessed a little dignity. The others obstinately stood their ground.

Jealousy and envy proliferated, and I feared for Mukerem Bey. It would be so easy to arrest him on trumped-up charges. His enemies went in and out of his house casually, ate at his table, spied, and snooped in every corner. Nesy, in her innocence, didn't see the dangers she had created. Fascists, communists, partisans, royalists, and even German Gestapo people met one another in her "salon." She liked the game. The princess laughed, had fun, flirted with everyone, and thought all were loyal family friends. Ekrem Bey warned me, but I had grown so fond of Nesy that I couldn't leave her alone.

The second time I saw the German officer at her place led to a fierce conflict between Nesy and me. The first time, he visited her uninvited, under the pretext that she was the most cultivated woman in Tirana. Secluded and culturally indigent as he was, he asked her if he might chat with her now and then. On this occasion he loaned her a book in order to ensure that his return would not seem obtrusive. Vain Nesy, flattered by his attentions, laughed and found the young German "amusing," just like most of her acquaintances. Mukerem Bey and I preached to deaf ears when we reproached her; she had to realize that we were in the middle of a war and that it wasn't fun for any of us. I threatened not to visit her anymore if she received the German agent again. "Don't you see that you're putting all of us in danger? Do you think that entertainment is more important than people's lives? In your stupidity, do you have to make yourself the center of interest for a band of informers? You don't think that you and your unusual guests are being watched from all sides?" I questioned her angrily.

She promised meekly not to receive the German anymore. The day he returned, Nesy, Mukerem Bey, and I were sitting in the garden. She wanted to get up to greet him, but I, enraged, held her back. Mukerem Bey opened the garden gate himself. "I've taken the liberty of visiting the princess," rattled the young officer. "The princess regrets," I heard Mukerem say, "that she isn't receiving visitors today. She doesn't feel well." Shocked, the visitor looked over to us in the garden. "Then I'll make a visit tomorrow or the day after tomorrow," we heard his bright voice snap. "The princess won't be receiving visitors then either," said Mukerem Bey as calmly and affably as ever. Finally the unwelcome guest understood what was going on. "I want to exchange a book that the princess so kindly loaned to me. I'm ready to leave you a deposit for it," he added foolishly. This was too much for Mukerem

Bey. "Neither I nor the princess owns a lending library," he said coolly. "I hope you understand." He accompanied the visitor politely to the door, and the two men bowed to each other. The German officer got into his vehicle, and the composed Mukerem Bey returned to us.

We didn't expect Nesy's outburst. Deeply offended, she screamed at both of us, showered us with vehement reproaches, and then suddenly had a crying fit. It was difficult to get her into bed. I resolved to stay away from her, and I stood by this firmly despite her many visits to my room. Then she became ill, and all of my resolutions were immediately cast to the wind. Serious liver ailments followed. She screamed from the pain, didn't eat anything, and came down with a high fever. Mukerem Bey asked me to help him. Once again I spent the night. Mukerem Bey and I couldn't leave her bedside without producing a scene. Sometimes she lay there half-conscious for hours, murmuring, "Je suis laide, je suis bête, je suis laide, je suis bête" [I'm ugly, I'm stupid, I'm ugly, I'm stupid], while she rolled her head back and forth. Then she would scream piercingly, "Mukerem Bey, Irene, don't leave me! I'm dying!"

The sultana was a profound nuisance at the time. With the greatest effort, she dragged herself up to Nesy's room on the second floor, poked us to the side with her large cane, and screeched like a parrot, "I'm going to report you to the police! My Nesy is dying! You've poisoned her!" If we wanted to feed Nesy in her presence, she knocked the bowl from our hands so that the soup spilled onto the bed. Nesy cried, the sultana screamed, and Mukerem Bey and I were at a loss. If the sultana saw me eating, she would stick her ugly, clawlike hands in my dinner, grab the meat, and throw it to her favorite cat, Rosalinde.

Since a midday meal no longer awaited them, the daily visitors now avoided the house. When Nesy was conscious, it was almost worse. She let herself be led to the bathroom, locked herself in, then bathed herself in the unheated room while Mukerem Bey and I stood in front of the locked door and implored her to come out. When she finally opened the door, she usually fell into our arms totally exhausted. Her fever then rose again to 41 degrees [Celsius]. Every day new doctors would come there. Nesy wouldn't let the doctor examine her if she didn't like him, or she would scream and insult him when he returned the second time with medicine that had been procured with much effort and money. She would refuse the medicine or would spit it out like a naughty child after we had talked her into taking it. We gave up, and to spite everyone, Nesy slowly began to recover.

On the first day the princess didn't have a fever, Mukerem Bey was arrested. Someone knocked on the door late in the evening, and Mukerem Bey opened it. Eight people had come to seize him. All were wearing civilian clothes, all carried rifles over their shoulders, and some wore old soldier's caps. They pushed the ancient sultana aside roughly and glanced lasciviously at the princess in her long, flowing dressing gown. However, they paid no attention to the nosy employees or to me. Mukerem Bey calmly said good-bye to us and whispered in my ear, "Nesy's friends have succeeded."

The night that followed remains etched in my memory. The princess couldn't be put to bed under any circumstances. She wouldn't even go to her room. She stood at the garden gate the entire night, hoping to see one of her friends or a hired car. She wanted to do something to rescue Mukerem Bey, but neither reason nor threats reached her consciousness. She had forgotten that there was a curfew at 6:00 P.M. and that we couldn't do anything until morning. She stood there, clinging to the garden gate. With her pale face and her flowing hair, she stared fixedly at every German soldier who went by, asking him in French if he could find a hired car for her. Luckily, not one German soldier understood the foreign language. However, one stopped, rattled the gate, and screamed: "Open up, doll, I've got a spare hour for you!" "The girl is seriously ill in addition to being mad," I scolded desperately. "Go away!"

I pulled Nesy away from the door violently, and she fell over. I wanted to take her to her room, but she slapped me in the face as hard as she could. "I want to rescue Mukerem Bey! Tomorrow morning will be too late. Let me go!" she screamed sobbing. "It will be all your fault if they shoot him tonight. Let me go!" Then she began to cry, falling exhausted into my arms. Morning came. We drove to Ekrem Bey and to another important relative of Mukerem's; they promised to help as quickly as possible. Two days later, in the evening, a pale-looking Mukerem Bey returned. Things had worked out once again. Nesy had a relapse and vowed to send her friends packing. Unfortunately, she didn't stick to her word.

On that same day, after another tremendous bill we couldn't pay was sent from the restaurant, I fired the cook, the housemaid, and the other daily thieves who had worked in the house. It had become impossible for Mukerem Bey to make the dangerous trips to his estate, so we slowly sold household objects for cash.

We now had a truly good friend at home: Marcello, the handyman. Marcello was a jewel. He was one of the many Italian soldiers who went from door to door and offered to do work in the house in exchange for room and board and protection against German captivity. Marcello was a young, rosycheeked farmer's boy, trusting as a child, and very proud of his cooking. He was loyal to all of us from the moment we met him.

Without him I couldn't have managed this muddled household and its difficult occupants. The sultana hated me from the depths of her soul. Nesy raged. I couldn't go away for a moment without Mukerem Bey needing me to advise him about financial matters or to help sell something. Both Marcello and I went together to sell any expensive objects and returned with food and the rest of the money. Nesy was getting better, but she was still very weak and had to eat. So we secretly took the condensed milk that the sultana had hidden away for her cats and fed it to our sick problem child.

Marcello had the imagination and talent of a great chef. Every day he put new dishes on the table, although the ingredients were almost always the same: cornmeal, canned meat, and now and then a green vegetable or an egg. He liked to watch how much each person ate, serving the meals on beautiful porcelain and silver, giving each person the exact same portions. The cook reluctantly gave more food to those who wanted it but made them aware that they would receive less that evening. Sometimes, to tease Marcello, we would disappear, but we could be sure that our evening meal on those days would be very meager.

Luckily, the sultana ate alone in her room. Marcello prepared other treats for her and the cats using the same ingredients. He cared for her as if she were his only child. He fed her, told her stories, and led her into the bathroom. Once when she didn't feel well for a few days, he slept in her room, and he changed the sheets by himself one night when there was a small mishap, despite her screaming opposition.

His earthy humor gave rise to many cheerful hours. Once he came down with a bad sore throat and a fever. I wouldn't let him get up, and I brought hot herbal tea to his bed. He apologized a thousand times for the inconvenience he was causing and wished the blessing of all the saints on me. I sat down on his bed for a moment to take his temperature. Above his head were pictures of bathing beauties, half-naked dancers, and similar kitschy subjects thumbtacked to the wall in fanlike fashion. "Nice, eh?" he asked me beaming. "Yes, Marcello, they're very nice. But tell me, why have you put Mary and the child Jesus in the middle?" I inquired. "So she will forgive me when I look at the beautiful women before I go to sleep," he answered innocently.

Marcello's greatest passion was the ties, elegant shirts, and suits that Mukerem Bey gave him. He washed and ironed everything with the utmost care and presented himself in his radiance each time the princess and I went out. The only users of Mukerem Bey's perfume, the last bottle of which was given to Nesy, were Marcello and the princess. He used it for hair tonic, and we let him have his way because he brought so much joy into our lives. One day the following incident happened, a nice little story we subsequently teased him about almost every day.

On my birthday I wanted to go first into Nesy's room, as usual, to say good morning to her and ask her how she had slept. It was the nicest hour of the day. Nesy usually waited for me to come, and when she saw me she would request almost immediately, "Tell me a story, but not the story about the princess and the pea—that's what I am." I usually told her something that had very little to do with a princess or pretty maids; instead, I tried to open her eyes to the world outside. I wanted to expose her to the war and its horrors and to turn her keen mind toward other things besides her own pleasure.

I was astounded to discover that she wasn't in her room on this particular morning. Mukerem Bey had also disappeared, and even Marcello was gone. I went to the kitchen but found the door locked from the inside and heard Nesy and Marcello talking excitedly. When they finally opened the door, there was a great surprise: Nesy had made a birthday cake for me. And where she managed to get the magic ingredients will always remain a mystery.[2] The cake was wonderful, and, full of pride, she reported that there were enough ingredients left over for a second.

A few days later a very important person came to visit, and in his honor we placed another cake on the table. Marcello had made the cake following the same recipe, but it tasted different this time. After the guest had left the house, I called our cook into the room and asked, "Tell me, Marcello, did you make this cake according to the given recipe?" "Certainly," he said. "I used just as much butter, just as much sugar, and just as many eggs as the princess had in the other cake; only I used twice as much flour," he admitted somewhat meekly.

He had shown a particular dislike for one of the daily guests who, if somewhat fewer in number, started frequenting the house again. Professor Viera, a famous Italian sculptor, arrived at ten in the morning and didn't leave before six in the evening. He wrote, read, sang, and ate in the house. In addition to this, he demanded that Marcello iron his pants while he stood in the bathroom under the shower. "Son of a bitch," swore our good Marcello softly behind the professor's back. One day he avenged himself for his fellow countryman's impudence by burning a large hole in his trousers. He showed it to me grinning, and I was amused by it as well. Marcello ruled this house unrestrainedly, and it was a blessing for all in this eccentric household to have a person with such a healthy farmer's attitude.

One day when there was no more wood and no money, Nesy couldn't take her hot bath. She wanted to procure some fuel quickly while there was still a chance to get some. She tried to get Marcello to chop up the dining room chairs for heating material so she could have hot water. Marcello flatly refused. "No, princess," he said obstinately, defying her command, "the furniture won't be put in the furnace. You're not the only person in the world who can't take a bath for a few days." He left the room without taking the slightest notice of Nesy's sulking—he got his way.

I still didn't live in the house all the time. Nesy was well again, and despite her request, I couldn't resolve to give up my room. Now and then, when the nagging sultana and her cats and the whole crazy scene there were too much for me, I would sleep in my tiny room and gather strength for the next few days in Nesy's home. Life without agitation and dramatic scenes was impossible there. Every day new intrigues were discovered or invented. One had the feeling that a catastrophe would break out at any moment—the house would be blown up, Mukerem Bey would be imprisoned or shot, the sultana would poison me, Nesy would be kidnapped by one of her good friends, or business people would appear with bills that hadn't been paid. In other words, we were sitting on a powder keg and naturally felt anxious.

The situation in Tirana and all of Albania intensified each day: the partisans made life difficult for German troops, we heard artillery fire at night more frequently, and bombs flew, sometimes hitting their residential targets. Inhabitants of Tirana's outlying areas were forced to leave their homes. To hinder the secret guerrilla penetration into the city, the Germans let entire streets burn down. Mukerem's younger brother who fought with the partisans had been shot to death, but we received no further details. It was rumored that the enemy would take revenge, and we feared for Mukerem Bey. All thought of escape. One of Nesy's acquaintances told us about British U-boats that were supposed to surface near Durazzo on certain nights in order to help the partisans and bring them needed ammunition and food. We made plans to travel to Italy on one of these clandestine ships.

Despite the danger, Mukerem Bey traveled to his estate to obtain money, afterwards giving a large portion of it to a middleman. Then we discussed how we would undertake the journey up to Durazzo: Mukerem Bey and I wanted to ride in a vehicle with Nesy; Marcello and the sultana would be in another. Marcello was the only one of the entire group who could successfully entertain the old woman during the dangerous operation. He would pass her off as his mad grandmother if stopped. We were conscious of the deadly game we were about to undertake. Marcello and the sultana would be allowed to know about our operation only at the very last minute. But our plans were in vain. The mediator disappeared one day with all the money. Had we been tricked by a swindler, or had the young man been caught in his dangerous game and given short shrift? Assuming the first, the loss of money is long past and forgotten. If the second came to pass, we did not mourn his execution.

I told Nesy to be careful in her conversations, seeing a scoundrel in everyone who entered the house. They were in reality the enemies of Mukerem Bey. Nesy's infirmity alone let us make excuses for her behavior. Mukerem Bey and I knew how much she loved us; we knew that she didn't want to hurt us and only wanted to "amuse" herself. We were the healthy ones, and we could leave or escape whenever we wanted to. We had our legs. The only thing Nesy had was a yearning heart, a lust for life, and a beautiful face. So in long debates we defended the shortcomings of our darling, our sweetheart who could cost us our freedom and perhaps our life. In these months of being together we learned the meaning of love in its fullest sense—understanding everyone and forgiving everything. We loved Nesy with all her faults and weaknesses and accepted her as she was.

The great battle for Tirana had begun.[3] That night I slept in my room, and around eight o'clock in the morning I went to my pupils as usual. My beginning students, the many children to whom I had taught German songs, lived in a narrow alley a long distance from the center of town. I didn't reach their house. Before I left, I had heard muffled artillery shots in the distance, but I couldn't afford to stay at home. My work was important: we had to eat. Mukerem Bey could under no circumstances take any more trips to get cash. At the time the sale of the most expensive objects was of no immediate interest, because people had other concerns besides buying old pictures or silverware for their homes.

I noticed that the streets were strangely empty and most of the stores were closed. The owners of a fabric store were in the process of locking up when a bomb hit in the immediate vicinity. I ran into the nearest house with a young man who was also on the street. "The partisans are already in Tirana, and they're fighting at the second crossroad. The fighting will last till this evening at the most. Then we'll be free," said the young man. "The guerrillas have penetrated the city from all sides, the Germans are surrounded," reported another. "They'll set the city on fire before they withdraw," opined the man of the house. "I think we should try to escape."

I stood there at a loss. The businessman who had run into the building with me became nervous. "I have to go home," he said. "My wife is alone with the children and she is scared to death." Despite the entreaties by the others to stay there because it was too dangerous to cross the street, he turned toward the door resolutely. Both of us left the house together, just as we had entered. Once on the street, we hurried in opposite directions, each heading for his own home. I huddled close to the residences on the road; I was the only person who raced along the strange empty thoroughfares. Gasping, I finally arrived home. My landlord and landlady had bolted the gate from the inside. I hammered on it with my fists until someone finally opened up.

I went into the kitchen to greet them and observed the landlady violently slamming the door to a cupboard. I wasn't supposed to see the stored canned goods, flour, salt, and other supplies. No one knew how long the battle would last. Probably thinking that they would be the next to starve, she warned me loudly, "Signora, make sure that you get some food. We have very little, and we can't help you."

An ordeal began for the residents of Tirana who lived from hand to mouth. If they didn't work, they didn't eat. The battle for Tirana lasted a long time. Every morning I went with many other people to the nearest or the next to the nearest bakery and waited there in a long line to buy bread. Other foodstuffs were difficult to obtain. Sometimes this or that store owner would open his shop for an hour, and each person would buy what he found there and could afford. The owners took advantage of the situation and sold all goods that were already spoiled, or expensive dill pickles in jars, or cinnamon and cloves, at outrageous prices. Everything was disposed of except flour, beans, rice, salt, and sugar, because if the owner had those supplies himself, he kept them for a good reason. We carried the expensive treasures home as quickly as possible. Once there, we were happy that the hazardous foray was over and we had once again escaped the artillery shells and bombs that whizzed past us right and left.

During these first few days I saw Nesy only one time. Entire blocks were evacuated one by one, depending on how far the battle had advanced. Mukerem Bey and I decided that it would be better for me to stay in my room so that if an emergency arose, the entire family could move in with me; or if the combat should enter my street, I could immediately move in with them. After a few days it came to that. The partisans were on a side street, and the Germans were on ours. Most of the old homes had chain exits,[4] so that one could often walk by six or seven homes without having to cross the road. The partisans, of course, made good use of this knowledge. They set the houses on fire when the Germans followed them. Those who could saved themselves. I took my few jars of food and ran to Nesy's house; she greeted me with tears in her eyes.

Mukerem Bey, Marcello, and I prepared a small room facing the court-yard as our communal bedroom. In it the sultana, Marcello, Nesy, Mukerem Bey and I spent the days and nights together. Because of the sultana's loud protests, the cats stayed there too. Splintered rock filled the other rooms daily. The windows were broken, the doors were full of holes, the explosions came closer and closer. Marcello, Mukerem Bey, and I took turns buying food. All of us but the sultana could withstand the hunger. She screamed and demanded soup, but we could only give her the most necessary nourishment, because we didn't have anything else. Her old body wasted away before our eyes. More and more often we returned from our dangerous searches for food empty-handed. Our money also ran out.

Once Marcello returned with a sack of cornmeal and a chicken with a broken neck. We asked no questions. He heated up the oven with the kitchen chairs, this time without the princess's request. For a few days the sultana received a hot soup at noon. The cornmeal that he put in front of us was divided up stingily in equal portions.

Then the day arrived when the meager provisions that lasted from one hour to the next became everything. We heard explosion after explosion in the nearest vicinity, so during a small lull I ran into the garden to see what was going on. The surrounding homes were burning, and panic-stricken people were running across the road. I opened the garden gate wide, and soon women and children streamed into the only house that still had a roof. They sobbed out their grief and told how the Germans had broken into their homes, shot all the men, and driven the females and children out. While the women stood on the street wailing, they saw flames shoot out their windows. With this new trauma, they almost forgot the first one and ran with their children up to our house or to another where the doors were open. They waited there until, once again, they met the same fate.

Marcello cooked cornmeal and stuffed the mouths of the bawling and screaming children. The sultana demanded that we send the uninvited guests away because she wanted to sleep and didn't need visitors. Nesy tried to console the women. Mukerem Bey and I looked at each other. What should we do? Should we wait till it was our turn? Should we allow Mukerem and Marcello to be murdered? What would happen to the two women who were ill and couldn't walk? We discussed these matters in undertones. It was getting dark and the battle raged more furiously than ever. All the frightened people sat moaning near one another on beds, on the floor, or wherever they could find a place in the small back room. Suddenly there was a terrifying burst, and the house shook to the rafters. The horrible screaming and wailing that followed intensified the general anxiety.

Marcello ran out the door. A bomb had hit the house. The top floor was open to the sky, and fragments lay everywhere. Nobody was hurt, but we were all seized with panic. "Out of the house!" screamed some of the women. The first packed up their kids and ran out onto the street aimlessly. The others soon followed. We were alone again, except for a friend of Mukerem's who by some miracle had managed to slip away when the Germans broke into his house. Afraid to go into the street, and shaking all over, he wanted to stay. No one refused him the hospitality.

The bombs and artillery fire didn't stop. We didn't know if we were in the partisan or the German zone. We awaited the Germans at any moment, expecting them to force their way into the house or set it on fire. Nesy demanded that Mukerem Bey, Marcello, and I flee, but we were of a different opinion. Could we leave our child and the old feeble-minded woman here alone? We decided to wait until the next day and then leave the house together the following morning. Mukerem Bey and I wanted to set Nesy on a large sheet and take her with us in a kind of cradle. Marcello offered to carry the sultana, and, as always, she protested screaming. If we were hit on the street, then so be it. Anything was better than waiting there idly. We couldn't do that anymore.

Late that night new homeless people appeared at our house. A young Jewish girl among them, whom I knew, described how she tripped over soldiers' corpses till she reached us. But she had lost her brother in the darkness when he ran into a house someplace. "He was around here somewhere," she said. "As soon as the sun comes up I will go look for him."

The night was terrifying. A second bomb tore into our house. Again no one was hurt. Morning dawned. There was so much noise on the street, but it was different from what we had been hearing for the last few days. Explosions, machine guns, and gunshots could be heard between the sound of motors and men's footsteps. No reasonable argument could keep the young girl from going out to look for her brother. We prepared ourselves for the escape, dressing the old woman warmly and knotting Nesy's sheet securely on both sides so we would be better able to carry her. We wanted to wait for the girl and her brother because it would be easier for all of us to manage our two invalids. It would be enough for us if the two young people could prepare the way through the fleeing throng. We had set a time limit: we wanted to leave the house at five o'clock at the latest. Now it was shortly after three. Everyone waited impatiently.

The two arrived sooner than we had anticipated. Impetuously, they burst through the open door. "The Germans are retreating! The war is over!" they screamed again and again, laughing and crying as they hugged us. We couldn't believe the miracle! We didn't laugh and we didn't cry—the girl's words were incomprehensible to us. Mukerem Bey was the first one who tried to speak logically. "Where did you hear the news?" he asked in his cautious manner. "Come outside and see for yourself!" said the girl excitedly. "The Germans are fleeing in tanks, in cars, and on foot. Don't you hear the clattering of German boots?" she inquired.

As a matter of fact we did hear the racket, whereas the bombs and shots occurred only sporadically now. Was this possible? Was it really happening? *Die Deutschen ziehen ab* [The Germans are retreating]. How simple it sounded. Do you know what this meant—The Germans are retreating? This meant no more deaths, no more burning homes, no more wailing women, no more hungry children, no more fear of the next hour or the next minute one breathed. Very slowly I began to realize the significance of these words, before I broke down and cried. Mukerem was the only one who understood my tears. He held me in his arms for a few moments and calmly stroked my hair. Marcello laughed and danced for joy. The old woman demanded something to eat immediately.

Nesy acted like a madwoman. She hugged and kissed everyone, hobbled up the stairs so she could see everything there was to be seen, and called down excitedly to Mukerem Bey and me. She fell over debris and overthrown furniture on the top floor, banged her knee until it bled, and cut her hands on the glass fragments lying around. Then Nesy broke down—she laughed and cried, quivered and trembled. We took her to bed. The excitement was too much for her weak body. We sat near her, and soon she became calm again. Our little Nesy was already making new plans. "Now that the Germans have left Albania," she said, "I'll travel to Egypt. I don't want to stay in this country anymore." "Yes," Mukerem Bey said sadly, "now the bird can fly again without our help, yet flying will become difficult for me." At the time I didn't understand his resignation, although his statement made such a deep impression on me that I can write it down today word for word.

On that same day, in the afternoon, Mukerem Bey and I walked through the streets. What a horrifying sight it was: dead German soldiers were lying in the road because no one had bothered to remove the corpses. Among other things, I saw a young man frantically holding on to a picture of a young woman with a small child in his rigid fingers. I pulled Mukerem Bey away. I had seen enough, I wanted to go home. It filled me with a profound sadness, not satisfaction. How senseless it all was. People killed, people were killed. Mothers lamented here, and mothers cried there. Were men born only to die like this? Was this the meaning of life?

How inadequate words are, how difficult it is for me to say what I feel. Do all of you reading these lines understand me? Does the story speak to your heart? This, and only this, is what it should do. The words should shake you up and keep the pain of the victims alive. Need I say more? I was never good at preaching. I can only describe it and be aware of it, and I want you to be aware of it too. And if you have forgotten it, just try once again, you mothers and fathers who have young sons. Try to imagine bringing them up, loving them, and expecting joy in your old age. Then one day in their youth they lie unburied on a street somewhere. Do you want to bring up both murderers and victims?

Albania was free. It had cost many lives on both sides, but it was free. The streets were cleared of human corpses and dead horses, and the rubble was cleaned up. Partisan fighters, who were most certainly tired of life in the mountains, returned to their cities and villages. The administrative boards and agencies now had new trustworthy employees. Many of those who didn't have a clear conscience fled their homeland at the last minute because they feared the retaliation of their countrymen, with good reason. There were plenty of melodramas in those days: trials ensued, imprisonment and executions followed. The day of reckoning had arrived for those energetic German collaborators. An Allied commission made up of a few Americans, a few British, and a few Frenchmen arrived in Tirana. Nesy went out alone and made secret visits. We thought she was trying to get exit papers from one of the foreign powers.

The Jews were beside themselves with joy. They made travel plans and organized the first transport back to Yugoslavia.[5] Everyone wanted to return home, and no one wanted to lose any more time. Perhaps one would return to Skopje or Belgrade and find the house intact, perhaps businesses and hidden valuables could still be saved, perhaps there was new work for the ones coming home. Two large trucks filled mostly with Yugoslav Jews soon followed the first transport. Nesy and Mukerem Bey talked me into waiting to see what happened. What would I do in Belgrade alone? We wanted to stay together until I received news from Bobby or another one of my family members. So for the time being I stayed in Tirana.

I moved in with Nesy. The house was soon filled with new people, and even these were up to no good. Nesy once again "amused" herself, and Mukerem Bey and I had more problems: we had less money than ever, Mukerem Bey's estate was confiscated, and I wasn't working. We sold what there was to be sold. Marcello didn't receive any more wages but didn't ask for any and did his job willingly and faithfully, as always. The sultana was sick. A young doctor whom I knew from Belgrade took care of her without charge as well as he could. He spent hours at our house, changed compresses, took her temperature, and gave the invalid medication that he himself had procured. Nesy's grateful smile was enough reward for his trouble.

I was filled with anxiety. I wanted to go away, but I didn't know where. Almost all the Jews had already left Tirana. The only ones remaining were those in the same situation I was in. That is, people who had lost everyone and everything, who expected no one and nothing, people without a homeland, without a family, without a home, loners who didn't care where they spent their time. Why move to Belgrade or Vienna? Wasn't Tirana just as good? The unrest in the world was great—does the end of the war necessarily mean immediate peace? Many had a brother, an uncle, or friends in America or Palestine and hoped to reach another country more quickly from Albania than from somewhere else. Others expected news from the displaced persons returning home. One assumed that they would first go to a neutral country, probably Switzerland, where they would be accommodated, registered, and cleaned up and could convalesce. One imagined how they would try to rush them so they could get home more quickly, despite all the difficulties and the bureaucracy. I belonged to those who had such fantasies. But days went by, followed by weeks and months, and still no news.

In the meantime, enthusiastic attempts were undertaken by the Jews to come into contact with the "Joint."[6] This large, helpful organization had already begun its work in Europe. We heard fantastic tales about the aid in the form of food, clothes, and money that was being distributed to our lucky fellow sufferers in Italy. We in Albania endured every kind of privation. Most of us walked around ragged, hungry, without a penny in our pockets, looking for a temporary job and waiting for a better tomorrow. The few who still had money at their disposal kept one or two others above water as best they could. Surely aid from the Joint would eventually reach the handful of Jews in Albania.

TOMMY

Chance, which had always played an important role in my life, intervened, and I became the mediator between the Jews in Albania and the Joint in Rome. Chance came in the form of a small, rotund American with merry eyes named Tommy. I met him in the following way. In order for us to get in contact with the Joint, our letters had to be forwarded by the resident "Americans" in Tirana. Under ordinary circumstances, the members of this small commission were two solemn, elderly gentlemen who spoke some English and worked in the "America House."

The meeting place for the emigrants in Tirana was still Cafe Berlin, where one could learn about the latest news and the most important events. Our committee, which consisted of a few sensible people, met here as well. On this day I walked by, as usual, to hear the latest news. Someone explained that our two emissaries had refused to deliver any more letters to the Americans and that two new people were to take over the job. An older gentleman, Engineer Labinski, had volunteered his services, but he wanted somebody to help him. Because I spoke a little English, someone suggested that I help him. I did, and my destiny was changed in ways I had dared not even dream.

Tommy welcomed us in the courtyard of the American Consulate, where the small commission was housed. He was the commander of the American group, and when we arrived he was inspecting something on his jeep. Engineer Labinski uttered our request in fluent English. Tommy, the American officer, took the letter and promised to settle the matter as soon as possible, chatting affably with the older gentleman. Enviously, I tried to follow the quick conversation. When the American asked me a question in English, I clumsily uttered something that made him burst into peals of laughter. I giggled along with him, and the foundation of our friendship was established.

Tommy tried to speak a little French and uttered some strange sounding words. My French was superior, and I teased him a little. I asked him if he could take me to Italy in an American plane, because I needed immediate attention; I was sick. He ostensibly took me seriously and asked what was wrong. I pointed to my head and my heart and said: "I feel weak here and here." He looked at me obliquely with his small merry eyes and said he would do everything possible and that he would inquire in Rome whether I could obtain an entry permit. When we left, he gave each of us a package of cigarettes and told us to return in a few days.

I proudly showed my treasure to Nesy and told her about my amusing adventure. When we visited the next time, Tommy had good news for us. He had spoken personally with the head of the Joint in Rome, who promised us immediate attention. Tommy asked us to send a spokesman for all the emigrants, so we sent Herr M., one of the few Albanian Jews.[1] What joy! Soon there was money, and the most urgent problems of the indigent were solved. We never learned whether the funds came from the Joint or from a private donor.

Tommy, the young officer, told me to come to see him the next day in his office, where he informed me that my request to travel to Italy for convalescence had unfortunately been denied. I went along with his serious tone and reacted as if I believed that he really had tried to procure an exit visa and regretted that I wouldn't be able to journey to "sunny Italy." We chatted for a while. I described my "war adventures" and finally my friendship with Nesy and Mukerem Bey. He showed great interest in meeting Nesy, having already heard about the ill, beautiful, and strange Turkish princess. He asked if she spoke English and if she was really as charming as people said. I invited him to come visit us, because I knew how happy Nesy would be to meet new people.

The next day Tommy came to tea with another officer. In honor of the Americans, I sold our most valuable possession, a radio, in order to give Marcello some money to buy ingredients for a cake. Our cook made every effort to create the greatest treat from the strangest raw materials. It looked better than it tasted, but our guests were comfortable. Nesy, as usual, charmed everyone who came near her. Mukerem Bey, true to his nature and upbringing, was the perfect gentleman. Of course, next to such unique personalities, I was not noticed and remained in the background. But despite this, I was the one whose life was profoundly changed by the subsequent friendly relations between the Americans and Nesy's household. My initial travel plans were intended to be comical, but they became serious.

I hadn't received any news from Bobby or from any of the other missing persons. Slowly, the horrifying truth leaked out. We heard about the death camps in Poland; we heard about those who had been beaten, shot, starved, and gassed. Allied soldiers who had witnessed evidence of the atrocities with their own eyes shattered the illusions we had about the work camps. We were told about lists of those who had survived the concentration camps, and we were assured that such registers were to be found in all Jewish communities in Italy. Every Jew in Tirana now ardently desired to go to Italy to look at these lists. They thought that perhaps they would be one of the lucky ones who would find a family member still alive. I was haunted by this wish day and night and spoke more often and more seriously with Tommy about the possibility of traveling there. At the time, the partisans were granting no exit visas, and the difficulties were tremendous. It was not easy to obtain a passage to Italy.

I made a strange suggestion to him: could he smuggle me secretly out of

Albania in an airplane? Tommy rejected all my ideas as impossible, even laughable. It wasn't in his power to help me. His position and his sense of responsibility wouldn't let him engage in illegal acts. I had no scruples about illicit border crossings or regulations that arranged an entry or exit visa for another country and would happily have walked across the border if it had been possible. Unfortunately, however, there was a sea between Albania and Italy.

Nesy also busied herself with travel plans: she wanted to visit her father in Egypt. She didn't remember him, because she had last seen him when she was a young girl. But she still seemed to long for new countries, new people, and new experiences. We knew that nothing more could hold her back, neither Mukerem Bey's love nor her crippled legs. She wanted to leave. Mukerem Bey was right: our little bird wanted to fly and no longer needed us. She filled out lengthy forms and had long conferences with a British officer. On his recommendation, Nesy sent away applications for important positions and waited for the miracle that would allow her to travel. Both of us were impatient, and we would have hour-long discussions about our chances of leaving.

Tommy didn't give me much hope and mentally prepared me for the return to Belgrade. I shuddered at the thought of going back to the city that still held so many memories for me. Would it be possible to return there alone, where I had lived together with Bobby? Where every street spoke to me? Where none of my friends and relatives lived anymore? I postponed the trip daily. I'll leave tomorrow, the day after tomorrow, I thought. Then I told myself that I would leave the next week; I couldn't bring myself to make a serious decision.

Once again I went to Tommy and asked him to help me. "I have to go to Italy," I pleaded. "Please understand me, I have to see the list of survivors. Maybe my husband or other members of my family are in a convalescent camp. Every day people from all over the world arrive in Italy." Tommy then asked me, "What would happen if you couldn't find anyone in your family?"

"Then I would still have time to go to Belgrade or somewhere else, or I would stay in Italy. It wouldn't matter to me where I spent the rest of my life. Perhaps I could go to America or to Palestine. I want to get out of here, where every stone is full of blood," I protested. On this day he made a serious promise to get me an entry visa and wrote down my personal data. A few days later Georgie, a young American soldier, told me to go to Tommy's office.

Without any comment, Tommy put a piece of paper in front of me. I read it. The letters danced before my eyes. What I saw in black and white couldn't be true—it was the entry permit for Italy, issued on 25 May 1945 and valid until 25 December! The city of destination was Rome, and the reason given was to contact the American Jewish Joint Distribution Committee. Speechless with happiness, I stared at Tommy. "Yes," he said, "it's true. Congratulations. You're the only one who has managed to do it. Almost all emigrants living here have tried to get to Italy, but only you have succeeded." I understood very well that it wasn't I who had succeeded but Tommy. Finally, I was able to express my appreciation and joy. "When can I go?" I asked him impatiently. "Relax, relax," he said. "There is still a small matter to finish concerning your papers. In addition to the entry permit for Italy, you need an exit permit for Albania. As soon as you get that, you'll be packed into the next airplane, and two hours later you'll be in the land of your dreams."

I wanted to run to the appropriate department immediately. In my naiveté, I thought that I could have everything accomplished in ten minutes, but Tommy dampened my spirits. "Just leave everything to me," he advised. "In the next few days I have a conference with one of the most important gentlemen in the department, and I'll take care of your matter right there." He made an appointment for me to return to his office three days later. I hurried home joyfully to tell Nesy and Mukerem Bey about the extraordinary events that had just transpired.

When I returned to the America House on the appointed day, Tommy wasn't there. I waited for his return with feverish impatience. Finally his car drove through the entry gate, and I saw him coming up the steps from the window of the small office. He opened the door, threw his hat on the table, and then caught a glimpse of me. "Oh, there you are," he mentioned in a somewhat unfriendly manner. "You might as well unpack your suitcase. Your exit permit has been rejected." And he added mechanically, "I'm sorry." I looked at him, totally devastated. I hadn't thought for a moment that this could happen. All my hopes and dreams lay in ruins before me.

Tommy cleared his throat. "Take it easy," he commented. "Come here, have something to drink." He gave me a glass, and I drank it quickly. The alcohol refreshed me, and my courage and composure returned. "Why has my request been refused?" I inquired. "I'm not an Albanian, so why can't I leave the country and travel where I please? What are the reasons for this?" "Reasons, causes, explanations," he said irritated. "How should I know why your exit permit was denied? Just forget the whole thing and stay here or travel back to Belgrade," he said.

But I wasn't going to give up. People had played cat and mouse with me so many times in the last few years that it had become second nature to me to find a way out. I remained silent and thought matters over. Tommy's annoyed comments whizzed through my head. Reasons, causes, explanations. Reasons, causes, explanations. To hell with it all! What reasons, causes, and explanations could there be? "Tommy," I said, thinking out loud, "please ask the reason why they won't allow me to travel, and demand an explanation for it. Tommy, please tell the gentlemen there that you need written proof stating why my exit permit has been denied after the Allied authorities had already given me my travel papers and assured a free trip. Tell them that you have to show this written document to your superiors."

Tommy listened very calmly to my increasingly impetuous suggestions but then exploded. "Leave me alone!" he screamed. "Go there yourself and ask them why you can't leave! I don't want to have anything else to do with it!" Defeated, I went home, where I found Nesy lying in bed. She had a fever again, and Mukerem Bey was sitting next to her. Luckily, there weren't any loathsome visitors in the house. The new state of affairs could be discussed and examined from all sides. Should I go to the ministry myself and try my luck? Could I be successful, when the commander of the American Military Commission hadn't been? What an absurd thought. Should I return to Belgrade? Should I wait and see whether Nesy would succeed in going to Egypt? Perhaps she could take me along as her traveling companion. Should I try to obtain false Italian documents and wait until I could smuggle myself into a transport plane full of Italians returning home?

While we considered every possibility, we heard a car stop suddenly in front of the house. Mukerem and I both ran to the door. Georgie, the young American soldier, stood in front of the gate and waved a large white envelope back and forth excitedly. "The exit permit! The exit permit! Irene, the exit permit has been granted!" he screamed. "The commander and everyone from the commission wish you luck!" he cried joyfully. Finally convinced that he was telling the truth, I got into the jeep, and we drove to his boss.

Tommy shyly refused my show of gratitude. He also didn't discuss how he had managed, an hour later, to have my travel permit in hand with the necessary signature. His entire face beamed and his merry eyes twinkled as he poured me a strong cognac for the second time that day. "Okay," he said. "Now just wait a little while, and in a few days you'll be leaving. I'll have Georgie come and tell you when they're ready to go. Be prepared, and be at the airfield on time. Otherwise they'll fly away without you," he yelled, laughing, as I walked through the large courtyard toward the exit. Two long weeks passed before I could leave. The date of my exit permit had already expired. Quite nervous, I ran back to Tommy. "You're leaving tomorrow or the day after tomorrow," he assured me. "Just don't get excited about it." "But the date, Tommy, won't they give me a lot of trouble about it?" I protested.

"Just extend the deadline yourself," he said. "I hope that you'll show me your papers tomorrow and that they'll be in good order." On the way home I went into a store and bought a little bottle of correction fluid.[2] The next day I went to his office and showed him my papers, which were in tip-top shape. The American officer said "okay" once again, and I thought it would be superfluous to discuss it further.

Two days later Georgie came by in his vehicle at seven o'clock in the morning. "I'm coming back to pick you up at 2:30 P.M. Take care of what you need to quickly; the commander wants to speak with you right now." We drove to his office, and Tommy gave me a cover letter that was for the director of the Joint. He hugged me and wished me luck. "Georgie will accompany you to the airplane," he said to me. "Unfortunately, I have a conference at two o'clock, so I can't go along." I thanked him once again and hurried to the Cafe Berlin. I was the sensation of the day. No one believed me when I told them I was leaving for Italy in a military plane that very afternoon. I promised them that as soon as I arrived, I would go to the director of the Joint to give a precise account of the Jewish situation in Albania.

Then I ran home quickly. Nesy and Marcello had packed my few belongings in one of Mukerem Bey's suitcases, while friends there marveled at the miracle. Professor Viera and other Italians asked me to take some letters along; Ekrem Bey Vlora's wife requested news of her husband and children and the extreme financial situation of her husband and brother-in-law. Everyone wished me luck, and all envied me from the bottom of their hearts. Finally, all had left, and the house was empty.

Mukerem followed me into my room, where I tended to the last minor details. "We have to say good-bye to each other now, dear friend," he said. "Later I won't have time to tell you what I would like to say now. I thank you, Irene," he declared, "for spending so much time and putting so much effort into keeping this house together. I want to thank you for the friendship that you showed the princess and me in every situation. I also want to thank you for your efforts, unfortunately in vain, to make Nesy my lifetime companion." He said sadly, "Nesy is going to Egypt. I'll await my destiny here. Today or tomorrow I will be given the *coup de grâce* by one of my enemies. Come what may, I have no strength to resist. I'm already a dead man." Ashamed, I took leave of my friend with pain in my heart. I will never forget his distinguished character, his noble spirit, his goodness, and his generosity.

Georgie was standing in front of the door at 2:00 P.M. I shook hands once again with those who had become so dear to me in the past months and then climbed into the vehicle. Nesy remained brave. I saw her standing at the gate smiling through tears for as long as I could look back. We both knew that a new stage of our life was beginning. It was painful, but the time had come. We had to part.[3]

At the airfield, the formalities were taken care of quickly. My slight alteration of the date was not noticed. In addition to me, the military plane had two Italian soldiers as passengers. We flew away, and Tirana disappeared from sight. Farewell, Albania, I thought. You have given me so much: hospitality, refuge, friends, and adventure. Farewell, Albania. One day I will tell the world how brave, fearless, strong, and faithful your sons are; how death and the devil can't frighten them. If necessary, I'll tell how they protected a refugee and wouldn't allow her to be harmed even if it meant losing their lives. The gates of your small country remained open, Albania. Your authorities closed both eyes, when necessary, to give poor, persecuted people another chance to survive the most horrible of all wars. Albania, we survived the siege because of your humanity. We thank you.

Italy

ROME

We arrived in Caserta as it was getting dark. While a young American officer looked over our papers, the two Italians were led into a room and I was told to wait. Soon the captain returned with his comrade. My papers were perused once again and then the two took me into a small office, where I was offered cigarettes, chocolate, Coca-Cola, and canned pineapple—all things that had long ceased to be a reality for me. Then one of the young people telephoned someone and spoke English very quickly. The only thing I understood was that they were talking about me, because they pronounced my name clearly, though incorrectly. Half an hour later the captain and I were on our way to Naples. I was accommodated in a hotel for American officers and slept wonderfully that first night in the new country. At 10:00 A.M. my comrade was up and ready to accompany me to an office where once again someone checked my papers and wrote notes on them. They told me that I would be sent to Rome the next day.

This gave me time to take leisurely walks in Naples and marvel at the well-stocked stores, the many Americans, and the city itself. Early the next day I rode to Rome in a large comfortable vehicle with two UNRRA [United Nations Relief and Rehabilitation Administration] officials and a young woman in uniform.[1] I was taken to the Esperia Hotel, which housed the officials of UNRRA and the Joint exclusively. Then someone showed me my room. Totally overwhelmed by the new impressions of the last two days and without thinking about what would happen tomorrow, I quickly fell asleep. I was in the land of my dreams.

There was strict adherence to meal schedules in the hotel because all the guests had to begin their office hours or other duties early. Breakfast was served at 7:30 A.M., and the dining room was empty at 8:30 A.M. Those who didn't come to breakfast on time went hungry. I don't know who was more astounded those first few days of my sojourn in the hotel, me by the abundance and selection of food or my meal companions by my unbelievable appetite. The marvelous things that appeared on the table were an irresistible temptation for my famished body, which had grown so accustomed to Marcello's cornmeal creations. I could eat as much white bread as I wanted. I also devoured coffee, milk, butter, eggs, ham, jam, hot cereal, and fruit juice early in the morning. I thought of the princess: how I would have liked to have her here with me! My little Nesy didn't eat as much in a week as I did here in one morning, let alone lunch and dinner. It was paradise.

But I didn't have a job. The first morning there I went to the office of the Joint to explain the situation of the surviving Jews in Albania and to plea for immediate aid. The director of the Joint was not in Rome, so I spoke with one of the gentlemen there, who read the letter intended for the director. He also made notes from my verbal accounts and promised to send material and spiritual aid to the Jews in Albania as soon as possible. The assistant intimated that I could stay in the Esperia Hotel until the director of the Joint returned from his trip. Because the reason for my entry was "contact with the American Jewish Joint Distribution Committee," the personnel of the "UNRRA HOTEL" didn't give me any trouble. Not only my wonderful accommodations but also my splendid meals were taken care of for the time being.

I lived as if I were on vacation in a spa, taking many walks and marveling at the beautiful sights in Rome. Of course, I also thought about what I would do when the splendor came to an end, because my stay in the hotel was only temporary. The cash I possessed amounted to seven thousand lire, and I knew it wouldn't last long. After I had found out how much a room cost and how expensive the food was there, I calculated my subsistence as fourteen days, or four weeks at the most. There were American supplies in the country, but the Italian people could only take advantage of this when they had enough money to buy American goods on the black market. Rented rooms cost a fortune. Because entire hotels and large pensions were occupied by

American and British officers, the landlords could demand any price for vacancies, and they got it.

I started to look around for a job. I asked the "housekeeper" of the Esperia Hotel if she could use my services. She refused. My knowledge of English was too meager to be able to work with her in the office; in addition, I was totally unprepared for this kind of secretarial work. There were enough Italian women who not only could speak English fluently but also typed very quickly. Why should they hire someone who was less skilled?

I visited Ekrem Bey Vlora, who was now living with his relatives. We talked for a long time. He couldn't help me now, because he presently needed help himself, perhaps less material help than spiritual. He had left his wife and children in Tirana and was very worried about them. Ekrem Bey Vlora expected it to be many years before he could see them again, maybe never. I thought about Bobby, Mile, Vida, and the others and couldn't give him much consolation. Although my loved ones were not listed among concentration camp survivors, I still couldn't believe they were dead. Every day new registers arrived, and every day freed victims came from Polish and German camps.

I went to Delasem and spoke with this and that person, leaving letters with important information about every member of my family to be forwarded to Jewish congregations in Belgrade and Skopje.[2] I made inquiries through the Red Cross and waited and hoped every day for good news. Each morning I went to a particular place and looked at the pictures that were on display. They were original photographs of survivors of the death camps, pictures of emaciated, ghostlike figures, skeletons of people still alive and those already dead, masses of them lying on top of each other in heaps, and hollow-eyed, naked children. I saw old and young people who had been carried to the piles on stretchers, placed between corpses, only to be pulled out at the last minute by American soldiers.

I viewed photos of others imploring with outstretched arms, afraid of dying before they were rescued. There was filth and death everywhere. So that was what the "work camps" looked like. The death camps with their horrifying methods of extermination: gas ovens, starvation, slaying, shooting, strangulation, being torn apart by wild dogs, being experimented on. There was no end to the different ways to die. There was variety in every kind of cruelty and perversity.

People were always stopping in front of the pictures. I wasn't the only one who stood there hoping to see a familiar face and cursing the murderers, all in vain. I awaited further news. It couldn't be that *all* of them were dead. How could they be? They were among the last ones [*Sie waren doch unter den Letzten*], so they must have survived.[3] It had been two years since that fateful night in March 1943. I nurtured hope in this manner and continued to wait. The only thing I could do was to find work and start saving money so that I could further assist those returning home.[4]

Those were my thoughts, because I had forgotten the dream and the last farewell. I waited, waited along with many other men, women, and children, all in vain. Refusing to give up hope, we would imagine our loved ones returning home the next day. Even today, after so many years, that hope is hidden and minute but still alive somewhere inside us. Our minds comprehended the bitter truth long ago, but our foolish hearts didn't want to believe it. In our final hours, long after we close our eyes, hope will flicker perhaps once more. This flame, large and luminous, will prepare us for a reunion in other realms and bear witness to our gathering.

The director of the Joint had returned. After I had taken care of the matter of the Albanian Jews, the hotel management urged me to look for another place to stay as soon as possible. I didn't have the right to live in a hotel for UNRRA officials. Sheer luck—that I couldn't talk to the director of the Joint immediately—allowed me to stay there as long as I did. Otherwise I probably would have landed in a displaced persons' camp, because I was almost destitute. That was still a possibility for me. In the meantime, I had registered at UNRRA and hoped that I would be given funds, as many other refugees had been, until I could adjust a little.

Thanks to the compassionate officer who questioned me, I was not transferred to a camp. It was something I was afraid of—I knew that my physical well-being would be attended to there, but that wasn't what worried me. I could endure hunger and bad living conditions but not the restriction of my freedom. I feared stagnation and the decline of my energy and vitality. The war was over. I didn't want to go back. I wanted to go forward, I wanted to work, I wanted to make up for all the years I had missed. I couldn't just stay idle again and wait around for what would happen to me. I had to be able to decide for myself, something I had learned in the years I had spent alone. I explained all this to the man at UNRRA, who listened, nodded, made notes about my qualifications, and promised that he would see to it that I soon found a job.

Meanwhile, my time at the hotel had run out. I was allowed to stay one extra night, but I had to have new accommodations by the next day. I still hadn't found a room, and I sat there and ate my dinner despondently. My fellow boarders had already finished their meal and left the dining hall while I was sitting there staring into space. A young American official was sitting at the next table eating her fruit dish. Then she tried to get her lighter to work so she could smoke a cigarette. I gave her a box of matches, she thanked me, and we soon got into a conversation. It wasn't long before she found out the reason for my melancholia.

I had known her by sight for a while. She was a small, plump woman with short legs and a round boyish face that was crowned every day with another impossible hairstyle. Her colorful blouses and dresses brutally screamed her *joie de vivre* to the world, and I almost always saw her in the company of one or more young men. The ladies whispering at the nearby tables didn't seem to bother her in the least. She proudly waddled through the dining room in her gigantic high heels, glanced self-confidently at her reflection in the large mirror, and conversed brilliantly with her admirers. I suspected that her female enemies furnished her with the substance for her loud, sarcastic laughter.

While I lamented my woes, however, she didn't laugh. She let her clever eyes rest peacefully on my face. I observed her thinking something over for a moment, and then she exclaimed: "How wonderful it is that there are happy-go-lucky women like me around! You see, if I didn't have something besides my hotel room, with my insufferable neighbors, and if I didn't have my small apartment, you would have to sleep in the park tomorrow night. But I'll sleep here in the hotel, although reluctantly, and you can sleep in my place until you have found something else. I hope it won't take too long, or my boyfriend will become impatient," she added roguishly with a twinkle in her eye.

So I suddenly had a charming little flat all to myself. It was on the top floor of an apartment building and had a tiny kitchen, a wonderful bathroom, and a splendid view of the city. I could lie in the hot bath for hours and think about my luck: life was beautiful, life had meaning. My happiness would have been almost complete if I had not had to rack my brains thinking about what I would live on in the near future.[5] But even this problem was solved. When I went to UNRRA again in order to inquire whether there was a job for me, I arrived at precisely the right moment. A few temporary female workers were needed in an American "rest camp." A little note was pressed into my hand, and I read that I was to report to Major L. in the Mussolini Forum. I set out right away. The Mussolini Forum was outside the city, so I rode the bus to the last stop on the line and then asked how to proceed further.[6]

A long, dusty alley led to the rest camp. On the way I saw no civilians, only American soldiers with packages under their arms shouting something funny or cheeky that I didn't understand. One grabbed my arm and tried to pull me away with him. "Signorina, chocolate, cigarettes," he cooed. I shook him away so fiercely that he reeled and cursed. But the incident hadn't made the slightest impression on his comrades, to whom he returned.

The Mussolini Forum was a city unto itself, surrounded by a temporary fence. There was rigorous inspection at the different entrance gates, and I was sent, slip of paper in hand, from one door to the next, until I was finally let in. Then I was taken to an officer who listened to me speak English, filled in my personal data on a piece of cardboard, and explained my job and hours to me. After that I was hired! I had a job and would earn money.

I could begin the next day, and the working conditions were excellent. Most of my colleagues would be Italian men and women, and I was supposed to be there at 5:30 P.M. We were led into a large dining hall with long tables and benches, where gigantic pots of hot food were brought in. Each person received about a half a loaf of bread, and our plates were heaped so full that the food almost ran over the side. Happy as children at a birthday party, these adults spooned up this tasty American dish. It had been a long time since one could afford [to eat like] this; Italy was now poor, poorer than ever. Most of the men and women chewing eagerly had forgotten how good a meal tasted when it was prepared with lots of oil and served with white bread. Those who had no money could only afford American delicacies such as canned goods, chocolate, and cigarettes when they had something to sell. Most of us were happy to have received a job with the Americans, especially here in the Mussolini Forum, where the "rest camp" was housed.

In this splendid and comfortable place, the Americans had put up a transit camp for their soldiers who were waiting to go home. Most of the people didn't stay in the camp for more than three to four days. All of their needs had been generously provided for by the American government. Nothing was lacking for those returning to the United States: large rooms to sleep in, good food, movies, and other distractions. We worked in a kind of amusement park. In the front part of the Mussolini Forum, stalls with refreshments were set up. A dance floor was built not far away, and movies and cabaret performances were accommodated in the large stone buildings.

My work began promptly at 7:30 and ended at 9:30. It was very simple: I worked in the beer booth, where I sat behind a small counter and gave out vouchers for drinks. My colleague, an Italian woman, sat on the other side of the booth. The soldiers stood in a long line in front of our counter and received their beer at the front of the booth. Each person received one voucher. My coworker had done a similar job for the Americans before and had some experience in getting tips. She showed me a small cigar box that she put near her window; almost all of the soldiers threw one or more cigarettes into the box. The next day I tried it too. It worked: no one went by without throwing something into the box.

Some cheated a little in order to get more than one bottle of beer. They stood in line three or four times, and I would recognize them. They would wink at me, and then instead of one cigarette they would throw an entire packet of cigarettes or a bar of chocolate into the box. I let them do it, and my conscience didn't bother me in the least. Just the opposite.[7] I waited impatiently for the end of the evening in order to be able to count my cash balance. At a quarter of four all personnel were loaded into trucks and driven to their front door. I would rush upstairs to count my cigarettes, because on such a night I often had between 100 and 150. I would sort them according to brand and sell them the next day to one of the street boys who traded them secretly. So now I had a warm meal every day, received a salary, and had rather substantial extra earnings.

My colleague had found me a room. I thanked my nice UNRRA friend many times and moved into an old, somber house on the famous Via Margutta. I liked my work—it was easy and provided me with lots of spare time and a good income. I would often go to the Mussolini Forum at four o'clock to walk around and look at the beautiful marble statues: hunters, swimmers, ball players, Amazons. I observed the splendid male and female figures created in glowing white marble and closely spaced at regular intervals, each one glorifying another sport, filling up the entire forum. I usually sat down at the edge of a fountain and enjoyed the magnificent surroundings.

Sometimes I had short conversations with the American soldiers. Once a young man asked me if I was Italian. When I said no, he promptly exclaimed, "Good, then we'll have lots of fun together!" When I asked him why he assumed this, he replied, "Tomorrow I'll drink coffee at your place when you're free." "I don't have any coffee," I teased, "nor tea, nor lemonade." "Why not?" he asked me naively. "Of course, I'll give you coffee and sugar, and I'll also bring canned foods and chocolate as well," he added enticingly. When I made it clear to him that I didn't want him to visit me, he stared at me for a moment totally astounded and then said, to my amazement, "What a pity. You are the first woman I've met in Italy who has nice clean teeth, and the day after tomorrow I'm leaving for America." Unfortunately I couldn't help him, but I laughed a long time about the disappointment painted all over his young, boyish face. Another young man asked me to go dancing with him, and as I gently made him aware that I was about twice his age, he consoled me quickly and concisely. "It doesn't matter. In America I had a girlfriend who was forty years old and still looked really good."

These young American men thought they were so irresistible and were quite surprised when a woman flatly refused them. In any case, they weren't entirely wrong. The starving European girls and women were easily bribed with the cigarettes, canned goods, soap, or even a few dollars that the charming young Americans gave them. I observed what was happening in the "rest camp." The Italian male and female workers stole anything in sight, because they were tempted by the abundance of food. It was needed either to feed the family at home or to sell for a lot of money on the black market.

You could find everything on the black market; the sales even took place in public. If an American policeman came by to check, then the goods were quickly stowed behind the nearest door and five minutes later were casually put up for sale. In addition to all kinds of food, there were also fine officers' shoes, entire uniforms, warm underwear, fountain pens, saccharin, penicillin, other medicine, and, most important, dollars. Fortunes went from one hand to the next as dollars were bought and sold. Some men who had never earned more than a daily wage their entire lives, became wealthy during this period. Everyone wanted to profit from the American wealth. The military and the government weren't the only ones who helped the process. Soldiers sold their rations, and warehouse keepers stole large quantities. Whoever wanted to could buy an entire case of beer or a whole wagonload of sugar, if he had the money. Some operated big, others small—that was the main difference. Unfortunately, the amusement park had been set up for three weeks only, so our jobs came to an end, and my cigarette sales ceased.

Once again I went to UNRRA, received my "package," and at the end of the month collected a small payment in cash. The "packages" were wonderful. Every fourteen days the emigrants who received support gathered in the basement of the large UNRRA house. It was like being in a large store where all sorts of customers shopped: elegantly dressed men and women in expensive fur coats, ragged and tattered youths, and girls and women in whose faces hunger and misery had drawn deep lines. There were also monks, nuns, Japanese, Mongolians, Jews, French, and Hungarians; people of all social classes and from all possible countries met here to receive their food. We acquired sugar, flour, oil, coffee, raisins, canned milk, soap, and sardines. Most of us would have slowly but surely died from malnutrition without this generous aid. We had enough to eat until the next "package" was ready.

My Italian landlady looked at me full of envy when she saw me come in with my expensive treasure. I usually gave her a bit of oil, flour, and sugar, because I knew that when I wasn't there she helped herself to my supplies anyway. The milk, coffee, and chocolate that we received now and then were the articles I sold in order to buy other items such as toothpaste or new soles for my shoes. Once in a while I would go to the hairdresser to get my hair cut.

I became vain again; I had met Tea. She gave me back my courage to face life. How could I describe her, the girlfriend who became so near and dear to me? The beautiful large woman with the elegant hands, the freckled arms, the strange round blue eyes, the high forehead, and the short strawberry-blond hair? Or shall I describe her as the serious woman with the keen, masculine judgment, the responsible colleague at UNRRA, the woman who knew how to give quick advice in tough situations? She was the friend who was always there when I needed help, who acted with cool deliberation and an empathetic heart to put the cart back on the right track. Or shall I describe her as the person with whom I could laugh again about the day-to-day trifles, about myself, about the entire world? Hasn't it been said that people who can laugh about the same things understand each other?

We laughed about the same things and we understood each other. Tea was also alone. She was separated from her husband, an Englishman, and had a boyfriend who caused her great worry and anxiety. In the early days of our friendship we didn't see each other that much, but we later lived together in the same house. Tea lived stylishly in the front part of the house in a nice first-floor apartment that looked out onto the street. I lived in the back with a view of an ugly, dark courtyard. A poor family with eight rude brats between the ages of five and fifteen lived there as well. In spite of the gifts of flour, oil, and sugar, my landlady on the Via Margutta had given me notice to leave!

The reason had been my cologne fabrication. Sam, one of Bobby's cousins, had shown up in Rome. The joy at seeing one of my husband's relatives alive was so great that I wasn't willing to listen to the rational arguments with which Tea remonstrated me. I saw Sam as one of the cleverest, best, most competent persons in the whole world. He was a chemist. Who better to fabricate cologne? We went together to buy the materials needed: essence, alcohol, filters, funnels, and large flasks, all purchased with Sam's money. Because he lived in a very respectable pension and didn't want to annoy his neighbors with the pungent odors, he thought it only natural to set up a laboratory in my room. My landlady was of a different opinion and sent me looking for a place once again.

After a long, exhausting, and totally useless search, I finally landed in a pension that was way beyond my means. The owner was a Polish aristocrat, and my room was between the kitchen and the storage room. Despite the elegance of the pension, it was teeming with bugs. The lady of the house, who emphasized ten times a day that she was of noble birth, owned no fewer than six dogs. They nonchalantly used half of my bed as a tree trunk, and one of them was most certainly on my bed every hour that I wasn't. They would growl threateningly when I tried to exercise my rights. Sam came every day for about ten minutes to look at our mixtures and left the rest of

the work to me. We had gathered all the old perfume bottles that we could find. I cleaned them inside and out as well as I could, filled them with our little water mixture, and then tried to sell them.

After three weeks I was ready to find a cheap room as quickly as possible. I desperately looked for another place, searching all of Rome and finding nothing even worthy of consideration. Sam remained totally oblivious. "You still haven't found a room yet?" he asked now and then. Otherwise he avoided me when possible. My day of grace expired without my having found another room and without my having won in the lottery—I couldn't pay my rent.

In my distress, I called up Ekrem Bey's sister-in-law, Madame X, and asked her for advice. Madame X lived with her small daughter in a furnished room as well. Her husband, an Albanian politician, had been put in a camp by the Allies. She immediately offered to let me stay there at night. For eight nights, I would creep into her room late each evening and share a bed with her. In the morning we would make the most complicated maneuvers to fool her landlady.

I would get up and dress myself completely, and then Madame X would accompany me noiselessly to the front door through the long hall that separated her room from the landlady's. We would ring the doorbell, greet each other loudly, and quickly run back to our room. Only then could I use the bathroom. Nevertheless, we aroused the owner's suspicion, and she surprised us one morning as we were coming out of the room. She told Madame X point-blank that the room had been rented to one lady only and that if I slept there once more without her permission, she would hand my papers over to the aliens' registration office for inspection.

I informed Tea about the matter. It was serious; I knew if I didn't find a room quickly, the only alternative would be the displaced persons' camp. By that evening I had found a room, thanks to Tea, who, as always, had had a good idea. She rang every doorbell of the large house where she lived, wouldn't let herself be scared away by refusals, and finally managed to convince Signor Milleri to let me live in a room in his small apartment. I cried tears of joy when I unpacked my little suitcase and paid half a month's rent in advance. Two weeks of peace. Nothing more could happen to me, I thought. Fifteen days was not much time to earn more money, but no problem, I could do it.

An unbelievable din reigned in the Milleri household. One child was always bawling, another bounced a ball against my door, others were always fighting, the oldest girl sang loudly and out of tune, doors were slammed, the doorbell rang shrilly, visitors came and went, and Signor Milleri tried in vain to suppress all the noise in his soft voice. The children's mother worked in an office, and Signor Milleri, who had lost his job as a bookkeeper, now was in charge of the household.

He was a small, mousy man, bald and hollow-chested, and he ran busily back and forth keeping up with his duties. He cooked, did the shopping, made the beds, swept out the rooms, cleaned the dishes, and washed and ironed the laundry for the entire family. Signor Milleri shyly asked me if I would like to have my things washed inexpensively along with the others. I said no. The children pestered him to death and his wife nagged him for hours in the evening, and he responded patiently and softly. The man of the house allowed me to prepare little snacks for myself in the kitchen, and I gave him this and that from my UNRRA packages in return. I had to sell the greater part of my food supply for cash: sugar, flour, oil, milk, everything but the canned fish. I even had to pay for my own room at the cost of constant hunger.

THE CASINO

Surprisingly, I had become a competent businesswoman. The food I could do without I sold to an emigrant, one of the many "dollar merchants" who did their business on the Piazza Colonna, which was not far from the stock exchange. I knew he had enough money and could afford every extra expenditure for his family, so, bashfully, I let him pay me the going black-market price for my milk and sugar. "Could you also get some bath soap for me?" he would ask. "I have two bars at home, and I'd be happy to bring them to you. I also have some coffee," I added, doing my best to earn some more money. I was in desperate need of a new pair of shoes. My acquaintance looked at me a little scornfully, or at least so I thought, and said, "Two bars of soap? Fine. But can't you get a little more for me? I would buy an entire box," he urged. While mentioning this, he opened his briefcase and to my astonishment took out a thousand lire, stating: "Now you have a little bit of capital. Buy some soap, milk, and sugar, or whatever else you can get for the money, and then give it to me."

I quickly walked to the black market, looked at the prices for the different goods, and finally bought food with the thousand lire and my remaining five thousand. The next day I had seventy-five hundred lire instead of six thousand! Thus began my brilliant career as a black marketeer in foodstuffs. The exercise was very simple: I would go to the market every day, spend my entire capital buying everything I could, and then sell it the next day for a profit. I would schlepp packages weighing ten to twenty kilos from one end of the city to the other. Most of the time I walked, because I was afraid that if I traveled in one of the small trucks, a policeman would ask me what I had in the large suitcase. In time I became so well known at the Piazza Colonna that new customers would freely ask me to deliver three kilos of sugar or ten cans of condensed milk to their home. I always said yes, and I would wear out the soles of my shoes finding what they needed and delivering the goods.

Once someone asked me to find saccharin for his sick mother. It was a difficult venture for two reasons: first, it wasn't available that often on the market, and second, it was very expensive and demanded great capital. I cautiously asked how many bottles my customer needed. "I'll take any quantity," he said arrogantly, "twenty, thirty, fifty bottles. Buy as many as you can get your hands on." I tried my luck. Someone gave me the address of a man who had obtained saccharin from his relatives in America and wanted to sell it. They were right: the man had twenty bottles of tablets. In the meantime my funds had grown to fifteen thousand lire. Excited, I lay my entire fortune on the table for the bottles, because I intended to earn five thousand lire from this one sale. I went quickly with the expensive goods to the Piazza Colonna, but my customer wasn't there. Nor was he there the day after, or the day after that. I never saw him again. Had he left? Had he been arrested? Had he died? Whatever happened, he was never seen again, and I sat there with my saccharin. No one in Rome seemed to need it. I imagined myself years later telling my grandchildren the sad story that took place in 1945 as they sweetened their tea with saccharin. I could tell them what came to pass in a melancholy tone: "Yes, a difficult period began for me then. Saccharin doesn't taste so good by itself and has no nutritional value, so I became emaciated and had many, many troubles."

I slowly recovered from my business setback. Tea loaned me three thousand lire, and I was able to increase my small capital to seven thousand because a great opportunity arose. A young man whom I had seen many times on the Piazza Colonna spoke to me one day in the following manner. "Frau Irene, I have a business proposal for you. Would you have thirty minutes for me?" Of course I had time. We sat down in a quiet corner of a popular coffee bar, and he began, "I don't know whether you know that I saved Herr Jovanovic's life during the war." This fact was known neither to me nor to Herr Jovanovic, but that didn't matter at the time. So I nodded my head slightly and let the young man explain.

"Well," he continued. "Now the time has come when he wants to show his gratitude. Herr Jovanovic is the owner of a club, and in the next few days he is moving to a new and very large locale. He wants to hand over the kitchen management to me, out of gratitude, mind you. You will understand that as a young man I'm not able to cope with such work, and I'm asking you to help me with the job." His reference to "club," "kitchen," and "assistance" didn't make sense to me. The entire story seemed a bit confused.

Slowly I began to comprehend the connection; he was describing a casino to be opened in a grand fashion. In addition to the spiritual pleasure it would offer, a little corporeal refreshment would be made available to the guests. About thirty thousand lire was needed for the undertaking: to pay for cups, plates, glasses, and the necessary foodstuffs, as well as cigarettes and chocolate. The opening would be in two days, so we had to make a quick decision.

I promised to give him an answer that same day. We ran quickly to Tea's office, disturbed her in the middle of an important task, and demanded her immediate attention. "What's there to think about?" she questioned. "You can't lose more than half of your seven thousand lire." She added cautiously, "The other half I will put in safekeeping so that in case of a fiasco you will at least be able to pay your rent." My saccharin business had made her skeptical. It seemed that she hadn't heard my argument: I didn't need thirty-five hundred lire, but rather fifteen thousand, for my contribution to opening the business. She was in a hurry to return to her work and said good-bye to me and my future business associate.

He waited impatiently for my answer. I knew that it meant a lot to him to have me as a colleague. The young man didn't think he was able to prepare a cup of tea or a ham sandwich for a guest and seemed to be thoroughly convinced of my housewifely talent. I didn't destroy his illusion, but rather stated casually, "I've decided to work with you. Shouldn't we make up a list right now of the things we need to buy?" We created a provisional inventory of dishes, wine, coffee, and baked goods that would cost over thirty-five thousand lire. "What about the cigarettes and liquor?" he asked. "Fine," I added. "We'll go shopping early tomorrow morning." I asked him, "Do you have enough cash to be able to pay for half of the specified items?" "Of course," he replied. "I have enough in my pocket." "Good," I said. "Then we'll buy as much as we can for fifteen thousand lire. I can't pay my share for a few days, because my money is locked up in merchandise. I'll probably be able to turn it into cash after three days." I felt like such a shrewd merchant, because the great project actually turned out to be a success. At the very worst, I thought, I could also put my saccharin into the business and sweeten the coffee of the unsuspecting guests. At the very least, I had gained some time and meanwhile become co-owner of a bar.

The opening was two evenings later. Mario and I had been at our new place of employment since early in the morning and had worked diligently all day long. The club rooms were on the first floor of an old building not far from the center of the city. On the top floor of the same building was a large pension inhabited mostly by foreigners. A large sign on the entrance door of the first floor read "Fencing Club" in pretty gold letters. It wasn't meant to be a joke; the rooms, which formerly had been frequented by members of a respectable fencing club, certainly weren't being used much in these hard times. Herr Jovanovic had taken advantage of the opportunity and relocated his business here because of high rent elsewhere.

Opening night was a great success; about one hundred guests showed up. Mario and I sweated in our miniature kitchen preparing the orders: two coffees, four sandwiches, three cakes, hot dogs. We could hardly keep up with the guests' demands. We had to do three things at once, and if we couldn't remember whether someone ordered tea or hot milk, we panicked. Our small electric boiler had trouble keeping the brewed coffee warm. How could it overcome the difficult problem of producing coffee, tea, and hot dogs at the same time?

We were rewarded for our troubles, however. At seven o'clock in the morning Mario and I tallied our first cash balance: we had brought in sixty-eight hundred lire, of which we calculated two thousand lire to be pure profit. We were speechless. We couldn't believe our luck. Full of enthusiasm and good humor, we went shopping again in order to replenish our supplies. After that the two of us returned dead tired to our respective homes in order to sleep so we could brace ourselves for the second night.

The guests at the club were strange people. Men and women of every age met there and played for high stakes. They stood or sat nervously around the round table and won or lost a small fortune in the course of one night. The impatient ones came early in the evening to squeeze in a few hours of poker before the forbidden baccarat began. Groups of gamblers would arrive at about ten in the evening, and the table was soon full.

The police ostensibly closed their eyes to our fencing club, but the owners still took great precautions. The house gate was closed at 10:00 P.M. After that time, only the newly hired night watchman would open it, and then only if he recognized the person or if the visitor had an introduction. Another watchman was posted in the small room of the club where the uniforms and swords were kept. He remained on the lookout at the window the entire night to warn of possible danger. At the entrance to the club rooms stood yet another guard, who once again looked over every unknown guest from head to toe before he or she was allowed to enter the sanctuary.

Most of the players were Italians. They arrived punctually every evening and left for home every morning between four and seven. Win or lose—it didn't matter what the night had brought them—they remained devoted to our "Fencing Club." Soon Mario and I got to know every guest: we knew who wanted his coffee with a lot of milk and who loved his eggs soft-boiled. We observed each male and female player from our own point of view and got to know the idiosyncrasies of each one. Herr X wanted to eat goulash every morning at three, whether he had won or not. Madame Y only ate something when she won. Herr M bought cognac for thirty people when fortune smiled upon him. Herr and Frau B brought sausage with them and insisted that they be cooked and served with mustard. Herr A took his wife the leftover cake for breakfast when he went home at seven, driven by the club chauffeur.

Our business had grown. In addition to another electric boiler and a few new cups and glasses, we now had a waiter and a young man who washed dishes. Mario didn't work at night anymore; he went home at 10:30 at the latest. He needed sleep so that he could study during the day, or so he said. Because he was Herr Jovanovic's favorite, I couldn't do anything about it and worked the entire night with just the other two employees. Everything would go well until two in the morning; after that an almost insurmountable fatigue would set in. I wasn't a night owl: I loved to go to bed at around ten. So I would keep myself awake with strong coffee the rest of the night. The young, seventeen-year-old dishwasher would sometimes take a nap, and he slept so soundly and peacefully that it hurt me to wake him up. So in the early morning I did his work as well.

When I would finally arrive home at 8:00 A.M., I couldn't sleep, despite the darkened room. Signor Milleri worked and sang, the radio in the neighboring apartment whined, the children played and shouted loudly, and someone was always beating the rugs in the courtyard. Oversensitized, I heard every noise three times louder than it actually was. At five in the afternoon I would finally get dressed again and go back to my job. Tea usually came to visit me there at six and ate her supper while I made some strong, hot coffee and breakfasted.

Because she helped me with the preparations, we usually had enough time for a little chat until the guests arrived. Most of the time our first customer was a small, fat man who would greet us merrily from a distance. "A hot coffee and two ham sandwiches, please, but only if I'm allowed to drink the coffee in the kitchen!" he would shout in his funny German with a Hungarian accent. The gentleman would sit down in our small kitchen and consume his first breakfast at 8:00 P.M., sometimes bringing a small bouquet of flowers or a pastry. Soon everyone considered him my most devoted admirer. I, however, viewed him only as my best customer. His weekly bills were so handsome that he was the only one allowed to dine on credit. I buttered his bread very thickly, and he showed his appreciation in the most noble way, by advertising our tasty cuisine in the gambling room, dragging people to the bar, then praising our cheese crackers and beer. If someone won a game, then he shamelessly urged him to buy coffee, cake, and liquor for himself and the ten people sitting near him. No one dared refuse. They didn't want to defy their luck or to be branded a miser.

My admirer was the first to come and the last to go. He would often take me home in his car and gallantly walk me to the door. Then he would kiss my hand and drive home in order to recuperate a bit, probably because he was just as tired as I was. He never declared his love to me, perhaps because his lifestyle left him no time for it: he slept during the day and gambled at night. Nevertheless, I knew that he felt deep affection for me. I had grown accustomed to his attention and viewed him as an honest friend. He got rid of pushy admirers, wouldn't let me lend money to customers, knew where one could buy cheap American cigarettes and lipstick, watched the waiter's fingers during his game to make sure no one cheated me too much, drank coffee with me in the kitchen every morning between five and six, and wouldn't allow me to take sleeping pills. In short, he became indispensable.

On Saturday evenings I only worked until ten. In answer to my vigorous complaints, Mario had agreed to work the night shift once a week. Usually Jack, a fellow refugee, would invite Tea and me to dinner on Saturday nights, when I would eat the only warm meal of the week at a nice restaurant. Now I subsisted exclusively on strong and yet stronger coffee. I made an unusual observation: if I suffered from lack of money, my appetite increased, but if I earned enough, then I wasn't hungry.

Every morning when I went home, I would waken Tea. "Yoo-hoo!" I would yell loudly. Tea would look out the window sleepily and return my greeting. Signora Milleri, who got up at the same time, and who usually ran into me in the hall, would greet me curtly and hostilely. She did believe that I worked at night, but she imagined something quite different from making coffee, washing dishes, and getting tired feet. Her husband, on the other hand, observed me with increasing pity. My thin cheeks and puffy eyes didn't appeal to him. "Forget about that unstable life, *cara signora*," he requested. "You'll become ill. A young woman like you can still marry. Don't waste your time with these Americans, who most certainly have wives and children at home."

I was too tired to get into long discussions. I would let him speak, and then I would go to my room and try to sleep. Sleep, sleep, sleep—it was the only thing I could think about. But sleep had become my enemy, because it escaped me. At any moment I would awaken from a restless half-slumber terrified by confused dreams. Finally I would get up at three in the afternoon and take a walk to get some fresh air before returning once again to the fencing club, with its heavy atmosphere.

I had been working there for about three months now. The tension I felt in the beginning had not abated, and I knew how dangerous it was to stay. If it came to a police raid of the fencing club, then the owners, the guests, and I ran the risk of embarrassing interrogations and probable imprisonment. Visitors who had lost all their money would threaten to go to the police every once in a while. Lately a few clubs similar to ours had been closed down, and not surprisingly the newspapers had gleefully seized upon the scandalous stories. All this put a strain on my nerves and health. Mario had also become uneasy. Even though our business was going well, he wanted to sell me his share. Jack wouldn't let me take over the business alone. "You'll just give Mario the money you have worked so hard to earn," he advised. "The guy is more cunning than you. Do it the other way around: leave him the business and make him pay you for your share." Mario wouldn't hear of it.

I noticed something funny going on. Herr Jovanovic worked less and less and now had a manager who assisted him. The gambling groups whispered among themselves, while the customers became worse and worse. All kinds of riffraff loitered about in the gambling rooms. Professional players and women of the demimonde were now in the majority. The businessmen, lawyers, and ladies of high society who had earlier indulged their passion for gambling played less and less often and gradually stopped coming altogether. Total failure wasn't far away. However, a few days before it came to that, I had a breakdown.

BREAKDOWN

The illness began harmlessly: a mild sore throat and a low-grade fever coupled with headaches and dizziness. I continued to work through the entire night, and the next morning Jack drove me home in his car. I woke Tea as I usually did and told her that I wasn't feeling well. She promised to come to the club at six. My sense of duty forced me out of bed at five—my legs were shaking, and I hardly had the strength to get dressed.

I went to the drugstore to get an anti-flu shot and hoped that that would be enough to fight the faintness. At the club, after Tea had observed me in my resplendent beauty, she spoke seriously with Mario, then grabbed me vigorously by the arm and forced me to go home with her. I fainted at the front door to the house. She and the terrified Signor Milleri dragged me up the stairs.

The doctor confirmed that it was the flu. "It's nothing serious," he advised soothingly. "Just rest in bed a few days, and everything should be better again." Tea and Jack visited me and brought me all kinds of treats. I couldn't eat anything. I lay there apathetically, staring into space or weeping from exhaustion. Most likely, I would have recovered in spite of everything if new troubles had not entered my life.

The club was closed down. Mario came, settled the accounts, and divided the pots, plates, and cups with me. He sold the rest of our cigarettes, liquor, and sugar and brought me the money. My savings of the last few months had given me enough capital to last for at least sixteen weeks. I looked at the future calmly: I knew that within this time period I could easily find a new occupation. Hopeless optimist that I was, I didn't get any gray hairs over the future and knew that the sun would always shine again. However, I didn't expect fortune's malice. In my eyes, my assets were not much less than those of the Rothschilds. Before I went to sleep, I quickly calculated that I could live parsimoniously for perhaps even six months.

The next day and the day after that I waited in vain for Jack's visit. I spoke angrily to Tea about his less than amicable behavior. Only when he didn't show up on the third day did I think that he could be sick and needed help. Tea telephoned his apartment, only to learn from the landlady that Mr. Jack hadn't been home for three days. We phoned one of his friends and found out what had happened. Jack was in jail. During a raid on the Piazza Colonna, he, along with forty other people, had been pushed into a police vehicle on the spot.

The police were hunting down currency traders. After a short interrogation, those who weren't carrying foreign money and who had valid residence permits were set free. But Jack's residence permit was in his briefcase, which was at home in a suitcase. He didn't even know which one it was in. At any rate, when it was finally found, it was ascertained that it had long since expired and that he was therefore living in Italy without permission. For that reason, Jack was considered a suspicious foreigner and held in custody. This was the information we got from his friend. Thinking of his kindness and his helpfulness, I forgot my illness and fever and went to the Piazza Colonna to learn more about the unpleasant story. I had to do something to get Jack out of jail, and it wasn't as simple as I had so naively imagined.

In contrast to the case in other countries, in Italy one went to jail for invalid identification papers more quickly than one got out—assuming that one let oneself get caught. I was annoyed that this stupid business had to happen to our innocent Jack. There were enough dangerous scoundrels at large in Italy who, of course, possessed legal residence permits. I cursed Jack's slackness, all bureaucracies of the world, and my damned illness, which had become so cumbersome. A lot of running about was in store for me. To begin with, I had to find out what possibilities existed for Jack's quick release. Then I had to take some food to the prison for this poor, unhappy man, who had no relatives in Rome. The following day, I smuggled in some news about his probable release with a food package. I put myself in his cheerless position and tried to bring some joy into his life. But the information I had did not sound encouraging at all.

The Italian government wanted to remove the undesirable aliens from Rome and spoke of interning them in a camp for political suspects. So I had to be quick. I ran to lawyers and shysters who succeeded in taking my money but failed to help me. By this time I had become so weak that I had to stop on the street to lean on a gate because I couldn't walk any further. I hailed the next taxi and rode home.

Tea wanted to help Jack and went with me to the foreign registration office. She knew the closest co-worker of the almighty Dr. L., the feared chief of this government agency. Tea pleaded for help and protection regarding Jack's case. "Unfortunately, I can't assist you," the nice young co-worker said to us. "Your friend's records are no longer with the police. They were sent to the Ministry of the Interior two days ago." He sat pensively for a moment and then continued. "Try your luck at the ministry. The man in charge is called Dr. R. Perhaps he'll be able to help you. It is within his power, at least."

We thanked him for his kind advice and left. On our way out he added, "Please don't inform Dr. R. that I told you. Otherwise I could get into trouble." Tea and I promised that we wouldn't mention it. Both of us decided that I should go alone to look for Dr. R. the next day, which was Saturday. Visiting officials in administrative agencies was not one of my strong points. The universal arrogance of the men sitting behind their desks had always made me uneasy. It's the same feeling one has for the dentist. One waits with a queezy feeling in the stomach; then after finally being admitted, one is forced to sit in the martyr's seat. Moaning and pleading don't help. The dentist is stronger; he drills until he comes to a sensitive nerve, and then he takes his pliers and pulls out your nice tooth.

Dr. R. was an expert in his field. When he finally received me after persistent urging, I didn't feel like a petitioner, but rather like a dangerous criminal who has been forced to confess during cross-examination. At first he let me stand in front of his desk for fifteen minutes, totally unnoticed, while he leafed through files, telephoned, and gave orders to his subordinates. They shyly knocked on the door from the adjacent room, walked through, and then humbly offered a bundle of files as a sacrifice to the mighty ruler.

Suddenly he barked at me: "What do you want here?" His rough tone intimidated me momentarily, and I hesitatingly told him why I was there.

"Dr. R." I began. "I'm asking you for the release of a Mr. Jack B., who was arrested for no reason during a police raid and since then has been kept in prison by mistake." I was made aware of my faux pas when the person opposite thundered back, enraged: "Arrested for no reason? What is that supposed to mean? In Italy no one is arrested for no reason and kept in prison by mistake! What are you presuming? Who are you? Are you the spouse, the sister, or any other relative of the man who has been put in prison for no reason?" He sat there with his pen poised and waited for my answer.

I realized that I had deeply offended not only the Italian government but also the angry gentleman sitting behind the desk. I admitted contritely and hesitantly that I was neither related nor married to the groundlessly imprisoned gentleman, but that I took on this matter out of friendship and humaneness because he had neither relatives nor close friends in Rome. I mustered all my courage and asked the administrator to look at the files—he would surely see immediately that Mr. B. was no criminal, but rather that he merely had failed to get his residency permit extended. "I have no files on this matter," he stated. "Imprisonment is not a concern of my ministry, but the police. Go there and plead your case if you think you are right." He bent over the file on his desk, seemed to read it intensely, and deigned neither to look nor to speak to me again. I understood that my audience was at an end.

Disheartened, I thought for a moment about Jack, who would probably be sent to an internment camp. I imagined him standing behind a barbed-wire fence guarded by soldiers with rifles, and this vision wouldn't allow me to leave. I knew that Jack's release lay within this man's power, and I wouldn't let myself go out the door. My tenacious fighting spirit, which had been somewhat intimidated by the official's thundering voice, was resurrected. To my astonishment, I didn't leave the room, but heard myself articulate loud and clear: "Doctor, the files are no longer at the police station; they were transferred to the ministry a few days ago. There is no point in sending me to the gentleman at the police. He sent me to you." I added persistently, "Mr. B's files are in your possession, and I'm asking you once again to look into the matter so that you will be convinced of my friend's innocence."

Uncannily composed, Dr. R. observed me for a moment. Then he replied slowly, "So . . . so someone sent you here to me; someone at the police said that I pass the final judgment on this gentleman to whom you are so devoted. Very interesting." Dr. R. picked up the telephone, requested to be connected with the police, then questioned why someone had sent me to him. After putting down the receiver, he gave me a penetrating gaze for a few seconds. Finally he arose with the greatness and dignity befitting his position. "You are a liar," he droned icily. "Dr. M. from the police knows neither you nor your friend. You have never been there, and no one suggested you come here to me. Go away, and leave the matter of your 'innocent friend who has run into misfortune' in the hands of the proper authorities."

Had I had good sense, I would have left. Perhaps then everything would have turned out all right. Alas, I couldn't listen to reason at this moment. The gentleman behind the desk had insulted me—he had had the impudence to call me a liar. That is why I replied loud and vehemently in a voice shaking with rage. "I am not a liar. Who has given you the right to insult me? The files are here. I was at the police station and found out there. It wasn't Dr. M. who told me this, but his assistant. I assume that you too have a superior. I'm going to complain to him about your behavior toward me."

With my head held high, all I wanted to do was leave the room and its unpleasant occupants. But it never came to that. Miraculously, another large man suddenly stood in a subservient pose next to my opponent. The arrogant bureaucrat ordered calmly, "Take this woman to Dr. M. at the police prison." He signed a small paper, and I took leave of the ministry accompanied by the man. My whole body was shaking with rage. I couldn't think clearly, and I also couldn't understand why I had been arrested. "I know how to get there by myself," I told the man. "You don't need to accompany me." Instead of giving me an answer, he pushed me into a car, and we drove to the police. Only when we were on our way did I remember that the young man at the police station had asked me not to mention his advice to visit the ministry. Well, I couldn't do anything about it now. I had lost control when the man there had called me a liar.

Wretched beast, I thought. Hopefully you'll soon be locked up, then you'll see what it is like. My desire for revenge was strong but hopeless. He wasn't the person being put behind bars. I was. The man at the foreign registration office admitted me immediately, and I was put on the list. Enviously, the people waiting in the long line outside watched me as I disappeared behind the door of the mighty ruler. This time the officials were waiting for me. I didn't need to say a word. My enemy from the ministry seemed to have given them a detailed account. Had the gentleman from the ministry screamed? Had he treated me in a hostile manner? It was nothing compared with the reception I received here. A roaring lion welcomed me; a beast gone wild gesticulated before my eyes. He was a raving lunatic.

"Who allowed you to enter the ministry using my name? Who allowed you to lie in my name? I don't know you. You were never here. Liar! You are arrested. Take this person to the police cell. Quickly! I don't want to look at her. She annoys me!" As he screamed, his voice cracked and his eyes bulged. Up until now I hadn't said a word. Neither my name, nor my nationality, nor my age seemed to interest the madman. I was arrested. They led me up two flights of stairs to the police prison, but I could hardly walk. My legs shook beneath me, my head reeled, my heart raced loudly, I breathed with difficulty, and I almost fainted. I managed to pull through, however.

When I arrived at the prison, I was first led to a small office. It was here that a policeman in uniform took my papers, counted my money, and then kept it. He also took my purse, my glasses, and my handkerchief. Then he pulled a large key ring from the desk drawer, and we went into a small, dark courtyard. He unlocked a heavy iron door, let me go in, then locked the door behind me. I was in jail for the first time since the liberation, despite all the dangers that I had experienced. Now I let my exhaustion, the weariness that I had kept in check for so long, take its course. I sat down on the bare wooden-plank bed and cried loudly. No one heard me, no one was witness to my hopeless situation. I sobbed and physically let go of the unhappiness— I was sick, helpless, defenseless, and alone.

The pain caused by sitting on the uncomfortable plank bed finally dried my tears. Mechanically, I looked for my handkerchief. When I couldn't find it, I energetically took my slip, blew my nose thoroughly, and began to think about my situation. I didn't get very far with reasoning; the tears came too easily, and I continued to cry. I cried out all the misery of my soul. And when I used my slip this time, there was nothing left in me but a strong, healthy rage. "Irene," I said to myself in an audible voice, "don't go insane here.

Don't get hysterical. Enough of the bawling. Better see to it that you get out of this cage." My own angry words were successful.

My peace of mind slowly returned, and I began to think. It was Saturday morning, and I had to get news to Tea as soon as possible: she was the only person who could help me. If I couldn't contact her before noon, then I wouldn't be able to find her in her office until Monday morning. I knew that she was going to visit a friend before noon, and she wanted to spend Sunday there as well. Unfortunately, I didn't know the name of the family. I figured it out. Saturday, Sunday, Monday—I probably wouldn't be able to get out of here before Tuesday. Very unpleasant. I was sick. I felt like I had a fever. I hadn't gotten over the flu. Would I be beaten here? Would someone bring me something to drink? I was thirsty, and I needed something to quench my thirst.

I got up, reeling, and knocked on the barred window of the door, which was covered by an iron door from the outside. Almost instantly the little window was opened. The policeman who had put my things away stood there. He was a young man with a good-natured face. We looked at each other through the bars. "Please, could you bring me a glass of water?" I stammered. My tears flowed again. I held myself up, clinging to the bars. I was very weak. The policeman brought me the water, speaking a few soothing words that I didn't understand. I only felt his sympathy. I smiled at him through my tears, and when I handed him the empty cup, he didn't close the barred window.

He slowly paced back and forth in front of the cell. He didn't speak. The regularity of his pace soothed me. I waited until he was once again in front of my cell and asked him again for water. He brought it to me. "Please," I whispered. "could you make a telephone call for me?" He shook his head. "It's not allowed," he whispered back. "Could you get someone else to make a telephone call? My girlfriend doesn't know that I'm here. I'm sick!" I added pitifully. "It's not allowed," he said again. "I'm on the job now, but I'm finished at one o'clock," came his half-promise hesitantly.

I quickly gave him Tea's name and number and asked him imploringly to call her. "Of course, I'll get out of here immediately if someone helps me. I have neither murdered nor robbed. I have been arrested groundlessly and arbitrarily. I want to get out of here. I'm going to complain; I will take legal action against your boss!" I flustered in my childish, naive rage. "Pst, pst, just calm down! You'll be prosecuted again for defamation of a public officer while on duty. What have you really done? No one is arrested groundlessly in Italy," he insisted. There, I heard it again. "I lied," I replied curtly. "Lied?" he inquired. "Yes sir, I lied," I reaffirmed. "First I lied to a man at the ministry, and then I lied to someone here at the police. If I had known that one gets thrown into jail for lying in Italy, then I wouldn't have done it." "Well," said my guard skeptically, "that depends on the severity of the lie. If, for example, you murder someone and then later assert that you didn't do it, then we have to lock you up and keep you there until we know for sure that you are innocent." His face became serious: his suspicion had been aroused.

I wanted to explain how I had been arrested, when I heard someone on the stairs. He hastily shut the barred window and left me to my thoughts of revenge. Sometime later the door was unlocked, and the official who had led me there stood outside. "Come with me," he said curtly. I walked out of the cell. "Where are we going?" I asked him. "You're being transferred to prison. Here you were only in police custody," he replied. "First you have to go to the boss," he added as we once again walked up the wide, ugly staircase. My heart began to beat loudly. So I had to see this raving lunatic again. What was he going to do with me?

A great surprise awaited me upstairs. I was led into another office where a few harmless-looking clerks were sitting. One of them offered me a chair. He probably noticed that I wasn't very steady on my feet. "You can leave here immediately. You're released," he said amiably. "Released?" I got up quickly and was heading for the door. "Just one moment, please," the young man smiled. "First, you have to sign this paper." He put an official looking piece of paper in front of me. I grabbed a pen and wanted to sign the paper. The only thing I could think of was getting out of there and back into freedom as soon as possible. The two hours I had spent there had given me enough of a taste of what being in prison was like.

The young man dampened my enthusiasm. "Please, read the paper first before you sign," he advised in a dry, bureaucratic tone. So I read it. My eyes popped out of my head when I read it. I read it again. Could I believe my eyes? Forbidden to enter the police building, forbidden to enter the ministry. Well, these two prohibitions I certainly didn't want to violate. But what did the third part mean? Obligation to leave the country within four weeks. Leave the country within four weeks? Was it an expulsion? Could it be? Where was I supposed to go? Did I have a passport, a visa, or money to let me simply travel to another country?

"I won't sign it." I stated flatly, shaking all over. "I'm a refugee; I don't have a country, I don't have a family, I can't go anywhere. I have to stay here in Italy. No, I won't sign it under any circumstances." The official grappled with feelings of derision and sympathy when he said: "Sign it. There is nothing else we can do except keep you in prison until the day of your eviction. After you sign it, you'll be set free. You can go home, and," he added softly, "you can apply for an extension." He didn't look at me when he uttered the last words. I took the pen and signed. "Thank you," I said mechanically as my purse, my watch, and my money were handed back to me. I left the police office in a daze. It was 12:30. All the things that had taken place in the last three hours! The ground I had been standing on had been pulled out from under me. New and unknown excursions awaited me. I walked into the next bar and drank a double cognac. Then I telephoned Tea.

When she arrived home, she found me already in bed. I had a high fever. The excitement had brought about a relapse in my weakened body. My teeth chattered as I told Tea about the day's incident. "Everything will be okay," she consoled me. "The most important thing is to get well." The doctor ordered the strictest regimen. I was to lie in bed undisturbed, except for the medication that Signor Milleri patiently and faithfully pushed into my mouth every two hours. I lay there apathetically for a few days and let come what may. Then when my fever fell to 37.5 [Celsius], I became impatient.

The expulsion caused me the greatest worry. Where could I go? There was no country that had opened its borders. And even if one had, what good was it to me? I didn't have a passport. I brooded and brooded over my dilemma. Tea wrote petitions to the head of the foreign registration office, to the ministry, and I don't know who else. She looked for personal acquaintances to gain support for my case. It was all in vain. My expulsion was not withdrawn. I got up and ran to the Joint and to UNRRA, but that didn't help either. I got up for one day, then fainted, then lay three days in bed, then got up, then fainted two or three times. My health alternated between heart attacks,[1] fever, and cold shivers. It got to where I passed out even when I went to the bathroom alone. I didn't eat anything. Tea was in her office. Signor Milleri usually brought me what I asked him to, which was mostly black coffee and a few cookies.

Tea arrived with another doctor. His diagnosis was total exhaustion, and he said that I was a physical and emotional wreck. He prescribed rest, injections, tranquility, and good food. The one thing I did was get injections. How could I lie there in bed when days went by and I didn't know where I would go? Could I make it to the Swiss border on foot? I wondered. Or could I make it to France? What was going to happen to my personal belongings? Would I have to leave behind the few clothes and underwear that I had worked so hard to buy? I left my bed again in order to go to this or that person to see if there wasn't a way out.

In the meantime Jack had been deported to a camp for political suspects. I went to UNRRA and asked that I be interned in a camp when my time limit ran out. I knew that my weakened body could no longer withstand the strain of a secret border crossing, because the fainting spells and heart attacks had gotten worse. Tea was very worried about me. If she came home late in the evening, she would yell "yoo-hoo!" I would then give a signal with the light. If I turned the light on and off once, that meant that I was still alive and things were going all right. If I didn't turn the light on and off, she would come up to see what was wrong. Once she found me sitting on the bed gasping for air. She called the first doctor she could find in the middle of the night. I received a camphor injection and things improved. I fell asleep.

I suffered from anxiety—I was afraid of dying when no one was there. This took away my only remaining peace of mind and kept me feverishly awake. More than ever I longed for a person who belonged to me, for whom it wasn't a duty to help me, a person who was afraid of losing me, who trembled when I was sick, who would make me eat, who would hold my hand and console me when the dark hours came. I longed for a person who was my friend, who laughed and cried with me. My strength had vanished. The blow that had finally robbed me of my health was the expulsion from Italy.

If it hadn't been for Tea, whose constancy and sense of humor had given me courage, I would probably have died of physical and mental indifference. Does such a thing exist?

One day Tea brought along Dr. Landau, an immigrant from Poland. Through some kind of miracle, he had obtained a work permit, and he was practicing medicine in a modest office in a working-class district of Rome. From the first day of our acquaintance he was more than a doctor: he was a friend. He deliberated how he could forcibly save another good friend from death. On that first day, he examined me thoroughly and then sent the obliging Signor Milleri to the nearest pharmacy and let him buy remedies, injections, drops, fortifying tablets, vitamins, and God knows what else. Then he sat down comfortably on my bed, took my hand into his strong, calm hands, and said, smiling: "Now enough of this woebegone face. Have you looked at yourself in the mirror lately? You probably look like your venerated grandmama when she was sixty years old. Amazing that a pretty woman like you would let herself go like that. I've always worshipped you a little from afar," he admitted with a twinkle in his eye. "To be sure you looked decidedly better then."

I laughed and looked at Dr. Landau a little more closely. How handsome and nice he was. How cheerfully his brown eyes shown—he couldn't have been older than thirty-five. With an involuntary movement I arranged my tousled hair and pulled the blanket up to my chin. He laughed loudly. "That's fine that you have decided not to die yet. Tell me a little about your life," he said. "I'm having such a nice time, and I have nothing to do this evening. My last fiancée left me, and I'm so lonely." He grinned with his roguish smile. I smiled back. "I believe that your experiences are more interesting than mine," I teased. "Tell me about your last fiancée."

Without further ado he narrated a quickly invented and highly dramatic love story. I enjoyed it immensely. Every now and then Tea would throw in a strange question. I laughed for the first time in a long while and had neither fainting spells nor heart attacks. Dr. Landau would often visit me in his free moments, giving me medication and sending Signor Milleri to buy cake and whipped cream, of which he consumed large portions. His good humor and his comradeship contributed more than anything else to my slow recovery. The monotony of my existence was broken, I was no longer afraid of dying, and I knew that I would live.

Curiosity about the future revived me. In what kind of a country would I most likely live? America? Africa? Asia? Would it be hot or cold in "my" new country? It was fun for me to imagine the most impossible things that I would do in the unknown foreign land. Dr. Landau and Tea would feed my fantasy. If Tea suggested that I should become a cake baker, then Dr. Landau proposed I be a shoe shiner in a men's salon, while I opted to be a traveling companion to a fantastically rich Indian.

Well, I thought more and more, fate will determine soon enough whether I become a shoe shiner or a traveling companion, as long as I don't surrender. Would it not be a great shame to give up, I mused, as I lay in my bed or when I sat at the window for half an hour and looked at the narrow, dark courtyard where the children screamed and the neighbors fought? Had my experiences worn me down? What were they compared with the horrors that millions had experienced? Was I not happier than the many nameless ones who were rotting somewhere? Was it not my duty to live, to fight, to tell about what had happened? When God had so often saved my life in such fantastic ways, why shouldn't I do my part and stay alive? The war was over. To die now would be almost ridiculous. No, I want to and will get well, I thought, even if only out of curiosity to get to know new countries, new cities, and, most important of all, new people.

FINALE

I received good news from Jack: he hoped to be released from confinement soon. Comrades of his had left the internment camp and gone overseas with exit visas and he asked me to take some steps to procure one for him. Santo Domingo was allegedly receiving immigrants, and Jack wanted me to go to the consulate. I went, was greeted warmly, and found out that it was indeed true that there was a possibility of being granted a visa for that country. My hopes were raised when I filled out two large questionnaires and when I was promised by the consul that I would soon receive an answer. Santo Domingo—how romantic it sounded. I went to the Joint and made inquiries whether the possibility existed of someone financing my passage. To be sure, the possibility existed!

Outside in the lobby I ran into an old acquaintance from Belgrade, who also wanted to obtain a visa. We conversed for a little while, and when I told him about my travel plans, he took me aside and whispered mysteriously, "Wait downstairs on the street for me, I can perhaps give you a good tip. I have a friend up here, and I think there is interesting news for us." Aware that I wanted to go overseas, no matter where, he asked me to wait for him outside, because he wanted to offer me a great chance to leave. "Perhaps I can smuggle you along with me into another country as a family member. Maybe to Argentina or to South Africa," he added dreamily.

I waited for him on the street, and as I watched him come out, I could discern, even from a distance, that he had interesting news. His entire face beamed, and he waved his arms passionately. I ran up to him. He couldn't keep his secret to himself anymore. "We're going to Brazil!" he gushed. "Just think, Brazil! What a country! What possibilities! What luck!" he raved. Enraptured, he looked at me without interrupting his deluge of words. "The fabulous trip; just think, Rio de Janeiro! We'll see the most beautiful city in the world. The city where no one gets cold, where no one goes hungry, where everyone can live and work freely without persecution." I held him firmly by the arm. "Herr Blumer," I said excitedly, "now calm down. Rio de Janeiro is certainly a beautiful city, but that doesn't interest us now. Tell me what your friend has told you." What Herr Blumer related then was indeed remarkable.

Brazil had opened its gates to immigration: not even the applicants' religion or race was asked for. Everyone who had a passport, a profession, and money for travel could go to the land of promise. It was unbelievable. Could it really be true? A country that asked about neither religion nor race? A country that let people in if they simply owned a passport? A passport, ... a passport ... [the words] went hammering through my brain. Aha! that was the catch. Who among us possessed a passport? We were happy that we had a head on our shoulders, that we had food and clothing, but a passport? No, I had a right to be skeptical. The passage to Brazil was hardly meant for me and my kind. "Neither Brazil nor Santo Domingo nor any other country would take us in," I said sadly. "There is nothing left for us to do but wait for years in an internment camp until our problem is finally solved."

My friend vehemently disagreed. "No, Frau Irene, we're going to depart," he said. The Red Cross will take care of us and issue provisional passports. My friend who told me all this wouldn't lie to me. He wants to go to Brazil as well and is sure that it can be done. I'll keep you informed and call you when I hear further details," he promised, before saying good-bye and running home to delude his family into believing wonderful dreams about their future.

Dr. Landau and Tea were less suspicious than I. Why should it not be true, after all? Tea made inquiries among her influential friends at the Joint and UNRRA. No one knew exactly what to report, but the probability that Brazilian immigration permits, unlike those of other countries, did not have questions about race or religion was confirmed everywhere. I tried my luck on my own and walked to the Brazilian consulate. After endless waiting it was my turn. Yes, it was true, there was a possibility of obtaining a visa. What could I do? Who was I? What profession did I have? Did I have relatives in Brazil? Did I have money? What valid passport did I own? The young woman behind the counter questioned me thoroughly. When she heard that I answered all her questions stereotypically and observed that I didn't have a passport, she shook her head regretfully and replied, "There is no point in applying for a visa. You do not fit the requirements of our immigration laws in any way."

Distressed but almost gratified, I left the consulate. Hadn't I known all along that it would be like this? To hell with Tea, Dr. Landau, Herr Blumer, and all the other optimists. That things could be as easy as all of them had imagined was nonsense. We're traveling to Brazil! How fabulous it is there: no persecution, no hunger, no frigid weather—a perfect paradise, I sneered. Nevertheless, we sailed to Brazil!

All the difficulties notwithstanding, Herr Blumer was right. First of all, the Red Cross took on our case. When I first discussed the matter with the Joint, I was sent to the building housing the Red Cross to apply for a passport. I wasn't the only one who was trying to obtain the priceless document; people from all over the world waited there patiently until they disappeared behind the closed door to state their case. The questionnaire was filled out, and no documents were necessary. Most of the petitioners were refugees who could not give proof of their identity. Of course, this gave rise to a lot of abuse. If Hitler or Göring themselves had appeared and stated that they were Adolf Engel or Hermann Friedlich, they probably would have obtained the document as well. The officials couldn't do anything else but fully believe the declarations made to them. Thousands of unfortunate people were helped through this, even though some criminals' plans were facilitated. Eight days later I was the proud owner of a Red Cross passport, which expressly stated, however, that it was valid for one trip only.

Now things transpired with great speed. Brazil's gates were opened, and the Joint made things easier for us. Two months after I had obtained my passport I received a permanent visa for Brazil. The Italian foreign registration office didn't bother me during this period, and it seemed as though the expulsion had been forgotten. My health improved—I was too excited to be sick: I was traveling to Brazil. It suddenly seemed to me that I had no other wish and no other goal than that of arriving in Brazil! I loved the country before I had even seen it. It was the land of my hopes and dreams. Long before I knew when I would leave, my suitcase was packed. My only regret was that Tea, whom I had grown so fond of, would remain in Italy. It seemed my destiny to always be alone and to have to start from the very beginning again. I had to go my own way to the end, regardless of how difficult or easy it might be.

Jack was released from the internment camp. He too had a Red Cross passport and was waiting for his visa. He hoped to be able to travel with me, but by the time I had my visa in hand something unlucky had happened. His passport had been inexplicably lost in the offices of the Joint. Unfortunately, by the time he received a new passport and applied for his visa, it was too late. The Brazilian consulate had received orders from its country not to grant any more visas for the time being.

My travel costs were provided by the Joint, and a place on the *Andrea-Gritti* had been reserved for me. The ship was to leave port from Naples at the end of December. On 27 December 1946, Tea, Jack, and Dr. Landau accompanied me to the bus heading for Naples. Jack wiped the tears from his eyes,

Dr. Landau used his handkerchief often to blow his nose thoroughly, and Tea held my hand tightly until the moment of departure. One more glance, one more wave, and then my friends disappeared from sight. Rome, the place where I had lived for one and a half years, the gambling club, the illness, the sorrow, and the joy that this city had given me were now already part of the past. My path led me forward. I was going to Rio de Janeiro! I was going to Brazil!

When we arrived in Naples, it was already getting dark; it was too late to go to the office of the Joint there. I quickly decided to take a car, and loaded my baggage with the help of the driver. He criss-crossed the strange and dimly lit city, and now and then he stopped in front of a hotel and shouted, asking if there was a room available. Everyone turned us down. The driver didn't look very trustworthy. I was afraid of leaving my baggage alone with him. If I bargained with a porter in the lobby of a hotel, he could easily disappear with all of my belongings. When I realized that we were still riding and it seemed to me as if we were going in circles, I told him that he should call out the owner of the next hotel that we stopped in front of. This time it worked. I was given a room for the night in the dirty, sinister-looking hotel, though I had to rent a room with two beds because "nothing else was available." The door didn't close either, but still, I could lie clothed on the foul-smelling bed with a light on and wait for the next morning.

I was in the office of the Joint very early. The friendly gentleman there gave me an allotment for a pension immediately. I was well accommodated there with other emigrants until the ship embarked. On the morning of 31 December our baggage was picked up. We were put into a bus and driven to the harbor, accompanied by an official from the Joint. The *Andrea-Gritti* rose large and gleaming white in front of us, but the bureaucratic formalities lasted forever. Hundreds of emigrants would be traveling on this ship. Our papers were checked once again, while a doctor looked us in the eye and pronounced us healthy. Someone told us that for some unknown reason the emigrants traveling under the jurisdiction of the Joint were not to be permitted to board the ship. There was a long hour of nervous anxiety and quiet supplication. But no, it was all stupid gossip of irresponsible alarmists.

One after another, we climbed up the narrow iron steps to the *Andrea-*

Gritti. A sailor showed us the way to our bunks, as we walked along the long deck to another set of iron stairs that went down. We entered a room with 200 to 250 beds, one on top of the other. Those who were lucky managed to get one near a window hatch. I occupied one of the upper beds in the middle of the large dark room. Our hand luggage was stowed away under the bed, and our combs, brushes, and all other necessary toilet articles were placed under the pillow. I walked up to the deck and looked around. It was teeming with third-class passengers, men, women, and children speaking every possible language, predominantly Serbian, Polish, and French.

The ship set sail at midnight. It was 1 January 1947. A new year and a new period of our lives had begun. Life on the ship offered many new experiences for me—I liked it, and everything made me happy. I got up quietly at 5:30 in the morning, when all were still asleep, to use the shower when it was still clean. One hour later it was already in an indescribable state. At breakfast we poured thin, bad-tasting coffee from a large pot into our tin bowls and drank the lukewarm beverage with a piece of bread. The food was extremely bad. Ten people sat together on a long bench, and the two persons who brought the kettle with the food received full dinner plates. The system was like that in a barracks; after the meal we rinsed out our tin plates and put them back under our pillows. Still, at times some couldn't find plates or silverware at mealtime because someone had stolen them for some inconceivable reason. Much was stolen.

All the time in our dormitory we could hear a woman's voice carping loudly that this or that article was missing. If she looked askance at her neighbor, there was a quick exchange of ugly words and often a brawl. Male visitors were strictly forbidden in our room. Nevertheless, there were always a few husbands and fiancés on hand, just as sailors looking for something to do would watch us unashamedly when we changed clothes. We got used to it and after a few days didn't notice it in the least. At night our communal room stank abominably. About 230 women and children, most of whom suffered from sea sickness, lay crammed together in the hot sticky dormitory.

In spite of everything, the trip was wonderful for me. No first-class passenger could have felt happier than I did. Most of the time I lay on the deck and stared at the water or at the blue sky. With the exception of a storm that lasted two days, the weather was fabulous. I wasn't seasick at all and enjoyed the trip and the relaxation twice as much, while dreaming of a beautiful future. On the morning of 16 January our ship arrived in the bay of Rio de Janeiro. All of us were already standing on deck before sunrise so we wouldn't miss the glorious view of the bay. The sun rose slowly and shone on the mountains in a radiant luster. We saw Rio de Janeiro. My eyes were transfixed by the indescribably beautiful picture as the *Andrea-Gritti* slowly glided into the harbor.

Rio de Janeiro—Brazil—what would it bring me? What adventures awaited me? My heart overflowed with joy. Brazil, Rio de Janeiro, will you bring me peace and happiness? I wondered. Are you the end of my difficult journey?

Begun August 1949
Finished 10 October 1950

NOTES

INTRODUCTION

1. Harriet Pass Freidenreich, *The Jews of Yugoslavia* (Philadelphia: Jewish Publication Society of America, 1979), 5–7.

2. Freidenreich, *The Jews of Yugoslavia*, 179–89.

3. Freidenreich, *The Jews of Yugoslavia*, 189. Ladino is a Judeo-Spanish dialect that evolved from fourteenth-century Castilian.

4. Freidenreich, *The Jews of Yugoslavia*, 182.

5. Freidenreich, *The Jews of Yugoslavia*, 187; Christian Zentner and Friedemann Bedürftig, eds., *The Encyclopedia of the Third Reich*, 2 vols. (New York: Macmillan, 1991), 2:1073.

6. Freidenreich, *The Jews of Yugoslavia*, 190; Zentner and Bedürftig, *Encyclopedia of the Third Reich*, 1:17, 64, 2:1073.

7. Barbara Jelavich, *History of the Balkans*, 2 vols. (Cambridge: Cambridge University Press, 1983), 2:237.

8. Jelavich, *History of the Balkans*, 2:247, 262.

9. Jonathan Steinberg, *All or Nothing: The Axis and the Holocaust, 1941–1943* (New York: Routledge, 1990), 32.

10. Steinberg, *All or Nothing*, 38.

11. Freidenreich, *The Jews of Yugoslavia*, 190; Jelavich, *History of the Balkans*, 2:267.

12. Raul Hilberg, *The Destruction of the European Jews*, 3 vols. (New York: Holmes & Meier, 1985), 2:683.

13. Christopher Browning, *Fateful Months: Essays on the Emergence of the Final Solution* (New York: Holmes & Meier, 1991), 49.

14. Ernst Wisshaupt, quoted in Browning, *Fateful Months*, 42.

15. Browning, *Fateful Months*, 48–49.

16. Browning, *Fateful Months*, 49, 55.

17. Hilberg, *The Destruction of the European Jews*, 2:742.

18. Hilberg, *The Destruction of the European Jews*, 2:754–55.

19. Alexandar Matkovski, *A History of the Jews in Macedonia* (Skopje: Macedonian Review Editions, 1982), 129.

20. Matkovski, *A History of the Jews in Macedonia*, 178.

21. Matkovski, *A History of the Jews in Macedonia*, 179.

22. Matkovski, *A History of the Jews in Macedonia*, 181.

23. Jelavich, *History of the Balkans*, 2:217; Hugh Gibson, ed., *The Ciano Diaries, 1939–1943* (New York: Doubleday, 1946), 43.

24. Charles Jelavich and Barbara Jelavich, *The Balkans* (Englewood Cliffs, NJ: Prentice Hall, 1965), 95–96.

25. Shmuel Almog, *Nationalism and Antisemitism in Modern Europe, 1815–1945* (New York: Pergamon, 1990), 126–27.

26. Primo Levi, *The Reawakening* (Boston: Little, Brown & Co., 1965), 31.

27. Susan Zuccotti, *The Italians and the Holocaust* (New York: Basic Books, 1987), 74–75.

28. Steinberg, *All or Nothing*, 1.

29. Steinberg, *All or Nothing*, 4.

30. Martin Gilbert, *Atlas of the Holocaust* (New York: Pergamon, 1988), 179; Hilberg, *The Destruction of the European Jews*, 2:704.

31. Hilberg, *The Destruction of the European Jews*, 2:704–5.

32. Anton Logoreci, *The Albanians* (London: Victor Gollancz, 1977), 76.

33. Stefanaq Pollo and Arben Puto, *The History of Albania* (London: Routledge & Kegan Paul, 1981), 237.

34. Logoreci, *The Albanians*, 69.

35. Jelavich, *History of the Balkans*, 2:275.

36. Logoreci, *The Albanians*, 78.

37. Fitzroy Maclean, *Eastern Approaches* (New York: Time Reading Program, 1964), 412–13; Logoreci, *The Albanians*, 79; Jelavich, *History of the Balkans*, 2:283–84.

38. Logoreci, *The Albanians*, 78–79.

39. Jelavich, *History of the Balkans*, 2:274.

40. Jelavich and Jelavich, *The Balkans*, 104.

41. James E. Young, *Writing and Rewriting the Holocaust* (Bloomington: Indiana University Press, 1988), 37–39.

42. Terrence Des Pres, *The Survivor: An Anatomy of Life in the Death Camps* (New York: Oxford University Press, 1976), 192.

43. Gitta Sereny, *Into That Darkness* (New York: McGraw-Hill, 1974), 183; Des Pres, *The Survivor*, 191–92.

44. Bogdan Denitch, *Ethnic Nationalism: The Tragic Death of Yugoslavia* (Minneapolis: University of Minnesota Press, 1994), 31–33.

45. Denitch, *Ethnic Nationalism*, 118.

46. Misha Glenny, *The Fall of Yugoslavia* (New York: Penguin, 1992), 181.

PRELUDE

1. Yugoslavia signed the Tripartite Pact on 25 March 1941. Two days later Serbian General Dušan Simović led a bloodless coup d'état in Belgrade and took over the government. Hitler decided to invade after hearing about the anti-German demonstrations in Belgrade. Grünbaum's reference to "revolution" is apparently to the putsch, although she dates it 23 March (see Freidenreich, *The Jews of Yugoslavia*, 190; and Jelavich, *History of the Balkans*, 2:236).

BOBBY

1. Kamenica is located about sixty miles southwest of Belgrade.

2. The main Yugoslavian troops were concentrated on the border; however, once subdued they did not resist further. Following Yugoslavia's capitulation to Germany on 17 April, a retreat to Salonika (Thessalonica) via Bulgaria was impossible. (In secret sections of the Tripartite Pact, Germany and Italy assured Yugoslavia that it would receive Salonika as part of the peace settlement.) This escape route was now cut off because the German army already occupied Bulgaria. To make matters even worse for Serbia, there was little if no resistance from Croatia and Slovenia (see Jelavich, *History of the Balkans*, 2:236–37).

3. The Tasmajdan was a concentration camp near Belgrade. Most Jews from the Banat region of Yugoslavia, north of Belgrade, were taken to the Tasmajdan camp and systematically shot in the camp itself or on the banks of the Danube. These daily executions continued until late summer, and by 20 August 1941 the Nazis proclaimed the entire Banat region *judenrein*, or purged of Jews (Gilbert, *Atlas of the Holocaust*,

58–59. For more on the systematic destruction of the Jewish population, see Hilberg, *The Destruction of the European Jews*, 2:683).

4. It is unlikely that this would have happened so early in the war. The conference for the implementation of the Final Solution did not take place until 20 January 1942 in Berlin (Am Grossen Wannsee #50/58) (Hilberg, *The Destruction of the European Jews*, 2:404).

5. After Yugoslavia surrendered, the Germans created occupied and satellite zones in this territory. Macedonia was divided into three parts: the largest section was given to Bulgaria, the smallest was given to Albania, that is, Italy; and Aegean Macedonia was occupied by Germany. After the Bulgarian army invaded Macedonia, about three hundred Jews fled from German-occupied Serbia to Bulgarian-occupied Macedonia, where they hoped for more humane treatment. Most lived illegally in Skopje (Matkovski, *A History of the Jews in Macedonia*, 97–98,127–28).

6. Grünbaum initially refers to her sister-in-law as Viola but later calls her Vida.

7. In November 1941 the Bulgarian police ordered all Jews to register. Only sixty registered. Of these sixty, forty-eight were arrested immediately and handed over to the Germans; they were then sent to Serbia, where they were shot in December 1941. Soon afterward, talks began between the Bulgarian government and the German representatives in Sofia about deportation (Matkovski, *A History of the Jews in Macedonia*, 127–28).

KATJA AND NATASHA

1. The agreement to deport twenty thousand Macedonian Jews was approved on 22 February 1943. The blockade was planned for 11 March, but some in the Jewish community heard the news before that date. Sadly, most Jews there either did not believe it or chose to stay because they wanted to be with their families. We know from a statement made by Pepo Moshe Alaluf after the liberation that some of the Jews of Skopje were informed: "As secretary of the Jewish community, I was in daily contact with Ivan Zakhariev, the hangman of the Jews, who was continuously accusing the Jews of Skopje of openly expressing their sympathies with the military successes of the USSR. . . . I know that A. Belev came to Skopje a few days prior to the blockade and that he held a conference with prominent local fascists and anti-Semites. . . . Dr. Toma Petrov kept telling me that we would not be sent away from Skopje and that the camp would be within the city itself" (Matkovski, *A History of the Jews in Macedonia*, 129–31).

BLOCKADE

1. It was 11 March 1943.

2. A concentration camp was set up for Macedonian Jews in the tobacco warehouse in Skopje. The conditions there were atrocious. Survivors reported severe overcrowding and filthy rooms; there was no water for bathing, and hunger pervaded. The guards beat the prisoners and took their valuables (Matkovski, *A History of the Jews in Macedonia*, 131,138–39).

3. Perhaps this was Berta Khaim Noakh of Skopje, who is mentioned by Matkovski as a camp inmate; she was released after eighteen days because she was a Spanish citizen (Matkovski, *A History of the Jews in Macedonia*, 139).

4. It was Treblinka, not Auschwitz. The three deportations from Skopje took place on 22, 25, and 29 March 1943. These transports consisted of Jews from Skopje, Bitola, Shtip, and Kavala. The first transport delivered 2,334 persons to Treblinka; the second, 2,399 persons; and the third, 2,399. The total number of people who passed through the concentration camp in Skopje was 7,320. Of these, only 168 survived. The temporary concentration camp in Skopje existed from 11 March to 29 March 1943 (Matkovski, *A History of the Jews in Macedonia*, 143,148–56).

5. Guards were posted along Macedonia's border with Albania to stop refugees from fleeing a few days before and after the blockade in Skopje on 11 March 1943. Those Jews who could fled to the Italian-occupied territories of Albania and western Macedonia, where Jews were not being persecuted (Matkovski, *A History of the Jews in Macedonia*, 127,131).

NAFI

1. *Bey* is a Turkish title used in reference to a gentleman.

2. *Effendi* is a Turkish word that corresponds to *Mister*.

DJEMILA

1. Tirana is the Italian name for Tiranë. Grünbaum primarily uses the Italian forms of placenames in Albania.

TIRANA

1. Grünbaum sometimes spells this woman's name as Sukriye Hanum, sometimes as Shukria Hamun. It was probably Sukriye Hanim, *Hanim* being a Turkish form of address corresponding to either *Miss* or *Mrs.*

2. The revolt of the Albanian people against the enemy became extensive in the latter half of 1941. Partisans attacked Italian soldiers, military barracks, ammunition depots, and the airport in Tirana. Patriotic groups cut telephone lines throughout Albania. The Italians retaliated in kind as soon as they realized how widespread the uprising was. They burned villages and executed sympathizers of the "communist bandits" (Ramadan Marmullaku, *Albania and the Albanians* [New York: Archon Books, 1975], 46).

CAVAIA

1. Cavaia, also spelled *Kavaja,* was a transit camp for Jews who had fled Serbia and Croatia. As Grünbaum describes, refugees there were well treated by the Italian occupying forces and by the local population. Some who stayed there were sent to Italy (*Encyclopaedia Judaica* [Jerusalem: Macmillan, 1971], 2:523).

2. This may be a reference to the deportations from Salonika, Greece, which had been in the German-occupied zone since April 1941. Of the roughly 80,000 Jews living in Greece, 50,000 lived in Salonika. This city had been the capital of Sephardic Jewry for almost five centuries. Eichmann's agents ss *Hauptsturmführer* Dieter Wisliceny and Alois Brunner arrived in Salonika in early February 1943 and immediately began to implement their plan to liquidate the Jews. The first transport of Jews left on 15 March 1943, and the last on 7 August; there were nineteen transports in all. According to the records kept at Auschwitz-Birkenau, of the 48,974 Jews transported from Salonika, 37,386 were gassed as soon as they arrived. In Salonika the Germans took the necessary precautions, closing all the foreign consulates except the Italian one, so that the news would not leak out to the world. The last deportation took place about a month before the Armistice (see Steinberg, *All or Nothing,* 96–100; and Matkovski, *A History of the Jews in Macedonia,* 187–97).

3. Whether this tale is true is not certain. Egon Kreiser, Ernst Alger's enemy, told the story. Also, the Germans usually did not keep their word in such cases.

4. The author is in error about the date. The Italian armistice with the Allies was announced on 8 September 1943. At that time, the people of Albania began to participate in the struggle for liberation on a grand scale. Partisan units disarmed portions of the occupying Italian forces; some Italian soldiers joined the Partisans, some joined the Germans, and some tried to flee Albania. The forces of the Balli Kombëtar joined the collaborators, and Abaz Kupi formed the Legality Party, which cham-

pioned the return of King Zog. The Germans had been increasing their forces in Albania since the summer of 1943, preparing to take over from the Italians. The Germans also claimed to support an independent Albania, the pretext being the "liberation" of Albania from Italian subjugation (Marmullaku, *Albania and the Albanians*, 51–52).

5. Dibra is the Italian name of the province of Dibër in northeastern Albania. There is a city with a similar name, Debar, near this province, in Macedonia near the Albanian border. Grünbaum does not specify city or province. The mountains and forests near Dibra made good hideouts for the Partisans, and organized Partisan units liberated part of the Dibra region in 1941 (Marmullaku, *Albania and the Albanians*, 46).

ROAD TO DIBRA

1. Presumably this Italian was one of those who joined in the fight against Germany even after Italy had capitulated and the Italian soldiers had been disarmed.

2. Unlike most of the partisans, Gafur Brangu was pro-German.

3. And there were many camps. After the Italian fascist regime collapsed, Albanian guerrillas attacked their enemies. The royalists, as well as other nationalist groups in the north, won numerous battles and successfully captured many towns. The communists in the south fought even more successfully. The nationalist forces of the Balli Kombëtar (National Front) limited their skirmishes to the area around the southern port of Vlorë (Valona). After the Germans marched in, however, the guerrilla successes were short-lived.

In this chaos the Italian occupation forces were no longer active; some fell apart, while some joined the Germans and others joined the Partisans. The British officers in Albania tried to organize and unite the various guerrilla factions in order to fight the Germans, but they were unsuccessful. Also, the communist partisans were determined to liquidate their Albanian opponents by the end of the war.

This gave rise to a civil war that began between the Albanian communists, or the National Liberation Movement (LNC), and the Balli Kombëtar. In the hostilities and confusion that followed, many of the Balli Kombëtar went over to the German side. This allowed the LNC to group the leaders of the Balli Kombëtar with the members of the quisling government in Tirana as traitors. The civil war lasted a year (1943–44) and took place mostly in southern Albania. The LNC emerged victorious for many reasons: they were well-organized; they were not afraid of murdering their countrymen for a future communist Albania; they enjoyed the backing of the Yugoslav communist party; and they were confident about fighting two enemies: their Albanian political opponents and the Germans. By late 1944, the communist Partisans controlled most of Albania, which would have been impossible without Western military arms (Logoreci, *The Albanians*, 76–82; David Smiley, *Albanian Assignment* [London: Hogarth, 1984], 102).

4. See "Tirana."

TIRANA REVISITED

1. Scutari (Shkodër) is located about eighty miles northwest of Tirana and is one of the larger cities in Albania.

2. See "Cavaia."

3. The German rhymes.

4. See "Tirana."

5. Valona is the Italian name of Vlorë, a seaport in southwest Albania.

6. Grünbaum probably did not know the Muslim term.

DR. K.

1. See "Cavaia."

2. The author never mentions Dr. K.'s nationality; however, it seems unlikely that he was German. Had he been German, he probably would have had her arrested immediately. Perhaps he was a Serbian-speaking Albanian or a Serbian working for the Nazis.

3. On 20 October 1943 the collaborationist Constituent Assembly elected a Regency Council, headed by Mehdi Frashëri. This government was in reality a coalition of the nationalist Balli Kombëtar, the monarchist Legality Party, the Roman Catholic clergy, "independent" nationalists, and Gestapo agents. Perhaps the regent the author refers to is Frashëri, who was a well-respected politician and a former prime minister (see Pollo and Puto, *The History of Albania*, 237–38; Logoreci, *The Albanians*, 76).

4. Very little is known about the Jews' situation in Albania during the German occupation. After the capitulation of Italy, the Germans marched in and filled the power vacuum. Although the guerrilla forces increased in size, they were not successful in unifying and fighting the enemy. Eventually, a civil war broke out between the communist partisans and the nationalist partisans, spreading terror throughout the country. In April 1944 Albanian collaborators in Priština (Kosovo) arrested three

hundred Jews, who were deported to Bergen-Belsen. In such confusion it would have been easy to target a literate Jewish woman as a communist or a spy. Grünbaum was really at the mercy of the people who protected her.

THE PRINCESS

1. Sultan Abdul Hamid II was the autocratic leader of the Ottoman Empire from 1876 to 1909. He was known for both his cruelty and cowardice, and the epithet "Red Sultan" alludes to the blood of his victims. The leitmotifs of his long reign were war and financial catastrophe. Albania was under Ottoman rule from the sixteenth to the nineteenth centuries and proclaimed its independence from the Turkish yoke in 1912 (Andrew Wheatcroft, *The Ottomans* [London: Viking, 1993], 191–207).

2. It was 2 April 1944. Following the example of the Yugoslav communist Partisans, the Albanian communist Partisans met in May 1944 in the southern town of Përmet. Enver Hoxha was elected chairman of the provisional government and commander of the LNC. In the meeting, the communist Partisans reaffirmed their commitment to fight against the collaborators, the royalist guerrillas, the Balli Kombëtar, and chieftains of the northern clans. At this time the civil war still raged in the south of the country, although the situation in the north had become very confused (Logoreci, *The Albanians*, 79).

3. By the end of October 1944 most of Albania had been freed; the exceptions were a few towns in the center and north. The final phase of the liberation began on 25 October, when the German headquarters was moved from Tirana to Scutari (Shkodër), in the north. This left the capital with fewer soldiers to defend it, the plan being that the last units from Greece would soon join their brothers in Tirana. The battle for Tirana began on 29 October. As Grünbaum describes, it was fierce and bloody, and many of the local inhabitants took an active part. The combat lasted twenty days. A German column from Greece tried to reach Tirana but was defeated in the hills outside the capital. Partisan units led by Mehmet Shehu had to capture the streets and buildings one by one because the Germans were well armed and put up a strong fight. After days of bloodshed and Albanian partisan attacks on enemy tanks, Tirana was liberated on 17 November 1944 (Marmullaku, *Albania and the Albanians*, 56; Pollo and Puto, *The History of Albania*, 240–42).

4. The word Grünbaum uses, *Kettenausgänge*, refers to a type of door indigenous to the region with which I am not familiar.

5. The Germans had started to withdraw from Yugoslavia in the summer of 1944. In September, Tito had flown to the Soviet Union without telling the British government his plans. Once in the Soviet Union, he conferred with authorities on how to prepare for liberation. The partisans took Belgrade in October 1944 with Soviet assistance (Jelavich, *History of the Balkans*, 2:271).

6. The American Jewish Joint Distribution Committee, which Grünbaum always refers to as "the Joint," was established in 1914 as an overseas relief agency. After the Nazis came to power in 1933, the Joint focused on helping European Jewry with economic support and emigration. During the Holocaust it had offices in New York and Lisbon and local offices in Nazi-occupied Europe. Global expenditures were $26.8 million in 1945. For further information, see Israel Gutman, ed., *Encyclopedia of the Holocaust*, 4 vols. (New York: Macmillan, 1990), 2:752–55.

TOMMY

1. According to a census taken in 1930, there were 204 Jewish inhabitants in Albania. In 1939, some Jewish families from Germany and Austria emigrated to the safer cities of Durazzo and Tirana (*Encyclopaedia Judaica*, 2:523). As already mentioned, three hundred Jews were deported from Priština (Kosovo) in April 1944.

2. The word used by Grünbaum was *Tintentod*; it probably was used in the same way as the modern product.

3. Unfortunately, Grünbaum doesn't tell us what eventually became of Mukerem Bey and Nesy.

ROME

1. Grünbaum calls it UNRA, which could only have been UNRRA. I use the latter form in my translation.

2. Delasem was the acronym for Delegazione Assistenza Emigranti Ebrei, a Jewish service agency founded in Italy in 1939. Although Italy was an anti-Jewish state, Delasem helped many Jews before and during the war by providing food, clothing, shelter, living expenses, and medicine. It also helped Jewish refugees emigrate. Delasem was funded by contributions of Italian Jews, the American Jewish Joint Distribution Committee, and the HIAS-ICA Emigration Association, or HICEM. HICEM was founded in 1927 when three Jewish migration agencies were joined: the Hebrew Immigrant Aid Society of New York; ICA, or the Jewish Colonization Association, of

Paris; and the Emigdirect of Berlin. HICEM is the acronym for the three (Zuccotti, *The Italians and the Holocaust,* 65; Gutman, *Encyclopedia of the Holocaust,* 2:657,752).

3. It is not clear what the author means here. There were three transports to Treblinka in March 1943.

4. Presumably she means her family returning home.

5. Although it may seem insensitive of Grünbaum to talk in this way while still uncertain about her husband and family, it is important to remember what she had gone through and what she still had to face as a refugee in Italy.

6. In 1932 a new highway was built between Rome and the sea at Ostia, the ancient port of Rome. The Mussolini Forum was built in the Farnesina quarter; it was a sports facility and a fascist academy for training physical education teachers.

7. The black market was a means of survival for many refugees during and after the war.

BREAKDOWN

1. Grünbaum uses the word *Herzanfälle,* which I translated as "heart attacks." It probably wasn't myocardial infarction; it was most likely syncope or something similar.

Grünbaum, January 1962, São Paulo, Brazil.